THE ASSOCIATION FOR SC

NUMBER S

Comparison of
Thistle a distorted ... –
distorting forces – inequalities,
injustices
religious prejudices
etcs.

One of the most important part of the
human self is the erotic – Freudian
link, sublimation instinctive forces
express themselves indirectly (pg 40)

THE ASSOCIATION FOR SCOTTISH LITERARY STUDIES

ANNUAL VOLUMES PUBLISHED BY SCOTTISH ACADEMIC PRESS

1971 James Hogg, *The Three Perils of Man*, ed. Douglas Gifford.
1972 *The Poems of John Davidson*, vol. I, ed. Andrew Turnbull.
1973 *The Poems of John Davidson*, vol. II, ed. Andrew Turnbull.
1974 Allan Ramsay and Robert Fergusson, *Poems*, ed. Alexander M. Kinghorn and Alexander Law.
1975 John Galt, *The Member*, ed. Ian A. Gordon.
1976 William Drummond of Hawthornden, *Poems and Prose*, ed. Robert H. MacDonald.
1977 John G. Lockhart, *Peter's Letters to his Kinsfolk*, ed. William Ruddick.
1978 John Galt, *Selected Short Stories*, ed. Ian A. Gordon.
1979 Andrew Fletcher of Saltoun, *Selected Political Writings and Speeches*, ed. David Daiches.
1980 *Scott on Himself*, ed. David Hewitt.
1981 *The Party-Coloured Mind*, ed. David Reid.
1982 James Hogg, *Selected Stories and Sketches*, ed. Douglas S. Mack.
1983 Sir Thomas Urquhart of Cromarty, *The Jewel*, ed. R. D. S. Jack and R. J. Lyall.
1984 John Galt, *Ringan Gilhaize*, ed. Patricia J. Wilson.
1985 Margaret Oliphant, *Selected Short Stories of the Supernatural*, ed. Margaret K. Gray.
1986 James Hogg, *Selected Poems and Songs*, ed. David Groves.
1987 Hugh MacDiarmid, *A Drunk Man Looks at the Thistle*, ed. Kenneth Buthlay.

THE ASSOCIATION FOR SCOTTISH LITERARY STUDIES

GENERAL EDITOR—DOUGLAS S. MACK

Hugh MacDiarmid

A DRUNK MAN LOOKS AT THE THISTLE

An Annotated Edition
edited by
Kenneth Buthlay

SCOTTISH ACADEMIC PRESS
EDINBURGH
1987

First published in Great Britain, 1987
by Scottish Academic Press Limited,
33 Montgomery Street, Edinburgh EH7 5JX,
for
The Association for Scottish Literary Studies.

ISBN 0 7073 0425 3

The Association for Scottish Literary Studies
acknowledges subsidy from the Scottish Arts Council
towards the publication of this volume.

British Library Cataloguing in Publication Data

MacDiarmid, Hugh, 1892-1978
A Drunk Man Looks at the Thistle.—
(The Association for Scottish Literary Studies; 17)
Rn: Christopher Murray Grieve I. Title II. Buthlay, Kenneth
III. Series 821'.912

ISBN 0-7073-0425-3
ISBN 0-7073-0541-1 Pbk

Typeset at Oxford University Computing Service.
Printed in Great Britain by Bell and Bain Ltd., Glasgow

CONTENTS

THE ASSOCIATION FOR SCOTTISH LITERARY STUDIES

The Association for Scottish Literary Studies aims to promote the study, teaching and writing of Scottish literature, and to further the study of the languages of Scotland.

To these ends, the ASLS publishes works of Scottish literature (of which this volume is an example), literary criticism in *Scottish Literary Journal*, scholarly studies of language in *Scottish Language*, and in-depth reviews of Scottish books in *SLJ Supplements*. And it publishes *New Writing Scotland*, an annual anthology of new poetry, drama and short fiction, in Scots, English and Gaelic, by Scottish writers.

All these publications are available as a single 'package', in return for an annual subscription. Enquiries should be sent to:

ASLS
c/o Department of English
University of Aberdeen
ABERDEEN
AB9 2UB

PREFACE

THIS edition of *A Drunk Man Looks at the Thistle* aims at catering for the needs of those who come to the work with little or no knowledge of Scots language or literature, while at the same time making a contribution to scholarship on the level expected of a volume in the Assocation for Scottish Literary Studies series in which it appears. A result of this dual aim is unusually heavy annotation and glossing which may not make for the most elegant of books, but it is hoped that the widest possible range of readers will find what they want in it, and tolerantly pass over the rest.

MacDiarmid's explicit references to *The Waste Land* indicate that he had Eliot's poem in mind when writing *A Drunk Man*, and one respect in which his work rivals Eliot's is its extreme allusiveness and tendency to incorporate material from other writers. He did not supply his readers with notes as Eliot had done in *The Waste Land*, declaring in his aggressive 'Author's Note' to the first edition that he had deliberately excluded all such 'handrails'; but one reason for that was no doubt the enormity of the task if once he had embarked on it seriously. For a relatively short, earlier work, the original version of 'Gairmscoile', he had felt the need to supply sixteen footnotes, none of which dealt with the primary difficulty of the poem, which was lexical.

The difficulty of the Scots vocabulary deployed in *A Drunk Man* is not excessive, although it does contain a few set-pieces which were constructed on an armature of unfamiliar words assembled in the course of the poet's imaginative exploration of the Scots dictionary. It is rather unfortunate that the dedicatory poem to F.G. Scott which precedes the work happens to be an extreme example of this procedure which is liable to alarm some prospective readers. But most readers of poetry themselves tend to be word-fanciers to a sufficient extent to overcome the occasional obstacle of that sort which will confront them in the work itself, provided that their social and educational formation has not induced too rigid a prejudice against the very idea that forgotten Scots expressions are capable of imaginative revival in poetry of modern sensibility. If any writer can overturn such preconceptions it is MacDiarmid, and giving him a chance to do so can have rich rewards.

Those readers with a special interest in the vagaries of MacDiarmid's linguistic usage will find that the running glossary provided in this edition directs attention to some of the more curious examples, signalled by '(MacD)'. His principal lexical source, Jamieson's *Etymological Dictionary of the Scottish Language*, is identified by '(J)'. The authoritative resources of the *Scottish National Dictionary* (SND) and the *Dictionary of the Older Scottish Tongue* (DOST) were not of course available to the poet at the time.

The glossary is critical in the sense that the poet's usage of Scots expressions, and indications of their meanings in his own glossaries or elsewhere, have not been taken at face value. MacDiarmid's memory was not infallible and, like other poets, he would occasionaly give words a meaning he wanted them to have, regardless of received usage. Also, *A Drunk Man* was prepared for publication in 1926 under great pressure, and there are signs of this in the glossary MacDiarmid supplied for it, such as the inclusion of the word *scount*, which does not in fact occur in the text as published. I have not indicated the demarcation of regional dialect forms, since for the vast majority of readers it is sufficient simply to know that the poet in practice ignored such distinctions. However, I thought it worth departing from this rule on a couple of occasions to note examples of Shetlandic usage occurring long before residence in Shetland stimulated MacDiarmid's interest in that dialect. A holograph manuscript exists of a loose English translation of *A Drunk Man* which the poet made in 1967, and I have been able to consult this, thanks to the good offices of Kulgin Duval.

The notes, printed for greater convenience on the pages facing the text, are to a large extent concerned (like MacDiarmid's own notes to the original version of 'Gairmscoile') with the extreme allusiveness which has been found in practice to be the most difficult aspect of the work for most readers, including students specialising in Scottish literature. This is not only a matter of identifying specific allusions and quotations, of which there are a great many, but also of supplying subsidiary material which it is hoped will help towards a fuller understanding of what the poet had in mind in writing a particular passage, either because he showed a specific awareness of this matter elsewhere, or because it was 'in the air', the cultural ambience to which he responded at the time.

Some examples of material from other writers which was used in *A Drunk Man* are also included in the notes. MacDiarmid's reworking of such material is sometimes of much interest from a technical point of view, particularly in his 'adaptations', through English cribs which I have discovered, of poems by modern European writers. Where the professional translators were guilty of some execrable 'translatorese' in their English, the poet transformed this into excellent Scots, and, in almost total ignorance of Russian, produced versions of Blok and Hippius which were much admired by the foremost authority on modern Russian literature, D.S. Mirsky, who congratulated MacDiarmid on having produced 'the only real re-creations of Russian poetry' in any form of 'English'.

MacDiarmid's manuscript of *A Drunk Man* does not appear to have survived. It is likely that it was destroyed shortly after publication of the first edition in 1926, in accordance with the usual practice of many publishers at that time. In the absence of the manuscript the present text is based on the first edition, which was published by William Blackwood & Sons of Edinburgh and London.

All differences between the text of the present edition and that of the first edition are recorded in an appendix. They include spelling changes, mostly aimed at a more consistent use of the apostrophe as a convention of Scots orthography, which were made or confirmed by MacDiarmid in the edition of *A Drunk Man* published by K. Duval & C.H. Hamilton (Falkland, 1969). On the author's instructions, the text of that edition was followed for the *Complete Poems 1920-1976*, edited by Michael Grieve and W.R. Aitken (London: Martin Brian & O'Keefe, 1978), where he also authorised some additional changes.

From my own experience of editing with his approval some of MacDiarmid's Scots prose, I believe it would accord with the author's wishes and intentions—in the spirit, if no longer susceptible of confirmation in the letter—to regularise a few spelling inconsistencies which escaped the revision process in *A Drunk Man*. However, the principles laid down by the General Editor of the ASLS series prohibit this, even if all such changes are scrupulously recorded, because 'improvement' of the author's text is not acceptable. Readers will therefore find that a word may not always be spelled in the same way. Also, forms such as *wha's* (= whose), *ha'en* (= had) and *ga'ed* (= went) are preserved in the text as approved by MacDiarmid, despite the fact that these forms contradict the principle he followed whereby an apostrophe is inserted into a Scots form specifically to indicate where it lacks a letter present in the spelling of the standard English cognate. Ironically enough, while the poet himself was still with us, his attitude towards the problems of Scots spelling was such that he turned the entire text of *A Drunk Man* over to John Weston to be re-spelled more consistently in accordance with a different system—a procedure which Weston incorporated in his edition of 1971.

In the *Collected Poems of Hugh MacDiarmid* (New York: Macmillan, 1962) the text of *A Drunk Man* was divided into sections to which titles were assigned. Though in my opinion highly undesirable in the text itself, these divisions can be useful for detailed discussion of the work and for teaching purposes. They are therefore indicated by bold type in the notes, together with the relevant line-numbers.

INTRODUCTION

I
The Writing of the Work

THE most sympathetic reception for MacDiarmid's earlier ventures in Scots came from critics connected with *The Glasgow Herald*, and it was in that newspaper that he managed to place a piece of advance publicity for *A Drunk Man* on 17 December 1925 (p.4):

> Mr Hugh M'Diarmid has now completed a gallimaufry in braid Scots verse, entitled 'A Drunk Man Looks at the Thistle'. It is, in fact, a long poem of over a thousand lines split up into several sections, but the forms within the sections range from ballad measure to vers libre. The matter includes satire, amphigouri, lyrics, parodies of Mr T.S. Eliot and other poets, and translations from the Russian, French, and German. The whole poem is in braid Scots, except a few quatrains which are in the nature of a skit on Mr Eliot's 'Sweeney' poems, and it has been expressly designed to show that braid Scots can be effectively applied to all manner of subjects and measures.

The length had been reduced from 'over a thousand' to 'over 600 lines' when the poet offered it to his publishers, Blackwood's, on 12 February 1926, for publication in the autumn, saying that he was anxious to keep it by him 'for a little yet, at any rate, for final revision'.[1] The next day, six extracts from the work appeared in the *Herald*, prefaced by an explanatory piece similar to the advance publicity quoted above. The main difference, apart from the change in length, was the additional statement that the work was 'a complete poem . . . deriving its unity from its pre-occupation with the distinctive elements in Scottish psychology which depend for their effective expression upon the hitherto unrealised potentialities of Braid Scots'.

The six short extracts are described as 'representative selections, which can be read as separate poems, although in their proper context they form essential parts of the development of the scheme of the book', and MacDiarmid explains that the first of them ('Hurricane') belongs to a section designed as a 'Homage to Dostoevsky'. 'Hurricane', with a significant additional stanza, was to be called 'Farewell to Dostoevski' (ll. 2216-2235) when MacDiarmid supplied titles for the divided text of *A Drunk Man* printed in his *Collected Poems* (1962). It contains the statement 'I ken nae Russian', which might be taken as a sort of alibi for the 'translations from the Russian' mentioned in the publicity. The fifth extract is 'The Thistle' ('The Gothic Thistle', ll. 309-316) 'from the Belgian [*sic*] of George Ramaekers'.

Three of the other extracts are separately titled poems which were merged into what was called 'Ebb and Flow' (ll. 369-400) in 1962; and the final piece, 'The Skeleton in the Cupboard', was also to lose its title and become the second half of 'The Emptiness at the End' (ll. 2327-2334). It is worth noting that even these short specimens indicate that the poet had already at this stage developed his own peculiar symbolism of moon and thistle—the featuring of the moonlight as leprosy and the thistle as a skeleton is specially significant—and that he had adopted a characteristic device exemplified by the sudden switch from satirical portrayal of contemporary Scottish sterility and banality to a projection of the poet as a lonely voyager in metaphysical seas. The importance he attached to Dostoevsky is established by the choice of 'Hurricane' as 'representative' and by the mention of the section of 'Homage' to the Russian writer. And when MacDiarmid states that the work derives its unity from its preoccupation with 'distinctive elements in Scottish psychology' there is ample reason to associate this with the 'Caledonian Antisyzygy' which is indeed a main source of such unity as the final version was to possess.

It seems a reasonably inference, then, that this version of *A Drunk Man* in over 600 lines had a good deal in common with the work as published at 2684 lines, including the aim of restoring a European context to poetry in Scots through links with Dostoevsky and recent European poets some of whose work had been 'adapted'. The poem 'fixed up with the publishers at 600 lines', and regarded as needing so few final touches that on 12 March the author invited William McCance to 'do me either a frontispiece or some cuts or something', was then reported to various correspondents as 'swelling' to 'over 800' (22 March), 'upwards of 1200' (13 April), 'almost in final shape' at 'well over 2000' (25 May)—and *apparently* not only finished but in proof by 10 June.

That date, '10/6/26', is accepted in *The Letters of Hugh MacDiarmid* (p.318) as the date of a letter which MacDiarmid wrote to Pittendrigh Macgillivray enclosing a proof of his preface for the completed *Drunk Man* and responding to suggestions made by Macgillivray after reading the proofs of the work itself. Since this would have MacDiarmid answering a letter which was in fact written about four months later, one may assume a misdating and postpone consideration of this material for the time being.

On 22 June, in letters to Neil Gunn and Macgillivray, MacDiarmid stated that the length of the work now 'finished for the publishers' was 2600 lines, and to Macgillivray he added: 'I had an extraordinary spate of inspiration to finish with—writing at break-neck speed, and pulled off some extraordinary things, I think'. He did not, however, send his manuscript off to the publishers. Writing to Blackwood's on 9 July he said:

> I had hoped to have sent "A Drunk Man, etc." to you before this: but I am very conscious, if I may say so without immodesty, that this is or has all the makings of being one of the biggest things in the whole range of Scottish literature and I am determined not to let it out of my hands until I am absolutely certain that I can make no more of it.

Nevertheless, he was anxious to have it published in the autumn as planned, and hoped that this would still be possible if he delivered the manuscript by the first week of September.

On 6 August, although writing to Blackwood's to say that he would forward the manuscript 'very shortly', he also told George Ogilvie that he was

> up to the neck in proofs of "Contemporary Scottish Studies" and—worse—in rewriting, against time, . . . one of the main and most difficult sections of "A Drunk Man". . . .
>
> I realise fully the importance of what you urge in regard to the "Drunk Man". It will either make or finish me so far as Braid Scots work, & Messrs Blackwood's, are concerned. I dare not let them down with a work of such magnitude. As it now stands it'll be at least six times as big a book as "Sangschaw"—some risk for any publisher these days. I've let myself go in it for all I'm worth. My friend Scott, (the composer) and I afterwards went over the whole thing with a small tooth comb. But we both felt that the section I've been rewriting—which comes about midway in the book and should represent the high water mark, the peaks of highest intensity, could be improved by being recast and projected on to a different altitude of poetry altogether—made, instead of a succession of merely verbal and pictorial verses, into a series of metaphysical pictures with a definite progression, a cumulative effect—and that is what I've been so busy with. It's infernally intractable material: but I've spared no pains and put my uttermost ounce into the business. I'm out to make or break in this matter. There are poems in the book (which is really one whole although many parts are detachable) of extraordinary power, I know—longer and far more powerful and unique in kind than anything in "Sangschaw" or "Penny Wheep"; but that's not what I'm after. It's the thing as a whole that I'm mainly concerned with, and if, as such, it does not take its place as a masterpiece—sui generis—one of the biggest things in the range of Scottish literature, I shall have failed.

A week later, MacDiarmid told Macgillivray that he was going to have 'an intensive fortnight' working on *A Drunk Man* in the absence of his family, after which he duly sent off his manuscript to Blackwood's on 28 August. He was worried about its safe delivery, as he had no copy of 'a very large part of the poem'. And he reported soon afterwards to Macgillivray that he was totally exhausted:

> The fact is that I seem to have overdriven myself badly. The final stage of "The Drunk Man" took every ounce out of me. Since then I have been very much in the trough of the wave—in the grip of a species of impotence bred of pure exhaustion. . . .
>
> I should have valued it immensely if I had been able to go over "The Drunk Man" with you before I sent it off. But until the very last moment it was a hopeless jumble of scraps of scribbled and cross-scribbled M.S.S. I sorted it out by a last effort into some kind of order (re-writing no more of it than I could possibly help)—the comps will curse: it is just barely an intelligible MSS. However, I hadn't a scrap of strength left.—But it is a big thing. It is me in every way—satire, lyricism, and all the rest of it: beauty and fun and savagery and objectionable elements all mixed just as they are in me. . . .
>
> Thank you for your offer to help with the proofs. It is exceedingly good of you and I shall certainly be greatly relieved and proud to accept your offer. (6 September 1926.)

The proofs were supplied by the publishers in instalments, and MacDiarmid sent them to Macgillivray with some misgivings as to what he would make of 'the appalling fescennine, blasphemous, Scots Sinn Fein, and generally rebel character of my production'. He accepted most of the small corrections suggested by Macgillivray in the first batch of proofs, but said it was now too late to take his advice about changing the title to 'In Vino Veritas', 'although I quite see your point with regard to the existing title of which I am not specially enamoured either'.

Macgillivray got the remainder of the proofs on 27 September, and he dictated a letter the next day, indicating that he was worried by 'a lack of such plan and construction as would make fairly clear what you would be at, through the "drink", and your "thistle" symbol'. The letter continues:

> In this lot of proofs I have not come across so many little flaws as in the first section. But for various reasons, I have suggested a number of small deletes. They are such things as one writes in the heat of the evening and burns in the cool of the morning—I know them! . . .
>
> I have been wondering if you . . . could not do something illuminating in the way of a proem on your subject or its objective; giving a hint of your idea, motive, or plan, somewhat in the manner of the old masters. And then, I am inclined to suggest that you should have an epilogue in which your "drunk man" wakes up on a

> hillside among the heather and bracken in the sunshine of a lovely morning and sees great beauty in the thistle, its roses and spikey leaves all decked with diamonds of dew, and then indulges in wondering comments on the nightmare of ideas he has slept through. Show that nature in spite of all those dreadful nightshade things and harassing impressions which are but as dreams—is beautiful—everlastingly beautiful—as indeed she ever is to the healthy, if frankly and naturally accepted.
>
> Then having rounded off so—dispelling all clouds—you might go home, kiss your dear and affectionate little wife, and play with laughing little Chris till tea is ready, and afterwards sleep so sound that even the Lord, passing in the heavy boots of a "bobby",[2] would never be heard.

MacDiarmid's letter dated 10/6/26, as mentioned above, was surely written in reply to this, so that a re-dating to 6/10/26 might be acceptable. In it, he says:

> Your last letter with proofs gave me a bad time. I considered the matter very thoroughly: and took the views of other friends too. I quite saw all your points and agree that the excision of certain passages would make the work more harmonious etc: but it would be a false harmony—not true to my intention—depending upon the ignoring of essential elements and aspects of experience which are compatible to the psychology of the hypothetical toper (putatively identified with myself). My own first idea was the one you suggest of the Drunk Man waking up in the glory of the morning. I deliberately abandoned it as untrue. I cannot give that sort of happy ending. Nor, with all respect to your judgment, can I delete the passages you suggest. If I did I would from my point of view falsify the whole thing. But what I feel is perhaps best put in what another friend writes, and you may be interested in seeing how just what you object to is valued by him: He says:— "You have completed in my opinion the greatest poem ever produced by a Scotsman. . . . I'm perfectly satisfied with the architecture of the boat. I've had doubts at times about certain passages, but I can't now find a word to say against them. *I* mightn't have included them but then I'm not *you* and it's exactly for this reason, that the whole thing bodies forth the living image of C.M.G.[3] that I have come to see it as the masterpiece it is, for what man in ten generations succeeds in getting outside his own skin".

The seventy-year-old Macgillivray evidently did not take too kindly to this rejection of his advice, and the poet wrote him a placatory letter on 8 October, saying: 'I hated not being able to agree to your suggested deletions. I thought and thought over them, and tried alternative verses and poems copies of which I will send you'. He had made only two small changes requiring fresh copy in the first proofs, which he had returned to Blackwood's on 1 October. The publisher sent him the second proofs on 19 October, and he wrote to Macgillivray on 1 November, explaining that there were two copies of these:

> I made a few corrections on one of them and have returned it. The other I have kept by me a few days longer: and have been reading and re-reading it, and, along with it, your letters. I am now sending it to you: and you will see that I have made several alterations and have acted upon many of your suggestions. . . .
>
> But as to your major suggestions . . . I had to turn all of these down. . . . But I was tremendously touched by what you said when suggesting that I should end with a Sunny Morning Epilogue—the *real* beauty of the thistle—and turn to enjoy life again with my wife and baby. And this was subtly and strongly reinforced by the beautiful note and prayer and poem on Mrs. Macgillivray's death which I herewith return as requested. . . .I tried (although admittedly I was not in a good state for versifying and, if I had had time, your idea of an Epilogue might have come to something satisfactory) to give expression to the Epilogue idea: and here's the utmost I was able to make of it.
>
> And yet gin I could fa' asleep
> To wauken here at fresh o' morn
> Hoo bonnie micht this thistle seem
> Wi' jinglin' dew on ilka thorn!
>
> Fu' weel I ken that frae sic thochts
> As mine the nicht a'e side o' truth
> Is wantin', when it needs a' sides / them a'
> To see things richt—altho' forsooth
>
> They're ill to see thegither and,
> Compared wi' a' I'm seein' noo
> The pink and green at brak' o' day
> Micht seem owre bonnie to be true
>
> Yet a' that maist men dinna see
> —Or winna see—is needs worth mair
> Than a' they wull or aiblins can
> Gin use—or *that*—gars't seem maist fair!
> *Or*: Gin that sae seems mair true and fair!

These hirpling lines were offered only as a sop for Macgillivray, to whom MacDiarmid showed a courtesy and deference that were in fact quite typical of the private man, despite his public image. Mercifully unencumbered with any additions of that quality, *A Drunk Man* was published on 22 November. Perhaps the most striking piece of information about its composition, however, was yet to be conveyed—in a letter from MacDiarmid to Ogilvie on 9 December in which he said: 'At the last moment I excised lyrics etc. which aggregated at least a third more than its published bulk'. This is equivalent to at least 32 pages of text as published, and suggests that, on the basis of a line-count, the bulk of his manuscript may indeed have come close to being six times as big as *Sangschaw*, as he appeared to claim, *after* F.G. Scott and he had gone over the whole thing with a small-tooth comb. But regardless of whether the massive cutting in question was performed with Scott's active participation or—as seems to be suggested—afterwards, it is clear that the poet accumulated a very substantial amount of additional material between 22 June ('2600 lines') and 6 August ('at least six times as big . . . as "Sangschaw"'), and that he cut out something approaching the same amount of material before sending his manuscript off to Blackwood's on 28 August.

It is in the same letter to Ogilvie that MacDiarmid gives a precise account of how he saw *A Drunk Man* not long after its completion but subsequent to his period of post-natal exhaustion. This is in my view by far the most revealing thing he ever said about it, contrasting it with the new work he is planning, which he tells Ogilvie is to be complementary to *A Drunk Man*:

> Where the Drunk Man is in one sense a reaction from the "Kailyard", Cencrastus transcends that altogether—the Scotsman gets rid of the thistle, "the bur o' the world"—and his spirit at last inherits its proper sphere. Psychologically it represents the resolution of the sadism and masochism, the synthesis of the various sets of antitheses I was posing in the Drunk Man. It will not depend on the contrasts of realism and metaphysics, bestiality and beauty, humour and madness—but move on a plane of pure beauty and pure music. . . . It will take infinite pains—but along these lines I am satisfied that, if I cannot altogether realise my dream, I can at least achieve something well worth while, ideally complementary to the Drunk Man—positive where it is negative, optimistic where it is pessimistic, and constructive where it is destructive.

There remains to be considered the part played in the composition of *A Drunk Man* by F.G. Scott. MacDiarmid, in his 'Author's Note' to the first edition, said that Scott 'suggested it', and Scott himself said twenty years later that he 'outlined the plan and supplied the title of the poem'.[4] Nearly all the early correspondence between them has disappeared, or been destroyed, and for this and other reasons it seems impossible now to determine how much, or how little, should be understood by 'the plan' Scott said he outlined. As the completed work stands, the term would have to be applied to it in a very general sense indeed. Maurice Lindsay takes it to mean that Scott 'thought out the idea of the *Drunk Man*'—begging the question of what the idea *is*—and adds that 'there is supporting evidence that could be interpreted as backing up his claim' in a fragment of a letter from Scott to William McCance. (The letter should be dated rather later than Lindsay indicates, around 5 March 1926.) In this fragment, says Lindsay, 'the theme of some of the sections presumably of the unfinished and still unassembled *Drunk Man* are paraded by Scott to McCance for some undefined purpose'.[5] The purpose in question was probably connected with a project for 'creating some Scottish ballets' in which MacDiarmid said he was collaborating with McCance and Scott, with the poet 'doing the libretti'.[6] And as to the 'theme'—this turns out to be a string of references to satirical targets such as 'the Harry Lauder ilk and the crooked nibby and the London Scottish, Caledonian Societies etc., not omitting Kirkwood and the politicians, nor J.M. Bulloch, Will, Barrie, and the Kailyard generally'. One could hardly assume that everything MacDiarmid wrote on these familiar topics—and that was a great deal—emanated from Scott. But even if this could somehow be shown to be the case, the appearance of some of these topics in a few pages of *A Drunk Man* would not be very convincing evidence that Scott 'thought out the idea' of that multifarious work.

As to the title, which many people have found off-putting, it is based on a common formula of the time. MacDiarmid himself had used the rubric 'A Scotsman Looks at His World' for a series of articles in 1922-23, just as the then editor of *The Century Magazine* had used 'An American Looks at His World'; and books with titles like *An Irishman Looks at His World* by George A. Birmingham were common enough. If making this Scotsman drunk gives the title a comic slant, it might be thought somewhat reminiscent of the sort of music hall caricature of his countrymen that MacDiarmid elsewhere deplored. But his 'Author's Note' implies that what he actually had in mind was Gregory Smith's observation that Scottish writers frequently offered alcoholic intoxication as an explanation for manifestations in their work of the 'Caledonian Antisyzygy' (exemplified in one of his illustrations as the unexpected juxtaposition of 'thistles and thistledown'). Smith saw this tactic as a tongue-in-cheek device:

> a quizzing of those prosaic and precise persons who must have that realism which presents everything as sober fact, within an ell of their noses. The poets seem to say: 'Here is fantasy strange enough; if you, drunkard of facts, must explain it, do so in the only way open to you. . . . Be satisfied, if you think it is we who are drunk'.[7]

The thistle had been used with pub-associations by MacDiarmid before, in the title 'At the Sign of the Thistle'; and possibly, as suggested by Owen Dudley Edwards, there is a connection between the circumstances in which the Drunk Man is confronted by the Thistle and 'the rolling English drunkard' who made 'the rolling English road' in Chesterton's poem, about whom we learn that 'the wild rose was above him when they found him in the ditch'. Perhaps more probable, given the evidence of MacDiarmid's special interest in Alexander Blok, is a reminiscence of the latter's lyrical drama, *Neznakomka*, which opens in a pub from which the Poet is kicked out for getting too drunk and dumped in a snowdrift off-stage.

Scott's contribution to the actual manuscript of the work has become legendary. Both William Johnstone and Benno Schotz have testified that Scott told them that the event took place in Glasgow, with the addition in Schotz's case that the poet was accompanied by his future second wife, who said that he had bits of the manuscript stuffed in all his pockets, from which they were transferred to a bed, where Scott proceeded to demonstrate his principle that 'a work has to have a beginning, a middle, and an end'. 'I feel sure', says Schotz, 'that Grieve was not prepared for such an analysis right away, but F.G. was so taken with the poem that he felt he had to edit it'—which he began to do by selecting a 'vital' poem for the beginning, a 'powerful' one for the end, and one 'like an andante' for the middle.[8] By Johnstone's account, however, the poet was sunk in alcoholic slumber while Scott spent the night in editing and putting in order the 'fragments' of his work. These consisted of 'short images', and Johnstone (a painter) describes them as 'motifs in search of a vernacular'. By 'unifying them into a complete whole', Scott ensured that 'a masterpiece was born'. He also wrote 'the final lines'.[9]

These are, however, the recollections of old men. Earlier accounts are agreed that the event took place at MacDiarmid's home in Montrose—in which case the poet must have gone there sometime in July or the beginning of August from St. Cyrus, where he and his family were spending the summer. The first printed version of Scott's account of the event was given in an article contributed anonymously by Maurice Lindsay to the *Scots Review* (January 1947), where it was said to be 'common knowledge to his [Scott's] friends' that he received an urgent call to go to Montrose, and 'it was late at night when the composer arrived with his wife and family'. By daybreak the 'fragments' of the poem were set in order—and Scott 'claims he is "pretty certain" that he supplied those last two lines which bring the poem to its conclusion'.

Lindsay tape-recorded a conversation with Scott in the early Fifties which became the basis for another article in the *Saltire Review* (Winter 1954). He reported that the composer then added 'one or two details, and these were incorporated in my final version in my book *Clyde Waters*'.[10] This version ran, in Scott's words, as follows:

> One Friday night, when I was in Glasgow, I got a telegram from Grieve asking me to come up to Montrose immediately. When I arrived, Grieve was surrounded by innumerable bits of paper about six inches long out of which the poem was finally made up. There was no order or arrangement about the bits of paper.
>
> With the aid of a bottle of whisky, Grieve and I settled down to the task of going through the material. 'What about this one?' Grieve would ask. 'Put it in the waste-paper basket', I'd say; or 'I think that might go in'. By early morning, we gradually got the thing into order, and by four o'clock, we were almost finished. But there was one problem. 'How should we finish it, F.G.?', Grieve asked me. By this time the whisky was done, and I was exhausted. The last line of the final poem before us was: 'O I ha'e silence left'. So I said: 'Put down—
>
> "And weel ye micht",
> Sae Jean'll say, "eftir sic a nicht" '.
>
> Grieve wrote that down, which is how I came to be the author of the last two lines of 'A Drunk Man Looks at the Thistle'.[11]

It will be observed that Scott's wife and family have dropped out of this version (as has a reference by Lindsay in the *Saltire Review* article to MacDiarmid's first wife, Peggy, as 'Jean'), but there are important additions: the bits of paper were about six inches long, and they were in *no* order or arrangement when Scott arrived to banish Chaos and Old Night. (As MacDiarmid's handwriting varied considerably in size, it would be rash to hazard a guess at the number of six-inch-long bits of paper required for the approximately 3500 lines of verse that were presumably reduced to about 2500 by 4 a.m..) Also, there is no longer any hesitation about Scott's claiming of author's rights in the last two lines. However, it should be noted that there is a discrepancy between Scott's account of what stood before them in the form of the last line written by MacDiarmid himself and the holograph of the relevant passage sent to J.K. Annand on 2 June 1926, which ends: 'O I ha'e Silence left, the croon o' a' '.

This was not after all to be the final word which Lindsay provided. Included in an exhibition at the National Library of Scotland in 1980 was a letter from Scott, dated 20 May 1945, which the library had acquired amongst other papers from Lindsay, and it was clear that this letter had supplied the information used in the original article. Lindsay printed the relevant passage from it in his book on Scott that year, and again in his autobiography, *Thank You For Having Me* (1983), as follows:

> I outlined the plan and supplied the title of the poem during a rainy hike on a night in Glen Clovis Hotel. Christopher usually wrote his poetry in snatches: he never had any sense of form and after some months of scribbling on the backs of envelopes and odd bits of paper, he sent to Glasgow an urgent call for me to come for a weekend and see the litter (and mess!) he'd been making of my bright idea, as Blackwood's were asking for the MS and there *was* no MS. It was late at night when I reached Montrose and after his wife and youngsters[12] went off to bed, we sat down to a table, a great heap of scribbled bits of paper and a bottle of whisky. I can still see Christopher's face when I was indicating the shape the poem, or for that matter a musical composition, ought to take—he was literally flabbergasted either by the extent of my knowledge or by the whisky—it's anybody's guess! We spent until day-break sorting out the items worth keeping, Christopher arranging them on the table like a pack of cards in the order that I indicated as likely to give the best sequences, climaxes, etc. My plans necessitated a pianissimo close, after so much bustle ('The Stars like Thistle's Roses flower') to be followed by ('Yet ha'e I Silence left, the croon o' a') and I'm pretty certain I supplied the last two lines to bring the thing to some kind of conclusion.[13]

Reflecting on the statement that MacDiarmid 'never had any sense of form', it seems remarkable that Scott was nevertheless inspired to set to music such a large number of his poems, thereby producing some of his own finest work. It is true that, in the architectonic sense expected of very large-scale projects, the poet's feeling for form was not his strong point—but in *A Drunk Man* it is difficult to imagine where else he could have thought of placing 'Yet Ha'e I Silence Left', or for that matter the pages which began the work, establishing the setting and the key-symbols to be used throughout. If Scott was responsible for the entire formal sequence of the work, however, his credit is not greatly increased thereby, since it is this aspect of *A Drunk Man* that has been most severely criticised ever since it first appeared. And rightly so. One source of irritation to a reader who gets to know the work well is his realisation at certain points that MacDiarmid had seen two items as inter-connected but the reader has not registered this before, with consequent loss of comprehension, because the items in question have been separated by far too many pages of disparate material. And the reader has an urgent need of all the links he can find. Although he will see significance and positive value in some cases where a given item is followed unexpectedly and even disruptively by something of an extremely different order, there are too many instances where the sequence will strike him as being quite arbitrary, and this becomes increasingly counter-productive, whatever critical angle he may adopt. Without access to the extensive material discarded on Scott's advice, it is rather academic to debate instances where changes in sequence might have produced a more satisfying result; but that does not alter the irritation one feels at certain points with the sequence which *was* arrived at as constituting the main weakness of the work. Another weakness occasionally encountered is a tendency towards verbosity, though this is much less the case than in some other of MacDiarmid's long works. Still, its presence here is indicative of weak editing.

Such deficiencies are not, however, surprising if Scott was the real architect of *A Drunk Man*'s structure. As a writer, he himself never succeeded with anything of any size, and Maurice Lindsay's judgment of his music is that he was 'a miniaturist, a minor composer' who showed himself 'unable to develop extended ideas architectonically'.[14] What MacDiarmid gained from him on the level of technique, during the period when he could share a common wavelength with his friend and former school-teacher, was constant practical criticism on matters of more or less detail: criticism which he usually accepted, and was right to do so. Scott also represented for him an intransigent arbiter of the standard his poems would have to measure up to if they were to be critically respectable, and he did not question the appropriateness of Scott's criteria till well after the time of *A Drunk Man.*

It seems reasonable to suppose from all this that the main weight of Scott's contribution to *A Drunk Man* would fall on his advice about what should be excluded from it on grounds of quality, and that he played an important role in ensuring the work's great basic strength: the technical excellence of the verse from which it never diverges for too long throughout its formidable length. Where the structural sequence is concerned, the result achieved is not impressive, and one might conclude that the main advantage Scott had to offer MacDiarmid in this respect was the fact that he could stand back from the material more readily than the author could.

In any case, MacDiarmid was by no means reluctant to acknowledge his debts to Scott in this or in any other regard. He dedicated the work to him with a complimentary poem, planted a reference to him in the work itself, and in the 'Author's Note' saluted him extravagantly as the friend who had suggested it and to whom 'during the course of writing it, I have been further greatly indebted for cooperative suggestions and for some of the most penetrating and comprehensive of modern European criticism'. The repetition over many years of various versions of the legendary night's work in Montrose carried the implication that there was more to it than MacDiarmid would ever admit to, but his own account of the event seems generous enough:

> When I wrote the "Drunk Man" working on my own I had got to the point when I had ceased to be able to see the forest for the trees.

> I found the necessary imaginative sympathy in F.G. Scott and handed over the whole mass of my manuscript to him. He was not long in seizing on the essentials and urging the ruthless discarding of the unessentials. I had no hesitation in taking his advice and in this way the significant shape was educed from the welter of stuff and the rest pruned away. . . . I cut out and consigned to the fire forthwith a high percentage of what I had written—with incalculable gain to the whole. . . . I was, of course, particularly lucky in having at my elbow such a determined artist as Scott who in his own practice is wont to eliminate to the last degree and concentrate, at no matter what sacrifice of pet material, upon the highest ordering.'[15]

He wrote that in 1955, and repeated it in 1966, with the rider that 'while Ezra Pound did something very similar to Eliot's *Waste Land*, what happened in my case has been widely misunderstood. All it amounted to was that Scott read the great mass of verse I'd written, advised me to scrap a good deal that he thought repetitive or inessential, and suggested a more effective placing in order of what remained'.[16] Two years later, in a review of the revised edition of MacDiarmid's *Collected Poems*, Douglas Young exclaimed: 'How I wish somebody would get the facts straight about F.G. Scott's share in the arrangement of that masterpiece'. He too had been told by Scott about the night spent in 'sorting the work out from the odd bits and pieces that Christopher had accumulated; but just how much Scott did to organise it all I did not gather'.[17] Not surprisingly, MacDiarmid wrote to enquire what Young wished to imply by that. He repeated the gist of what he had already published twice, and added that 'Scott had nothing to do with the actual writing any more than Edwin Muir (who was also privy to what I was doing, and saw various portions of my manuscript as I wrote them). There is, despite Dr Young's insinuation, nothing further to be learned'.[18]

Nevertheless, in a recorded interview with MacDiarmid published in 1979, Alexander Scott raised the matter again, and elicited the following:

> *MacD*: Scott was invaluable to me, there's no question about that at all. . . . I had written a great deal more than appeared in the final text, and a lot of it was below par, below the level of certain other things, and he helped me by suggesting that this and that and the other should be left out and the whole thing strengthened on the basis of the best, what he regarded and what I came to regard as the best things in the text.
> *S:* Well, I believe he is also claimed to have provided the last two lines of the poem.

MacD: He claims that but I don't remember that as a matter of fact. I am quite willing to allow him the credit for that.[19]

—'And weel ye micht,'
Sae Jean'll say, 'efter sic a nicht!'

II
The Fixed Point

PERHAPS it reflects a certain lack of progress on my part, but the most useful approach to *A Drunk Man* still seems to me the one I originally put forward as long ago as 1954, in a review of the second edition in which I drew attention to the importance of the idea of the 'Caledonian Antisyzygy' to this work.[20] MacDiarmid found the idea in Gregory Smith's *Scottish Literature: Character & Influence* (1919), where Smith invented the term to identify what he saw as a distinguishing feature of that literature, and especially poetry in Scots: the coming together of contraries or opposites.

> Does literature anywhere, of this small compass, show such a mixture of contraries as his [the Scot's] in outlook, subject, and method; real life and romance, everyday fact and the supernatural, things holy and things profane, gentle and simple, convention and 'cantrip', thistles and thistledown? . . . There is more in the Scottish antithesis of the real and fantastic than is to be explained by the familiar rules of rhetoric. The sudden jostling of contraries seems to preclude any relationship by literary suggestion. The one invades the other without warning. They are the 'polar twins' of the Scottish Muse. . . .
>
> This mingling, even of the most eccentric kind, is an indication to us that the Scot, in that medieval fashion which takes all things as granted, is at his ease in both 'rooms of life', and turns to fun, and even profanity, with no misgivings. For Scottish literature is more medieval in habit than criticism has suspected, and owes some part of its picturesque strength to this freedom in passing from one mood to another. It takes some people more time that they can spare to see the absolute propriety of a gargoyle's grinning at the elbow of a kneeling saint.[21]

Although Smith was inclined to trace this antisyzygy back to the medieval world, the exciting thing for MacDiarmid was that he saw it writ large in contemporary trends of European thought and art. He could say of the terms in which Smith described it that they 'sum up the essential tendencies of the most advanced schools of thought in every country in Europe to-day'. Hence, the more he could revive and redeploy the Caledonian antisyzygy—'the great vital characteristic of Scottish literature—a distinguishing faculty, which it can only shape forth poorly in English, but which is potentially expressible in the Vernacular to which it belongs'—the more his work would be in tune with up-to-date European developments.[22]

By the time he wrote *A Drunk Man*, the concept of antisyzygy had become what he desribed as a *point fixé*: 'Most omnivorous readers know how curiously any theme that impresses itself upon them will run through all their subsequent reading until another supplants it; how everything one reads at such a time will throw some new light or yield some additional information, or bear in this way or that on that *point fixé*.'[23] One can see why that might well happen in this case because, regardless of the claim for a specifically Caledonian variety of it, antisyzygy had long been identified as a basic function of the imagination, which as Coleridge put it, 'reveals itself in the balance or reconcilement of opposite or discordant qualities'[24]. And behind this is the ancient idea that the world itself exists in the tension between polar opposites, a concept which is found appropriately enough in both Eastern (for example, the Taoist *yin* / *yang* duality) and Western thought. They meet in what may be called theosophy in the wide sense of the term: the ancient mystical tradition from Pythagoras and Plato through the Gnostics, Plotinus, Meister Eckehart, Bruno, Boehme, and Schelling, turning into theosophy in the narrow sense with the founding of Blavatsky's Theosophical Society in 1875. An important contribution to the broader mystical tradition came from the Cabbala, of which MacDiarmid's friend Denis Saurat made a special study—and it is as easy to find evidence of the principle of antisyzygy, or *coincidentia oppositorum*, in the Jewish Cabbala as in the Protestant mystic Boehme with his conception of reality as an interplay of opposites. Coleridge's shorthand for this principle—'extremes meet'—is used by MacDiarmid to indicate the Drunk Man's philosophical position early in the work, as if by way of a warning to the reader that, whatever the appearance to the contrary, this will turn out to be a philosophical poem. And some of the implications he had in mind are suggested by another of Saurat's special interests, Blake:

> Without Contraries is no progression. Attraction and Repulsion, Reason and Energy, Love and Hate, are necessary to Human existence. From these contraries spring what the religious call Good and Evil. Good is the passive that obeys reason. Evil is the active springing from Energy.[25]

Saurat apart, MacDiarmid's interest in the mystical wing of the *New Age*, where the influence of the religious philosopher and poet

Solovyov had become prominent, and in the theosophical studies of A.E. and Yeats, meant that stimuli from that long and richly variegated tradition were often prompting his thought and imagination at this time. Yeats's visionary handbook, *A Vision* (1925), is based on the principle of antisyzygy, and his tracing of this all-pervading principle in terms of light and darkness may be glimpsed behind MacDiarmid's more powerful development of that imagery in *A Drunk Man.* Although MacDiarmid dismissed *A Vision* condescendingly in the *New Age* (15 July 1926), that did not prevent him from appropriating the Great Wheel symbol from it via A.E's review of the same book, introducing it unexpectedly towards the end of *A Drunk Man*, and exploiting it at great length.

It is useful in reading this work to bear in mind the metaphysical as well as the aesthetic aspects of antisyzygy. Taking it on the aesthetic level can be most helpful in the earlier parts of the work, though it has to be conceded that there will be moments when the 'routh [abundance] o' contrairies' confronting the reader is no longer felt to be controlled by the imagination in Coleridge's sense but is producing diversity almost at random. At these points, the inebriety of the Drunk Man ceases to be acceptable as a metaphor for the imaginative inspiration of the poet and is felt rather to be an alibi for incoherence.

In the later parts of the work, the metaphysical aspect is dominant as the poet's speculative flights are sustained at much greater length. Some of these will take one into very strange regions where it is difficult to find one's bearings, but in my view it is the more sustained passages that give this work its stature as a genuine modern long poem. The sequential placing of certain items, big or small, still has its irritations, but the increasingly large-scale effects, fitfully at first but with greater assurance from the section called 'The Thistle's Characteristics' onwards, demand a large-scale response. If the reader accepts, as this reader does, that the long discursive passages entitled 'Metaphysical Pictures of the Thistle', 'A Stick-Nest in Ygdrasil' and 'Letter to Dostoevski' are successful, it is as writing of major stature that he must judge them to be so. And such sections as 'The Goal of Scottish History' and 'The Great Wheel', which are by no means entirely successful, do nevertheless convey a sense of major talents working at a highly ambitious pitch. Most criticism of *A Drunk Man* does not suggest that these are among the immediately appealing parts of the work, if only because so little is actually said about them, but they are certainly among the parts which most repay re-reading and pondering.

One wonders which of the 'main sections' MacDiarmid could have had in mind when he told George Ogilvie (6 August 1926) that he had been trying to bring it up to 'the high-water mark, the peaks of highest intensity' by projecting it on a 'a different altitude of poetry altogether'. Alan Bold is certain that the section in question 'must be' what he describes as 'the long evocation of a modern miracle of nativity' (ll. 571-723), though the relevant imagery actually changes from that of birth to resurrection, misread by Bold as 'growth'.[26] But there can be no 'must' about it: the identity of the passage MacDiarmid was referring to in his manuscript at that time is a matter for pure speculation—in which one is happy to join by hazarding the guess that he was thinking of the section to which he later gave the title 'Metaphysical Pictures of the Thistle' (ll. 2056-2183).

This is the culmination of a process which the poet began by seeing the thistle as an emblem of specifically Scottish antisyzygy in which high national aspirations are yoked to a mere weed—itself an uneasy combination of skinny, prickly leaves with rotund blossoms and volatile thistledown. From this, the thistle expands to encompass a series of prickly psychological and philosophical problems, suggested in terms of pairs of contraries: lust (the thorn in the flesh) and love, body and soul, passion and intellect, beauty and ugliness, matter and spirit, life and death, the real and the ideal, God and man, chaos and cosmos, oblivion and eternity. Thus, the Drunk Man, whose Scottish problem is how to 'pluck figs from thistles' or bring to fruition the abortive growth of his native Scots tradition, also has a metaphysical problem. He has to try to make sense of the thistle in its cosmic form as Yggdrasill, the Tree of Life that joins heaven and hell—and of which he is himself an infinitesimal part. His conclusion is to dismiss this monstrous thistle as a cosmic 'sport' spreading 'eternal mischief' through the universe. But a new set of 'Metaphysical Pictures' is still to come, in the section referred to.

Here, the romantic agony of the thistle as 'a symbol of the puzzle of man's soul', racked by the contraries of spirit and matter, culminates in defiance of the God of this world, a policeman with a taste for torture, who is opposed to the Unknown God of occult tradition. Life is seen as a disease that has been spawned in the poisoned drops leaking from eternity, and man in this mortal life labours only to give birth to his skeleton, from which in turn a cancerous light is given off: 'Disease o' Daith-in-Life and Life-in-Daith'. Other polar opposites, the Dark of chaos and the Light of creation, are brought together, and it is the Dark that is perceived as being not only primary but positive to Light's negative. 'Licht thraws nae licht upon itsel'', we are told, and

> only in the entire dark there's founts o' strength
> Eternity's poisoned draps can never file,
> And muckle roots thicken, deef to bobbies' feet. . . .
> —Darkness comes closer to us than the licht,
> And is oor natural element. We peer oot frae't
> Like cats' een bleezin' in a goustrous nicht

> (Whaur there is nocht to find but stars
> That look like ither cats' een),
> Like cats' een, and there is nocht to find
> Savin' we turn them in upon oorsels;
> Cats canna.

As this long passage develops, the poet does succeed in projecting the verse on to a 'different altitude', and it is hard to think of a modern poet who can outdo MacDiarmid in sustaining speculative thought throughout such constellations of images as one encounters here. It is rather like Milton or Dante looking through the other end of the metaphysical telescope:

> "Let there be Licht," said God, and there was
> A little.

This raises the question of the status of some of the speculative ideas, from antisyzygical cosmogony to Dostoevsky's 'Russian Idea', which are deployed with such panache in *A Drunk Man.* It may seem intellectually disreputable, if not morally irresponsible, to adopt pretty well any idea which might lead to the production of poetry of quality. But the poet's view at this time appears to have been that his art could afford to take such liberties at the cost of the downright scepticism, or Nietzschean nihilism, which underlay his position. When explaining to Pittendrigh Macgillivray that he cannot accept that the 'true' view of the thistle (ultimately the mystery of existence) is 'that seen in the sunny morning' (by the light of reason, or faith?), he goes on to say:

> In scores of directions I find two very different impulses animating me—1/ to avoid coming to any conclusions on certain fundamental matters: i.e. moral and ethical problems; and 2/ to experiment with the artistic expression of every different attitude to them I can conceive, i.e. to make every different attitude as wholly mine at a given time as I possibly can and find to what extent I can make a "convincing" poem of it.[27]

This in its way is not unlike Dostoevsky making novels in which, as Bakhtin observed, all ideas can take part 'with completely equal rights'. And MacDiarmid is uneasy about the pressure being put on him to 'take sides in regard to such questions instead of, as so far I have done, playing with them or watching them playing with me'.

Over thirty years later, despite his long-standing Marxist viewpoint, he answered John C. Weston's queries about some of the religious imagery in *A Drunk Man* by admonishing him that 'the point is not to be logical, but to deal with a diversity of ideas shooting from all directions on an intoxicated mind and be concerned only in dealing with them that poetry is made of them'.[28] The 'intoxicated mind' of the Dionysian poet can be irritating when used as a means of opting out of responsibility for his own work; but it seems to be the case that C.M. Grieve did at times create by letting the manic 'Hugh MacDiarmid' (or whatever name was given to the other self) have his head, regardless of Grieve's more sober use of that valuable property. There was no telling what the other self might get up to, but it was there, he felt, that the spark of genius might lie, and since that was wholly unpredictable, the only way to foster it was to allow it total freedom.

Yet this poet was a genuine intellectual—at least as excited by ideas as the average sensual man by sex, sport, violence, or money—and his playing with ideas or watching them play with him can be a genuine enough source of satisfaction in large parts of the work before us. It was in this sense that he set about the intellectualisation of poetry in Scots, which had reached such a vegetative state in the Kailyard—the main target of satirical attack in the work—and this was one of the main reasons why he was committed to writing *long* poems from *A Drunk Man* onwards.

The ideas that exercised his mind are rarely original, and they tend to come in other people's words, along with the attitudes he made his own at any given time, so that the influences which pervade *A Drunk Man* are legion. Nevertheless, the master-concept of antisyzygy can be seen as a fixed point in relation to many of these diverse influences. This may be illustrated in a number of instances, including a trio named by the poet himself:

> . . . there's Spengler,
> Or gin ye s'ud need mair than ane to teach ye,
> Then learn frae Dostoevski and frae Nietzsche.

Dostoevsky should come first, since he is featured as MacDiarmid's great hero and soul-mate in *A Drunk Man*, and is clearly a supreme exemplar of the combination of opposites. This point was made most emphatically by Stefan Zweig, who hailed Dostoevsky as 'the most perfect example of antinomy, the greatest dualist, that art, and maybe humanity, has ever known'.

> Dostoeffsky can only be understood in the light of this polarity. He is . . . not only the captive of his own duality, but also its missionary. In art as in life he desires to bring extremes together, to wed the most horrible, naked, cold, and foul reality with the noblest and sublimest dreams. He wishes us to find the divine in all things earthly; to discover in reality, fantasy; in sublimity, vulgarity; in transcendental spirit, the bitter salt of this world; and he wants us to experience these contrasted states and emotions simultaneously.[29]

MacDiarmid's chief mentor in Russian literature, D.S. Mirsky, also notes Dostoevsky's 'method of evolving a new style by the *fusion* of extremes'; and in 1925, the year when *A Drunk Man* was begun, there were two publications which expanded on this theme. The English translation of André Gide's book on Dostoevsky appeared, with its emphasis on the dualistic psychology of his characters and his ability to nurture the most discordant elements side by side, so as to produce 'an extraordinary wealth of antagonisms'; and Virginia Woolf included in *The Common Reader* her essay on 'The Russian Point of View' with the following reflections prompted by her reading of Dostoevsky in particular:

> When . . . elements of the soul are seen, not separately in scenes of humour or scenes of passion as our slower English minds conceive them, but streaked, involved, inextricably confused, a new panorama of the human mind is revealed. The old divisions melt into each other. Men are at the same time villains and saints; their acts are at once beautiful and despicable. We love and we hate at the same time. There is none of that precise division between good and bad to which we are used.[30]

According to MacDiarmid, the Caledonian Antisyzygy with its 'swift transitions' provided a similar, much-needed corrective for 'slow English minds' and those of Anglicised Scots. Dostoevsky, for his part, claimed that the ability to accommodate contradictions, and enter synchronically into diverse attitudes, emotions, and situations which Europeans could only take one at a time, was a Russian characteristic destined to produce the *Vsechelovek* (the 'Universal Man' of l. 1654) who would take over from a Europe exhausted by national and social conflicts originating in Western compartmentalism, specialism, social and moral rigidity. Caledonia, however, was well placed to cooperate in this process, since MacDiarmid maintained that the Celts, like the Russians, were poised on the edge of Europe where West and East could meet.

He also saw Herman Melville as an ally who could help him to an understanding of 'what this Russian has to teach'. It is in emulation of *Moby Dick* that the Drunk Man sets out on his voyages of speculative thought. And why is *Moby Dick* Melville's greatest work? Because for Melville, man is caught 'between apparently eternal and autonymous opposites such as good and evil, heaven and hell, spirit and matter', and 'in the white whale and the tremendous actions he sets off, the polarities that preoccupy Melville are for once magnificently expressed.[31]

Nietzsche is another pervasive influence on *A Drunk Man*, not least because of Zarathustra's remark that even the wisest of men are still 'only a discord and hybrid of plant and of ghost'—a phrase not used by MacDiarmid in so many words, but highly relevant to his way of seeing the thistle as a symbol of his own and other men's predicament. Nietzsche the poet-philosopher is so thoroughly antisyzygical that a recent analysis of his thought proposes 'thinking in antinomies as being itself Nietzsche's methodological principle' and sets out to examine 'the antagonism between art and knowledge in the light of contradiction as a fundamental principle. A whole list of antithetical concepts and images in Nietzsche's language seem to indicate a deep-seated antinomianism of thought and imagination'.[32] At the head of the list must come the dark Dionysian forces that are opposed to the bright Apollonian elements so as to produce 'a plethora of dualities and antagonisms'. And there is a memorable account of this by A.R. Orage, whose books as commentator on Nietzsche and anthologist of his aphorisms were, I think, better known to MacDiarmid than the original works themselves:

> In their larger aspects they [Apollo and Dionysos] are symbols of oppositions that penetrate the very stuff of consciousness and life; they are its warp and woof. Thus Apollo stands for Form as against Dionysos for Life; for Matter as against Energy; for the Human as against the Superhuman. Apollo is always on the side of the formed, the definite, the restrained, the rational; but Dionysos is the power that destroys forms, that leads the definite into the infinite, the unrestrained, the tumultuous and passionate. In perhaps their profoundest antithesis, Dionysos is pure energy (which Blake, a thorough Dionysian, said was eternal delight), while Apollo is pure form, seeking ever to veil and blind pure energy.[33]

As Orage pointed out elsewhere, Nietzsche was anticipated in this respect by Coleridge when he said in his lectures on Shakespeare that Dionysos was 'that power which acts without our consciousness in the vital energies of nature—the *vinum mundi* [wine of the world: for the Drunk Man, whisky, the water of life]—as Apollo was that of the conscious agency of our intellectual being'.[34]

Spengler, of course, followed Nietzsche and applied essentially the same antithetical principle to what he called the 'Apollonian' and the 'Faustian' in the historical cycles of his *Decline of the West.* That MacDiarmid made an explicit connection, however strained, between this and Gregory Smith's Caledonian Antisyzygy is demonstrated most clearly in his 'Theory of Scots Letters' of 1922-23. There he insists that Spengler was not concerned with the 'downfall' of the Western world:

> The idea he seeks to convey is rather "fulfilment"—the end of one civilisation and the beginning of another—the emergence of a new order. . . . Of the many antitheses out of which Herr Spengler builds up his thesis—which is destined to have an incalculable

> influence upon the future of human literature—that which predominates in every chapter is the distinction he draws between the "Apollonian" or classical, and the "Faustian" or modern type. . . . What is the cause of Doric [Scots] desuetude—of the absence of Doric drama and prose—but lack of fulfilment in the Spenglerian sense? What is this distinction between Apollonian and Faustian types, but just another way of phrasing the contrast between the false Scot—the douce travesty, the methodical level headed self-conscious creature of popular tradition—and the true Scot, rapid in his transitions of thought, taking all things as granted, turning to fun and even profanity with no misgivings, at his ease in both rooms of life.
>
> The canny Scot tradition has been "fulfilled" in the Spenglerian sense; and the future depends upon the freeing and development of that opposite tendency in our consciousness which runs counter to the conventional conceptions of what is Scottish. In other words, the slogan of a Scottish literary revival must be the Nietzschean "Become what you are".[35]

Which takes us back to Nietzsche, who like MacDiarmid overemphasized the Dionysian principle as against the Apollonian (which should have equal status in the conflict and interaction between them), because of the historical circumstances of the time and country in which he found himself placed. It will also take us back to Dostoevsky, because, in the account of Spengler used by MacDiarmid, we are told:

> Only in arts and letters can it be said that there are few or no possibilities of achievement. . . . Western Europe, with America, has exhausted her creative energies as Greece, Rome, Assyria, Babylon, exhausted their energies before her. She can add nothing to the sum of vitally new human knowledge, of fresh and adequate channels of self-expression. We must wait for the inevitable end or rather the new beginning which will come from a civilisation other than ours. . . . Already in Dostoevsky is to be found the first delineation of that new world. . . . Comparing Tolstoy and Dostoevsky he [Spengler] says: "beginning and end meet here. . . . The next thousand years belong to the Christianity of Dostoevsky".[36]

Spengler's attempt at a *Morphologie der Weltgeschichte* (morphology of world history) is linked with the expressionist movement in a passage of *A Drunk Man* (ll. 351-352) where the poet indicates that his poem shares the 'subjectivity' of contemporary German thought and art which was actually under attack in the review from which he lifted his German terms.[37] It could be said that expressionism is represented in *A Drunk Man* by Else Lasker-Schüler, whose poem 'Sphinx' he adapts for his own purposes a couple of pages later. Certainly she appeared in all the expressionist anthologies, but this seems to owe less to the qualities of her poetry than to the fact that she was married to Herwarth Walden, the leader of the *Sturm* group, and closely associated with other avowed expressionists. Perhaps in her role as 'the black swan of Israel' she could be said to represent the eastern wing of the movement. In any case, it is worth noting that MacDiarmid was attracted to her poem by the whiff of antisyzygy which he unerringly detected in its last line. And this despite his not having access, as it would appear, to the original German with its *Kampf mit Widerspruechen* ('struggle with contradictions').

There is perhaps a parallel between the relationship of imagism to expressionism and that of MacDiarmid's early Scots lyrics to *A Drunk Man*. Both imagism and expressionism in poetry are characterised by a condensed deployment of juxtaposed images, but with more scope for symbolic interplay in the latter. The extreme concentration on the individual image which was a feature of imagism, reflected in MacDiarmid's short lyrics, would seem to be a formidable obstacle for a poet aiming at a large-scale work like *A Drunk Man*. But the way out of that dilemma was suggested by Ezra Pound: 'The image is not an idea. It is a radiant node or cluster; it is . . . a *vortex*, from which, and through which, and into which, ideas are constantly rushing'.[38] This might look like a return to the suggestive attractions of symbolism through a back door, but it gives a very good indication of the way in which the master-images of *A Drunk Man* (the thistle, the moon, the whisky) function. The more fantastic strain of expressionist imagery also surfaces occasionally in MacDiarmid's work, where he seems to combine it with something of that special brand of 'wit' which had recently been rediscovered in the English metaphysical poets.

There are a number of other aspects of expressionism which might be paralleled in *A Drunk Man*. (1) Its preoccupation with extreme states of mind—a readiness to go too far in either direction, up or down—usually accompanied by distorted, grotesque imagery. (2) Its projection of the internal on to the external world, letting the irrational have free play. The imagery and logic of dreams have a special place in this, as in surrealism. (3) The consequent unstable, shifting subjectivity of the point of view which informs the whole work of art. (4) What was considered at the time to be a shocking preoccupation with sexual themes. (5) The hope that, through the violent destruction of traditional values, a new mystical vision would become feasible, even a new religion for modern man.

Of course, MacDiarmid shared in two of the major influences on expressionism, Dostoevsky and Nietzsche. And, sure enough, the expressionists had their own antisyzygy. As he reached the conclusion of his analysis of the movement, Roger Cardinal decided that 'the model I now need to work with is a conjunction of opposites', and he proceeded to illustrate, by reference to Dostoevsky's description of Myshkin's epileptic attacks in *The Idiot*, what he saw as 'a central Expressionist paradox, that extremes can combine in involuntary combinations which then take on meaning and necessity'.[39]

The poem which MacDiarmid adapted from Zinaida Hippius (ll. 353-368) is also antisyzygical, in that it scrutinizes with fascinated revulsion the oppressively physical, earth-bound image of a serpent only to end by seeing it as the soul. Mirsky says of her that 'like Dostoevsky's people, [she] oscillates between the two poles of spirituality and earthliness', but her sense of polarity is nothing to that of her husband, Dimitri Merezhkovsky. At the end of a long list of his works, Mirsky sums up as follows:

> All these writings are centred round one central idea—the 'polar' opposition of the Greek conception of the sanctity of the flesh, and of the Christian conception of the sanctity of the spirit, and the necessity of uniting them in one supreme synthesis. This central antithesis dominates a number of minor antitheses (such as the Nietszchean antithesis of Apollo and Dionysos), so that the general impression of his work as a whole is one of significant contrasts and relations. The identity of opposites and the synthesis of contrasts dominates all this world of interconnected poles. Every idea is a 'pole', an 'abyss' and a 'mystery'.[40]

There are moments when the Drunk Man is in some danger of being similarly obsessed, and one wonders if his creator took due heed of Mirsky's warning that Merezhkovsky's taste for antithetical thinking 'finished by ruining both himself and his style'. His influence was certainly pernicious in the case of Dimitri Mitrinović, with whose work in the *New Age*, under the name of M.M. Cosmoi, MacDiarmid would be familiar.

It was Mirsky also who observed of the other Russian poet adapted by MacDiarmid that Alexander Blok's work is 'akin to Dostoevsky's world of antithesis'.[41] It is Blok's *irony* that strikes one as his characteristic mode of antisyzygy—and the one which he felt best expressed the malaise of his own time. MacDiarmid is in tune with it when he writes of 'The grey that haunts the vievest green; / The wrang side o' the noblest scene / We ne'er can whummle to oor een' (ll. 1263-1265). But it was in a Scottish predecessor to whom he often paid tribute, John Davidson, that the metaphysical ramifications of the concept of irony can be seen most clearly:

> [Irony] is centric, the adamantine axis of the universe. At its poles are the illusions we call matter and spirit, day and night, pleasure and pain, beauty and ugliness. By it our enterprises are whirled

> away from our most resolved intentions. . . . Consciously, it is the deep complacence which contemplates with unalloyed satisfaction Love and Hate, the tiger and the nightingale, the horse and the blow-fly, Messalina and Galahad, the village natural and Napoleon. Unconsciously, it is the soul of the Universe. . . . Steep irony in Chaos, and the universe will string itself about it like crystals on a thread.[42]

Finally, there is one Scottish poet who is given a great deal of attention in *A Drunk Man*: Burns. The most pointed observation about him, for my purpose here, was made by Byron (himself the supplier in *Don Juan* of one of Gregory Smith's choicest illustrations in the text where all this began). Byron said of Burns:

> What an antithetical mind!—tenderness, roughness—delicacy, coarseness—sentiment, sensuality—soaring and grovelling, dirt and deity—all mixed up in that one compound of inspired clay![43]

Like the poet of *A Drunk Man*, 'a mongrel o' the fire and clay'.

III
Gallimaufry

THERE are many separable, fully formed poems in this work, but they drift, along with much else, on a stream of consciousness liberated by the whisky, ebbing and flowing with the moon, as the Drunk Man looks at the Thistle from every conceivable angle. Thistle and Moon are the poet's archetypal symbols around which figures of speech and patterns of thought and feeling constellate in astonishing profusion. Or, as suggested before, perhaps the best indication of how they function is to be found in Pound's words: 'The image . . . is a radiant node or cluster; it is a *vortex*, from which, and through which, and into which, ideas are constantly rushing'.

The inventiveness and vitality with which MacDiarmid responds to his key-images hold the work together, to the extent to which it *is* held together. For the rest, the inebriety of the Drunk Man is claimed, more or less humorously, as an extension of poetic licence. The poet is in effect the Drunk Man. The verse is *his*, as he observes succinctly to the reader: 'Hoo weel my verse embodies / The thistle you can read!' (ll. 1227-1228).

This leaves the reader with problems, the most awkward of which occur at points where a sense of humour (helpful though it is in other respects) will not mitigate the difficulty of discerning a significance in the sequence or inter-relation of the pieces, greatly varying in size, which are used as building-blocks in the structure of the work. Various attempts have been made to over-ride some of these problems, either by partition of the text or by tracing a thematic or climactic pattern which is seen as orientating the whole.

The building-blocks of *A Drunk Man* are separated from each other by the use of ellipses ('three dots')—a fact which remains unnoted throughout the most detailed consideration of its structure to date, in a dissertation by Ann E. Boutelle published in 1980. Boutelle states that the original format of the work has 'no division between the individual poems', thereby 'camouflaging the inherent pattern' which she would extrapolate from her perception that the work was 'conceived as a series of sections'.[44] She attempts to 'rediscover the lost sections' by taking the fifty-nine divisions made in the text of the work in the 1962 *Collected Poems* and arranging them consecutively in twelve groups. These groups are then called 'sections'—but if that is what they are, there is still no evidence to relate them to the sections in which the work is said to have been conceived. Where they can clearly be seen to have utility is in the breaking up of her long commentary into convenient parts.

Boutelle also provides some information about the titled divisions of the 1962 text, for which the publisher's editor was M.L. Rosenthal, the supervisor of her dissertation. It is known that another of Macmillan's editors, Emile Capouya, suggested to MacDiarmid on 26 February 1959 that *A Drunk Man* 'would be even more effective if it were divided into numbered sections, some of which, perhaps, might be given titles of your choosing. We feel that this simple device might help to avoid an initial embarrassment of riches'. And evidence is available to show that, nearly twenty months later, Rosenthal wrote to the poet saying that 'if you do divide up 'A Drunk Man Looks at the Thistle' as suggested, there will be no need to put it at the back [of the book]. Indeed it will be much more effective in its proper chronological place'.[45] However, Boutelle reports that MacDiarmid's correspondence with Rosenthal 'reveals that he readily accepted the suggestion to divide the sequence and that he quickly provided the titles'. This and a further statement that MacDiarmid 'consented to the breaking up of the sequence into individual poems' raises an important issue.[46] Does the mention of his accepting and consenting but not of his actually making the divisions indicate that it was not MacDiarmid who made them, or not MacDiarmid alone?

To the question who it was who actually made the divisions, Professor Rosenthal has given the following reply:

> Ann Boutelle's language is, actually, accurate. MacDiarmid raised no objections (his wishes would have been respected had he done so) but replied, and furnished the titles, with alacrity. They were

> his own titles, although of course he *may*—but I doubt it—have consulted with his wife, or friends like MacCaig and Smith in Scotland. It follows that the divisions, as well as the titles, were his own.[47]

But does it so follow? It seems to me that one might just as well conclude that MacDiarmid raised no objection to, and supplied titles for, divisions made by some one else.

A question-mark must therefore continue to hover over the matter in my mind at least, though this was not a factor in the view taken by the new editor, John C. Weston, who succeeded Rosenthal for the revised edition of the *Collected Poems* published in 1967. In his Preface to that edition, Weston urges readers to ignore as far as possible the titled divisions which have been allowed to remain, presumably for reasons of economy, in the text of *A Drunk Man*:

> One fault unavoidably remains in this edition, but mention of it by way of warning can to some extent lessen it. All the critics and admirers of MacDiarmid I know lament the breaking up of the masterpiece . . . into separate lyrics, each with its title. MacDiarmid now regrets that he did not persist in resisting the requests to do so.

And in the Preface to his own redaction of *A Drunk Man* (without the divisions) in 1971, Weston accepts that it was the poet himself who was

> unwisely persuaded . . . to break up the poem into parts and assign titles to each with the results that the unity of the poem is destroyed by the divisions—many of which obscure the real structure—and the effect of the poem is impaired by the banality of many of the titles.

Rosenthal has more recently, but not in my opinion convincingly, argued the case for the titled divisions in a book of which he is joint author, *The Modern Poetic Sequence* (1983). There, he does not consider the question of the effectiveness or otherwise of the titles supplied by MacDiarmid, and he follows Ann Boutelle in stating that 'in its original publication *A Drunk Man Looks at the Thistle* ran its 2685 lines of poetry continuously, without breaks to indicate that it was made up of fifty-nine separate poems'.[48] But the first edition of *A Drunk Man*, and all others, is full of structural breaks, indicated by the regular use of ellipses and by occasional changes of type-face, as well as changes in metrical form. What these indicate is, not indeed that the work was made up of fifty-nine separate poems, but that it was made up of at least ninety-four assorted items acknowledged by the poet to be structurally distinct—and internal evidence suggests that he could very well have added to that number. The supplying of titles in 1962 was mercifully confined to fifty-nine instances which are stated by Rosenthal to have been thereby given the status of 'separate poems', but clearly MacDiarmid could have gone on supplying more titles. In effect, he had already done that in 1925 and 1926 by giving titles to the items published in *The Glasgow Herald* and sent to J.K. Annand.

It may be observed that at every point but one where a division was made in 1962, MacDiarmid had already in 1926 used a structural ellipsis to indicate a break (as distinct from an ellipsis indicating a lesser interruption within a continuing unit). The solitary exception is the first of the 1962 dividing points (at l. 120), and this is the example on which Rosenthal argues his case for the desirability in *A Drunk Man* of 'what a poet does in numbering divisions, giving them titles, or using some other typographical indication'. Yet MacDiarmid had actually used such an indication in fifty-seven out of the fifty-eight instances relevant to Rosenthal's argument, though he does not take note of this fact.

The point is reiterated in *The Modern Poetic Sequence* that

> when MacDiarmid's *Collected Poems* was about to be published in the United States, in 1962, his editor suggested that American readers would be greatly aided by having titles for the separate poems, especially since very few knew Scots at all. MacDiarmid quickly accepted the suggestion, providing titles with such alacrity that it seemed he had thought of them from the start.[49]

But the letter from Rosenthal already quoted above indicates that MacDiarmid in October 1960, more than a year and a half after the suggestion had first been made to him, had still not divided the work in the manner suggested. And rather than viewing the operation as a matter of supplying titles for fifty-nine pre-existing poems or 'clearly separate, independent pieces', it seems that he then saw it as altering the nature of his work to such an extent that it could no longer take its chronological place in the corpus of his poems but would require to be relegated to the back of the volume, where the 'Hitherto Uncollected' items were to appear. If the poet subsequently provided titles with alacrity, this would be in accordance with his well-known ability to work at great speed, but it remains true that he had already had many months in which to think about the matter. On the other hand, the suggestion that these titles, like the separate poems, may have existed 'from the start' would have to be reconciled with the fact that MacDiarmid did supply titles for some parts of the work in 1925 and 1926, but they differ from the titles provided in the *Collected Poems*. For example, 'Creation's Whirligig' (1962) was in 1926 called 'The Hanging Judge', and it was extracted from a sequence entitled 'Twenty-Four Ways of Looking At The Thistle'. What, if anything, in the fifty-nine separate poems corresponds to that sequence?

The Modern Poetic Sequence is a survey of the genre to which *A Drunk Man* belongs, and the authors, Rosenthal and Sally M. Gall, mention MacDiarmid's work along with examples by Eliot, Pound, Yeats and Crane as contributing to 'the genre's full flourishing' in the Twenties. They approach the poetic sequence through what they call 'lyrical structure', this being seen as 'necessary for insight into the character of the sequence—its balancings of stress and interplay among its centres of passionate preoccupation'. The nature of lyrical structure, loosely associated with organic form, is hard for them to pin down, but they illustrate its function in a way which has a familiar ring to it: 'The ability to hold in balance conflicting and logically irreconcilable energies, and to identify their presence and intensity, is felt as mastery over contradiction, mastery by poetic conversion into a pattern of unruly but mobilized affects'.[50] Rosenthal and Gall miss the connection of this with MacDiarmid's antisyzygy, but the implication must surely be that the latter is peculiarly well suited to the characteristic modern form of the poetic sequence as they see it.

Their emphasis on 'lyrical' structure, however, results in an antagonism towards the 'discursive', and they summarily dismiss the 'more discursive stretches' of *A Drunk Man* because these are said to 'impose a factitious continuity of disputation' on the work. Consequently they turn to MacDiarmid's treatment of the sexual theme, which, though extensive, is not considered to be unduly discursive or disputatious.

Many critical accounts of *A Drunk Man* tend to concentrate on this theme, and it is useful to look at it for a moment in a historical perspective. In Scotland in 1926 it came as a severe shock to contemporary taste and mores. The ballad associations of much of MacDiarmid's verse (as of some of Yeats's) would have helped to make a degree of sexual frankness acceptable, but hardly to this extent. And when blatant sexuality invaded the territory of religion, only the obscurity of some of his Scots allowed him to get away with what would have been seen as obscene blasphemy. It was perhaps in this respect that MacDiarmid's work was most daringly, shockingly, 'modern'.

He was modern too in his Freudian attitude towards

> the physical basis
> O' a' life's seemin' airs and graces.
>
> It's queer the thochts a kittled cull
> Can lowse or splairgin' glit annul.
> (ll. 581-584.)

And like that 'Psycho-Somatic Quandry', the sado-masochist motif in his poem is an up-to-date version of the combination of opposites on a sexual basis. But along with his enlightened approach to sexual matters he retained much of the Puritan conviction of his upbringing that the flesh as such is shamefully degrading. Indeed his sexual psychology springs from a mixture of the two—and one might add that his combination of the enlightened celebration of sex with revulsion at its grosser side is perhaps commoner in human experience than now fashionable attitudes would lead one to believe.

Commentaries on *A Drunk Man* which highlight the sexual theme tend to oversimplify it, and they avoid its confrontation with other elements in the work such as the line of thought culminating in the conclusion that the life process which sex propagates is itself a mistake, a freak of nature, a disease of matter. It is not just the interest inherent in MacDiarmid's treatment of the sexual theme, or the perennial popularity of sex itself as a subject, which attracts so much attention to it in the work. There is also the fact that readers get tired of the proliferation of contrasts and sudden switches of attention when taken to such extremes, and they gratefully latch on to this theme as one which can be seen to run through a whole string of related items. It does so quite clearly, though some items are scattered widely apart from the others and there is sometimes a long wait before the thread can be picked up again. But the danger in much critical commentary is that some such thread may be presented as if it were *the* clue to the whole—conferring upon it indeed 'a factitious continuity'.

It would not have been difficult for MacDiarmid and / or Scott to have brought together the scattered items in which he explores his sexual theme, so that the reader could follow the thread without distraction throughout a whole long section or movement of the work. This would have obvious advantages. The disadvantages are that the unity of theme displayed in this case would reflect awkwardly on other parts where no such unified movement is possible, and it would continue for many pages without those startling interruptions and conflicting currents which (on the occasions when they are deployed significantly) contribute a good deal to the lively diversity of the work as it stands. But it remains true, I think, that readers would get greater satisfaction if there were more sustained sequences of linked items such as the one which begins at l. 571 (not six lines before, as the awkward division introduced in 1962 would indicate).

Criticism has tended to be enthusiastic but not very clear about this sequence, and especially its high-point, the celebrated poem 'O Wha's The Bride', which was a favourite of Yeats. It is certainly a mysterious poem, but the crux of it would perhaps emerge more clearly if more attention were paid to the piece which precedes it, 'In the Last Analysis' (ll. 604-11). This is a dialogue between a male who has old-fashioned, romantic notions about the 'purity' of the female—or at any rate the sort of female with whom he would envisage marriage—

and the girl herself. The male speaker is astonished that the revelation of his animal sexuality, of which he is abjectly ashamed, has had no apparent effect on the girl, whose 'bonny een / Are as they hadna seen'. But she retorts:

—Gin you could pierce their blindin' licht
You'd see a fouler sicht!

'Fouler' because his preconceptions about the 'pure' desires of 'nice' girls would lead him to regard the same animal sexuality in her as even 'dirtier' than his own.

Then follows 'O Wha's the Bride', in ballad form, with another dialogue between male and female, and traditional ballad imagery. Here, the bride, who is physically *virgo intacta*, nevertheless admits to the suspicious bridegroom that she has lost her virginity. She blames a man who died before she was born for doing 'this evil thing' to her, leaving her maidenhead 'as it were on a corpse'.

If this were indeed a traditional ballad, the reader might interpret the mystery in supernatural terms, remembering for example that revenants were popularly believed capable of returning from the grave and acting as ghostly lovers. But the theme of MacDiarmid's poem, like the previous one, is concerned with illusions about feminine purity, and especially the false values attributed by the male to virginity at least where his intended bride is concerned.

The 'evil thing' acknowledged by the bride is, I think, an allusion to original sin. Ever since Adam's fall brought sin and death into the human world, 'frae sire to son'—and from mother to daughter, and across the sexes—'we gang / And coontless corpses in us thrang' (ll. 1956-1957). Human life survives death only through sex, the act of procreation, which the Fall made shameful to Adam and Eve. And since life can only be continued through the *loss* of virginity, it is pointless to attribute positive moral value to virginity as such. The bride only has her being as a result of the loss of virginity by her parents, and their parents, and so on back to the original pair. She is physically a virgin, but her physical make-up is entirely the product of the sexual union of her fallen, mortal ancestors, so that their 'corpses' live on in her very cells. She cannot therefore be physically 'pure', and her bridegroom must forget his illusions about that and appreciate what she does have to offer him:

And on my lips ye'll heed nae mair,
And in my hair forget,
The seed o' a' the men that in
My virgin womb ha'e met.

In its wider context in *A Drunk Man* there is another dimension to this poem which is obscured when it is treated in isolation, as has so often been the case. By having the bride carry a bunch of white thistles the poet links her with his Scottish Muse, about whose real nature he has already suggested (through his adaptation of a poem by Blok) he is liable to delude himself. In some moods he may have been tempted to idealise her romantically as a pure, virginal figure, but the truth about Scotland, as about the bride in the ballad, is more complicated and a good deal less ethereal. (Blok may have felt something similar in his progress from the early 'Poems about the Beautiful Lady' to his later poems about Russia.)

The connection between the sexual and the blasphemous, which (like virginity) has lost a great deal in status since 1926, is largely due to MacDiarmid's mixing of apparently orthodox Christian elements with material from the occult sources of 'alternative', underground religion. Prominent in the latter is the explicitly sexual nature of the Deity that created the world by the union of its male and female aspects. MacDiarmid turns this idea in two directions. On the one hand, man in the sexual act is participating most fully in the divine creative power, as when the Drunk Man proclaims to Jean

> that sheer licht o' life that when we're joint
> Loups through me like a fire a' else t' aroint.
>
> (ll. 2030-2031.)

This reflects the close association (in the Cabbala, for example) of the light of creation with the seminal fluid—and the Drunk Man is capable of carrying his share of the divine seed to such lengths that he has his body confiding to his mind:

> 'I've been startled whiles to find,
> When Jean has been in bed wi' me,
> A kind o' Christianity!'
>
> (ll.572-574.)

On the other hand, from the idea that the feminine element is the lower of the two, and accountable for the gross world of matter, he turns the traditional Christian imagery into the following:

> Faither in Heaven, what gar'd ye tak'
> A village slut to mither me,
> Your mongrel o' the fire and clay?
> The trollop and the Deity share
> My writhen form as tho' they were
> A picture o' the time they had
> When Licht rejoiced to file itsel'
> And Earth upshuddered like a star.
>
> (ll. 1363-1370.)

Other elements of occult mythology are used to serio-comic effect in MacDiarmid's ambivalent symbol of the moon. The moon is associated with the 'eternal feminine' which he tended to link with Sophia, the divine wisdom (God's 'Other', in feminine form). But Sophia can be seen both in the radiant, celestial shape in which she appeared to Solovyov and (by way of the Gnostic account of her degradation in the material world) in the incarnate form of the whore from Tyre, Helena, who accompanied Simon Magus, and who was also called Selene, the Moon. The Moon in MacDiarmid's poem changes face in similarly startling fashion, and he stage-manages a dramatic confrontation between her and her bastard offspring, the Thistle.

The Thistle is what this whole work is 'about', as its title plainly indicates. But since the Thistle is ultimately 'the mystery o' life bewrayed to a wretched weed', it is not likely that the Drunk Man, however hard he looks at it, will come up with much that can be neatly categorised. Near the beginning of his monologue he explains that he has no faith in anything he can explain, and starts where the philosophers leave off.

If, as I have suggested, a main function of the thistle image is to embody the combination of contraries that confronts us in 'this puir transitory stage' of existence, the usual effect of this on the Drunk Man is for the contraries to tear him apart. And in his particular situation the negative elements appear as dominant over the positive. Amongst the strongest traditional associations of the thistle for MacDiarmid are those of the Bible, where its appearance is consequent upon the fall of Adam, to whom God says: 'Cursed is the ground for thy sake. . . . Thorns also and thistles shall it bring forth to thee'. Hence the thistle becomes the type of the weed in contrast to the fruit of the earth. Christ, in the Sermon on the Mount, asks: 'Do men gather grapes of thorns, or figs of thistles?'. And as Christ was to be crowned in mockery with thorns, so for the poet the thistle becomes an image of crucifixion.

Elsewhere, in 1923, MacDiarmid had addressed an 'Apology' to his Muse as follows:

> Ech, Muse, hoo I ha'e fa'en short!
> Twine the thrissel wi' the laurel,
> Since I turn frae payin' thee court
> Wi' gowks an' gomerils to quarrel.[51]

And towards the end of his poetic career, in 1958, he conceded only that

> The thistle is a handy thing
> If a barefoot foe comes trampling.
> Else, being a worthless weed, it's not
> A fitting symbol for a Scot.[52]

In *A Drunk Man* one might pick out two factors which tend to heighten the negative side of the poet's attitude: the animus of his satirical attack on the 'gowks an' gomerils' of contemporary Scotland, designed to scarify them into belated awareness of its abject decay, and his role as a poet in the Romantic mould, a patriot who is also an outsider, and a martyr crucified by his own feelings. For him, the specifically Scottish dimension of the thistle is rooted in the barrenness and perversity of Scottish life. 'But', he asks, 'will a Scotsman never / Frae this vile growth be freed?' Apparently not, on the evidence of this work—which is why he planned in its successor, *Cencrastus*, to show that it *was* possible in the end for the Scotsman to get rid of the thistle, 'the bur o' the world'. And naturally, in *A Drunk Man*, his animus is extended to the thistle in its universal symbolic form as the puzzle of the nature of life which confronts all mankind, a problem exacerbated by the fact that none of us 'ha'e the thistle's pooer / To see we're worthless and believe 't'.

The positive side of the thistle in the poem is relatively weak, and, unlike the negative side, it is never allowed to stand alone. In 'The Crying of the Fair' (ll. 455-476) the poet celebrates that splendid local specimen of the Cotton Thistle, said to be at least eight feet high, which was carried in procession on Common Riding Day in the Langholm of his youth (and indeed still is). In his imagined role as the bearer of the Langholm thistle, he declares that he will dance that night with the stars of heaven. Even so, he does not end on that exalted note but settles instead for Jean as his partner, not indeed as she is, but 'as she was on her weddin' day'. Then comes 'Man and the Infinite', in which the poet identifies with a cosmic force combining the symbols of world-serpent and thistle. In this rhapsodic mood he declares that the thistle will yet unite Man and the Infinite. But at the end of the piece, Man is confronted with the void left in his heart when the thistle flies off to become a phoenix in paradise.

The poet also tells us that there are moments when the moonlight seems to insubstantialise the 'grisly form' of the thistle. These moments are certainly high-points to him, but he is nevertheless aware that the grisly form is never really transcended, and that the light is surrounded by an ever-increasing darkness. Later, he juggles awkwardly with some lines in Italian to suggest that he is able to see the thistle as his own version of what Dante saw in the eternal light at the end of the *Paradiso*. But this is at once rejected as the siren song of the South which has held his Viking North for too long in its spell.

The Drunk Man confesses to a certain sympathy with the thrawnness or sheer bloody-mindedness of the thistle in remaining true to its own worthless nature, but he can make no sense of it, and the other aspects of the thistle featured in the poem are very largely repellent or derogatory. He sees it as though he were Dr Jekyll taking a good look at Mr Hyde. It is a Freudian complex, the Scots aboulia, a repulsive image of his own and his nation's soul, the secret contamination which humanity has tried to keep hidden, the blind, fruitless growth of human life: 'A' the uncouth dilemmas o' oor natur' / Objectified in vegetable maitter'. It is a pickled foetus or a corpse, an eaten and spewed-like thing, a skeleton abortively part-animated by a soul, a missing link, a creaking hinge between the dead and the living, a vegetable cat's melody, a spider's web, a ruined sail, a flaw or tragic crack in creation, a strangling rictus, a sterile spasm, a stricture in the groins of light, a gallows. It is the mind-forged manacles of morality, empty intellect, mortality itself. In a shift to political allegory, it is the plant which produces the unique blossom of the General Strike, only to end in self-crucifixion. It is the cosmic Tree of Life which seems to the poet merely to spread 'eternal mischief' throughout the universe.

As for the shoot of human life stemming from this thistle-tree, he sees it as a freak growth that is destined to be superseded, and he takes a perverse satisfaction in being able to see clearly that all beliefs which have placed a value on it have been delusions. The agony of crucifixion on the thistle can only be withstood by drawing on forces in chaos, the abyss, the Dark. If the poet is to escape 'the silly horrors o' oor fates', he will have to transcend all that mankind has yet amounted to.

At this point it is necessary to take note of some of the headier speculations in *A Drunk Man* which are generally passed by on the other side of the critical commentaries. In 'The Goal of Scottish History' (ll. 1640-1744), MacDiarmid declares his aim of joining forces with Dostoevsky in 'workin' oot mankind's great synthesis'. This is an allusion to the 'Russian Idea' of Dostoevsky's speech at the Pushkin memorial in which he claimed that Pushkin, the supreme national poet who could paradoxically identify himself with other nationalities, was the type of the Universal Man of the future: 'This Pan-Humanity is the national characteristic of Russia, and Russia's mission is to effect the final synthesis of all mankind'.[53] In 'The Great Wheel' (ll. 2395-2658), it is made clear that the Universal Man is needed because there is no future for man in his existing form. The vision of the Great Wheel of cosmic history reveals 'The horror o' the endless Fate / A'thing's whirled in predestinate', and this can be mitigated only if the poet can out-top all that men have ever sung or hoped, since

Nae verse is worth a ha'et until
It can join issue wi' the Will
That raised the Wheel and spins it still.

What is demanded of him is an expansion of consciousness to cosmic proportions so that through his poetry he will contribute to the evolution of the Universal Man—and beyond Him:

> And organs may develop syne
> Responsive to the need divine
> O' single-minded humankin'.
>
> The function, as it seems to me,
> O' Poetry is to bring to be
> At lang, lang last that unity.

The mind may boggle—but that no doubt goes to show that the mind in question belongs to one of those readers mentioned in the 'Author's Note' 'whose rational intelligences are all too insusceptible of realising the enormities of which "highbrows" of my type are capable—even in Scotland'. However, the grandiose vision of the Drunk Man is soon made to collapse under the weight of Scottish history and what he sees as its grotesque inheritance in present reality.

Until the advent of those apocalyptic developments in which 'The wheel'll tine its stature fast / And birl in time inside oor heids', the spectacle of existence is endurable only as an aesthetic phenomenon, as Nietzsche said. And in the drama our imagination makes of life, 'as stage by stage the play proceeds, Apollo must build continually more beautiful, more enduring forms, which Dionysos, in turn, must continually surmount and transcend. The drama of life is thus a perpetual movement towards a climax that never comes'.[54]

A Drunk Man seems to me to accord well enough with that view, though as a modern work 'beautiful' is too old-fashioned a word for its form. But there is a widespread tendency (recently endorsed by the authority of the *Oxford Companion to English Literature*) not only so see the work as building up to a clear-cut climax but to extract from it a pattern into which the climax is thought to fit. This line of thought seems to have originated in a less than careful reading of some remarks made by David Daiches in an essay published in 1962. Daiches there described the section of *A Drunk Man* entitled 'Farewell to Dostoevski' as

> a lyric whose rising elegiac rhythms draw the whole poem into a plangent sense of loss which yet, somehow, is related to a sense of hope:
>
> > *The wan leafs shak' atour us like the snaw.*
> > *Here is the cavaburd in which Earth's tint.*
> > *There's naebody but Oblivion and us,*
> > *Puir gangrel buddies, waunderin' hameless in't.*

> *The stars are larochs o' auld cottages,*
> *And a' Time's glen is fu' o' blinnin' stew.*
> *Nae freen'ly lozen skimmers: and the wund*
> *Rises and separates even me and you.*
>
> *I ken nae Russian and you ken nae Scots.*
> *We canna tell oor voices frae the wund.*
> *The snaw is seekin' everywhere: oor herts*
> *At last like roofless ingles it has f'und,*
>
> *And gethers there in drift on endless drift,*
> *Oor broken herts that it can never fill;*
> *And still—its leafs like snaw, its growth like wund—*
> *The thistle rises and forever will!*
>
> This seems to me to be the true emotional centre of *A Drunk Man.*

Having said that, however, Daiches immediately added:

> Yet MacDiarmid cannot allow himself such a simple slogan as 'The thistle rises and forever will' without raising the counter-statement. His nationalism does not go in for crude sloganising. So:
>
> The thistle rises and forever will,
> Getherin' the generations under't.
> This is the monument o' a' they were,
> And a' they hoped and wondered.
>
> Here the thistle is a gravestone as well as a symbol of hope, and we are left to make what we will of the conflicting meanings. The poem then plunges into another lively ironic account of the barren civilisation of modern Scotland.[55]

Returning to the same same passage some twenty years later, Daiches has emphasized that 'the sloganizing implications' of the line, 'The thistle rises and forever will', 'are immediately denied by what follows in the poem, a sardonic reflection that the thistle rises over the buried generations, a monument "o' a' they were, and a' they hoped and wondered" '.[56]

The point was in some need of emphasis in view of what others had made of this passage in the interim. In a pamphlet about *A Drunk Man* published in 1970, John C. Weston reached the surprising conclusion that 'the poem is very largely about progress'. He added that 'the validity of this view depends upon the Drunk Man's faith in the spirit of man', and that 'the longest section of the poem, on all mankind's predicament and progress', ends with 'the structural climax, the Drunk Man's assertion of faith . . . in the intrepid and indomitable spirit of man, "The thistle rises and forever will" '.[57] The following year, in a 'Critical Note' to his edition of the work, Weston again indicated a huge 'central section' (in fact nearly half of the entire work) as being 'about the process of mankind's development (ll. 1004-2243). Near the end of this long section on progress comes the ideological climax of the poem, when the Drunk Man affirms his belief in man's past and future progress in quite explicit and pointed terms: "The thistle rises and forever will" '. Not only is this for Weston the structural and ideological climax: it is also said to be the thematic climax of the work.[58]

For Ann Boutelle, too, 'at the centre of the poem, "the thistle rises and forever will", mysterious in its triumph and its ability to transform human agony into a kind of ecstasy',[59] but she gives a rather different emphasis to its connection with man's development:

> Just as earlier in the sequence, the phallus had risen in defiance of Jean's absence and in the presence of the 'strange Goddess', so the thistle rises here, indomitable, inexplicable, and insistent on its own vitality.[60]

Evidently this is also the sexual climax of the work.

It is, however, Alan Bold's presentation of the rising thistle that has achieved most prominence. In several books he has repeated his account of *A Drunk Man* as depicting the transformation of an inebriated defeatist Scot into 'a triumphant artistic redeemer—"A greater Christ, a greater Burns" '. What MacDiarmid says about the latter is that the most a greater Christ, a greater Burns will do is 'to gi'e bigger pegs / To folly and conceit to hank their rubbish on'. But Bold sees this composite national saviour as MacDiarmid himself, whose 'characteristics' the Drunk Man acquires, and this is said to give unity to the whole work: 'Holding together all the counterpointed images is the Drunk Man's increasingly steady vision of Scotland as a country with the potential to liberate itself from centuries of defeatism'. While the vision somehow holds all the images together, 'slowly the insobriety is replaced by a spiritual intensity as Scotland rises to rebirth'. Thus the grand climax is reached:

> Resurrection, rebirth, renaissance all come together in MacDiarmid's great work which is both universal in theme and insistently Scottish in origin:
>
> The thistle rises and forever will,
> Getherin' the generations under't.
> This is the monument o' a' they were,
> And a' they hoped and wondered.[61]

It is essential, however, to consider the significance of these lines in context, in the 'Farewell to Dostoevski' quoted in full by Daiches in the passage above. The wintry setting of the 'Farewell' is characteristic of MacDiarmid in that it is both cosmic and at the same time reminiscent in its concrete detail of a Highland glen that has been 'cleared' of its people so that only the ruined *larochs* of their cottages remain. In this desolate setting, the thistle is likened to a blizzard blowing through the broken hearts of the Drunk Man and his solitary companion, Dostoevsky. They are seen as beggarly tramps, wandering homeless in the storm, without even a language in common.

There is nothing there with which to associate the rising of the thistle but the rising of the blizzard, whether in the frozen wastes of the cosmos, Dostoevsky's Siberia, or MacDiarmid's deserted Highland glen. By continuing to rise forever—'its leafs like snaw, its growth like wund'—the thistle will hardly make a reassuring monument for the hopes and speculations of the generations buried under it. 'Oblivion' is not in the poem for nothing. And in the lines which follow immediately afterwards, the Drunk Man sees the thistle as representing what he most loathes and repudiates. It is 'the barren tree, dry leaves and cracklin' thorns' which he identifies with mere 'empty intellect'; a weed which has strangled the harvests of the sun and moon; a self-crucifying 'heraldic horror' rising in twisted religious form from the cancerous soil of Scotland; a secret tumour, associated with the slums of Glasgow, which spreads disease throughout the national life.

The reading which leads Bold to disregard all this and put in its place a vision of Scotland rising to resurrection, rebirth and renaissance, requires one to backtrack 1750 lines from 'The thistle rises' to 'The thistle yet'll unite / Man and the Infinite!' But even if one were to stretch a point and accept his interpretation of the latter, there is no reason apparent to me why it should be given a free transfer over 1750 lines to the former. And this manoeuvre is followed by a jump in the other direction, to the 'Great Wheel' section, where we are told:

"A Scottish poet maun assume
The burden o' his people's doom,
And dee to brak' their livin' tomb.

In his book *Modern Scottish Literature*, Bold ends his account of *A Drunk Man* at that point. However, what follows in MacDiarmid's text is:

Mony ha'e tried, but a' ha'e failed.
Their sacrifice has nocht availed.
Upon the thistle they're impaled.

This would seem to lessen the likelihood of a national rebirth. But when Bold does take cognisance of these lines elsewhere, his comment on them is: 'This time the sacrifice will be worth the effort; such is the poetic conclusion the Drunk Man comes to after exhaustively exploring the spiritual and cultural map of Scotland. There is nothing more to add. . . .'[62] MacDiarmid, however, does add the following:

> *You maun choose but gin ye'd see*
> *Anither category ye*
> *Maun tine your nationality."*

This whole passage, which we have now with some difficulty managed to retrieve, is to be understood as spoken by one of the poet's 'inner voices', telling him that the only way to avoid the grisly fate of being impaled on the thistle is to lose his Scots nationality. And the other 'inner voice' replies: 'Auch, to Hell, / I'll tak' it to avizandum'. That is, he will go off and think about it—thereby evading the question while the poet spends the next few lines looking desperately for a way out and finally has recourse to the ignominious device of a line of asterisks.

MacDiarmid does still manage to rescue his poem by the quality of his poetry on the final page, but it is worth noting that this includes a statement which again reveals the inadequacy of sloganising interpretations of 'the thistle rises':

> For aince it's toomed my hert and brain,
> The thistle needs maun fa' again.

It must be conceded, however, that the Bold version continues to flourish, since it is a paraphrase of this which appears in the new *Oxford Companion to English Literature.*

Perhaps a contributing factor to the view of *A Drunk Man* as depicting the evolution of a poetic saviour is the account of it given by MacDiarmid himself in 1958:

> The general (as beyond the particularly Scottish) theme of *A Drunk Man Looks at the Thistle* is to show 'a beautiful soul in the making'—to trace, that is to say, its rise through all struggle and contradiction till it stands out a self-conscious, self-directing personality—a purified person.[63]

Bold takes that 'straight', with no indication of unease about the extent to which it diverges from what actually goes on in the poem. But surely this is not MacDiarmid's own voice commenting on his own poem? If one knows one's MacDiarmid one at once suspects an unacknowledged quotation. But what could it be? An educated guess might conjure up a commentary on Dostoevsky's plans for *The Idiot.* Or maybe Shestov on Plotinus? But, as is so often the case with this crafty poet, it is extremely unlikely that one will make the right guess.

The answer to the question posed is: James Lindsay on Dante. The passage occurs in Lindsay's *Essays Literary and Philosophical* (Edinburgh 1896, p. 28). And Lindsay adds that 'the nucleus—the initial focus or dynamic centre—around which all this vast and wondrous conception of personality has for our poet gathered, is just the real and beautiful human personality of Beatrice'.[64] Evidently, in the 'powerful structure' of *A Drunk Man*, Tam o' Shanter's Kate and Leopold Bloom's wife, Molly, will have to give way to Dante's Beatrice.

The claim that *A Drunk Man* possesses 'a powerful narrative structure drawn partly from Burns's "Tam o' Shanter" (the reluctant return to a nagging wife) and partly from Joyce's *Ulysses* (the Odyssey towards a folksy Penelope figure)' awaits substantiation.[65] The parallels educed seem to me to be weak and in fact trivial.

There are, of course, specific references to 'Tam o' Shanter' in the section entitled 'The Splore' (ll. 811-860). But the effect of this is on the whole unfortunate because MacDiarmid's control of the sequence is shaky, his switching from the drink to the sex theme and back again is awkward, and the allusions to 'Tam o' Shanter' (a poem in which these two themes are handled with consummate ease) do not help. There is a bit of misplaced moralising in ll. 841-844 which is again unfortunate, because it is in marked contrast to the finely controlled irony with which Burns manipulates the moralising element throughout his poem.

As to *Ulysses*, the aspects of that work which seem to me to have less trivial significance where *A Drunk Man* is concerned are its employment of a 'stream of consciousness' and what at the time could be called 'expressionist' techniques, especially in the night-town section, together with Joyce's assault on the whole edifice of sexual censorship which MacDiarmid also felt had been built into literary English but from which he could gratefully and productively escape in Scots.

On the wide level of genre, there is clearly a broad base shared by MacDiarmid and Joyce. For the suggestion that the genre of *A Drunk Man* is 'Menippean satire' I am obliged to Peter McCarey, a Russian specialist who doubted, reasonably enough, if MacDiarmid had read Dostoevsky to any extent, but after reading Bakhtin on Dostoevsky's literary genre, came to the conclusion that the poet took the genre from the novelist. Some of the features of Menippean satire as defined by Bakhtin do indeed appear in *A Drunk Man*: for example, 'sharp contrasts and oxymoronic combinations, . . . abrupt transitions and shifts'. But of course this need not imply that MacDiarmid took the genre over from Dostoevsky. Rather, by placing Dostoevsky in relation to his categories of Menippean satire and, later, carnivalesque, Bakhtin reveals that there is a very long literary history behind the peculiarities of a Dostoevsky or a MacDiarmid which is relevant to both. On a similar basis, *Ulysses* and *The Waste Land* have been analysed in terms of Menippean satire.

I think it is the 'carnivalesque', however, that is most appropriate to *A Drunk Man*, because the drunkenness of the man is traditionally associated with the carnival spirit in which one finds '"life turned inside out", "life upside down" ("*monde à l'envers*")'. This involves blasphemous, obscene and parodic elements, since the hierarchial restrictions of normal life are suspended, and 'carnival brings together, unifies, weds and combines the sacred with the profane, the lofty with the lowly, the great with the insignificant, the wise with the stupid'. It is indeed yet another manifestation of antisyzygy, and Bakhtin's most striking characterisation of the 'carnival image' is as follows:

> It strives to encompass and unite within itself both poles of evolution or both members of an antithesis; . . . and the upper pole of a two-in-one image is reflected in the lower, after the manner of the figures in playing cards. It could be expressed thus: opposites meet, look at one another, know and understand one another.[66]

Drink, the Drunk Man's whisky, is the lubricant for the 'carnivalesque' freeing of inhibitions and reversal of established norms and conventions. And MacDiarmid was quick to associate himself with Joyce through a popular carnival tradition which is celebrated in the 'Abbot of Unressoun' material he extracted from Jamieson's Scots dictionary and used in 'Following Rebecca West in Edinburgh', one theme of which (in 1922, the year of *Ulysses*) was the need for a Scottish Joyce to do justice to the Scottish capital.[67]

Another writer who displays in overwhelming abundance the characteristics of Bakhtin's categories is Arno Holz, whose Gargantuan gallimaufry, *Die Blechschmiede* ('The Tinsmithy') attracted MacDiarmid's attention shortly before he wrote *A Drunk Man*. He adopted for his own work the term 'gallimaufry', used by H.G. Scheffauer to describe that extraordinary product of Holz's 'cosmic-lyrical boiler factory'.[68] In the normal meaning of the word, 'a heterogeneous mixture, confused jumble, ridiculous medley', this was of course misleading, since the vortices of MacDiarmid's key-symbols with their associated clusters of images and other linking devices of allusions and repeated patterns are present in the work precisely because he did try to hold it together as a whole, however loosely and at times precariously. However, the term has its uses as an advance disclaimer.

On the other hand, it is possible that in calling his work 'a gallimaufry in braid Scots' MacDiarmid had at the back of his mind a passage in Spenser which with a little adaptation could be used ironically to his advantage:

> He hath laboured to restore, as to theyr rightfull heritage such

> good and naturall English words, as have ben long time out of use and almost cleane disherited. . . . Now they have made our English tongue, a gallimaufry or hodgepodge of al other speches. . . . Whose first shame is, that they are not ashamed, in their own mother tonge straungers to be counted and alienes. The second shame no lesse then the first, that what so they understand not, they streight way deeme to be sencelesse, and not at al to be understode.[69]

MacDiarmid took a rather similar line in his 'Author's Note' of 1926 (included in this volume as an appendix). He was trailing his coat before those readers who were hostile to his experiments with 'synthetic Scots'—'synthetic' in the sense that its vocabulary was drawn from diverse historical and regional strata of the language—but he was also supplying ammunition which could be used against his work. By saying that his gallimaufry followed the logic of drunkenness, and suggesting that sober readers 'should avoid subtleties and simply persist in the pretence that my "synthetic Scots" presents insuperable difficulties to understanding', he was displaying, as usual, 'a fine sense of provocation'. But predictably enough, the reviewer in *The Times Literary Supplement* devoted most of his attention to inspecting the credentials of out-of-the-way Scots words, and said of the work itself that

> criticism of its meaning is forestalled by the title and the ironic preface. . . . It is idle to attempt a coherent account of a poem so deliberately and provocatively incoherent.[70]

Yet the vulnerability of *A Drunk Man* is partly due to the fact that it does not have the kind of obscurity characteristic of the modernist poetry of its day. It is clear to the reader what isn't clear in a given passage he is reading. Perhaps the poet would have done better to have prefaced his work with the following, from a writer he much admired at the time:

> If in that which follows you shall meet with arbitrary apothegms, brusque transitions, inconsecutive statements, veritable somersaults of thought, do not cry out that you have been deceived. We are about to enter—if it be that you wish to accompany me—upon a field of contradictions between feeling and reasoning, and we shall have to avail ourselves of the one as well as of the other. That which follows is not the outcome of reason but of life.[71]

KENNETH BUTHLAY

REFERENCES

1 All quotations from letters to and from MacDiarmid are taken from the collections of his correspondence in the National Library of Scotland. Most of the relevant letters by the poet are available in *The Letters of Hugh MacDiarmid*, ed. A. Bold, London 1984.

2 A reference to ll. 2059-2060 of *A Drunk Man*: 'And heard God passin' wi' a bobby's feet / Ootby in the lang coffin o' the street'. Macgillivray objected to the image: ' "God" and the "Bobby" are a hopeless conjugation; a sense of humour can't get past that! You might use the term "watchman", or you might delete the whole reference'.

3 The initials stand for Christopher Murray Grieve, MacDiarmid's real name.

4 Letter to M. Lindsay, 20 May 1945, said by Lindsay to have been received in 1946. See *Francis George Scott and the Scottish Renaissance*, Edinburgh 1980, p.55.

5 *Francis George Scott and the Scottish Renaissance*, p.57.

6 Letter to George Ogilvie, probably November 1925.

7 *Scottish Literature: Character & Influence*, London 1919, p.23.

8 *Bronze in my Blood*, Edinburgh 1981, p.171.

9 *Points in Time*, London 1980, p.73.

10 Letter to J.K. Annand, 30 May 1968.

11 *Clyde Waters*, London 1958, p. 130.

12 'Youngsters' as in the text of Scott's letter. MacDiarmid in fact had only one child at that time.

13 *Francis George Scott and the Scottish Renaissance*, pp. 55-56.

14 Ibid., pp. 155, 93.

15 *Francis George Scott: An Essay*, Edinburgh 1955, pp. 24, 26.

16 *The Company I've Kept*, London 1966, pp. 96-97.

17 *Lines Review*, no. 25 (Winter 1967-68), p. 28.

18 *Lines Review*, no. 26 (Summer 1968), p. 32.

19 *Studies in Scottish Literature*, 14 (1978), pp. 4-5.

20 'Call Me Anti', *Saltire Review*, 1, no. 1 (April 1954), 89-90.

21 *Scottish Literature*, pp. 20, 35.

22 'A Theory of Scots Letters—I', *Scottish Chapbook*, 1, no. 7 (February 1923), p. 182.

23 'Causerie', *Northern Review*, 1, no. 1 (1924), p. 3.

24 *Biographia Literaria*, chpt. 14.

25 'The Argument', *The Marriage of Heaven and Hell.*

26 *MacDiarmid: The Terrible Crystal*, London 1983, pp. 101, 105.

27 Letter to P. Macgillivray, 1 November 1926.

28 Letter to J.C. Weston, 21 August 1968, quoted in John C. Weston, *Hugh MacDiarmid's A Drunk Man Looks at the Thistle*, Preston 1970, p. 36.

29 *Three Masters*, London 1938, pp. 133, 175-6.

30 *The Common Reader*,London 1925, p. 227.

31 Richard Chase, *The American Novel and its Tradition*, New York 1957, p. 91.

32 Peter Pütz, 'Nietszche: Art and Intellectual Inquiry', in *Nietzsche: Imagery and Thought*, ed. M. Pasley, London 1978, p. 9.

33 *Friedrich Nietzsche: The Dionysian Spirit of the Age*, London 1906, pp. 34-35.

34 Quoted by Orage, *The Art of Reading*, New York 1930, p. 205.

35 *Scottish Chapbook*, 1, no. 8 (March 1923), pp. 213-14. (MacDiarmid there made use of reviews of Spengler in *TLS*, 27 October 1921, p. 690, and 25 January 1923, p. 59.)

36 Ibid., 213-14.
37 Review of C. Dyrssen, *Bergson Und Die Deutsche Romantik*, *TLS*, 4 January 1923, p. 13.
38 *Gaudier-Brzeska: A Memoir*, London 1916, p. 106.
39 *Expressionism*, London 1984, pp. 122, 124.
40 *Contemporary Russian Literature 1881-1925*, London 1926, p. 158.
41 *Modern Russian Literature*, London 1925, p. 107.
42 '"Irony"', *Speaker*, 22 April 1899, p. 455.
43 *Byron's Letters and Journals*, London 1974, III, p. 239 (13 December 1813).
44 *Thistle and Rose*, Loanhead 1980, pp. 94, 90
45 Letter, 14 October 1960.
46 *Thistle and Rose*, p. 94
47 Letter to K. Buthlay, 6 October 1983.
48 M.L. Rosenthal & Sally M. Gall, *The Modern Poetic Sequence: The Genius of Modern Poetry*, New York 1983, p. 276.
49 Ibid.
50 Ibid., p. 11.
51 *Complete Poems*, ed. M. Grieve & W.R. Aitken, London 1978, p. 1238.
52 'Tropaeolum Speciosum', *Complete Poems*, p. 1402.
53 D.S. Mirsky, *Modern Russian Literature*, p. 48.
54 A.R. Orage, *Friedrich Nietzsche*, pp. 35-36.
55 'Hugh MacDiarmid: The Early Poems', in *Hugh MacDiarmid: A Festschrift*, ed. K.D. Duval & S.G. Smith, Edinburgh 1962, p.44.
56 *God and the Poets*, Oxford 1984, pp. 198-199.
57 *Hugh MacDiarmid's A Drunk Man Looks at the Thistle*, pp. 25, 32.
58 *A Drunk Man Looks at the Thistle*, Amherst 1971, pp. 121-122.
59 'MacDiarmid's *Drunk Man*: Its Genesis and Structure', *Pembroke Magazine*, no. 7 (1976), p. 184.
60 *Thistle and Rose*, p. 148.
61 'Introduction', *Annals of the Five Senses* by C.M. Grieve, Edinburgh 1983, p. 11. *Modern Scottish Literature*, London 1983, p. 33. 'Introduction', *The Thistle Rises*, London 1984 p. xv. *MacDiarmid: The Terrible Crystal*, London 1983, p. 121.
62 *Terrible Crystal*, p. 121.
63 'Editorial', *Voice of Scotland*, 9. 1 (1959), p. 5.
64 Op. cit., pp. 26-27.
65 A. Bold, 'Literary Gospel and Heresies', *Weekend Scotsman*, 10 November 1984, p. 5. *Modern Scottish Literature*, p. 31.
66 Mikhail Bakhtin, *Problems of Dostoevsky's Poetics*, Ann Arbor 1973, pp. 101, 148.
67 *Scottish Chapbook*, 1, no. 3 (October 1922), pp. 69-73.
68 *The New Vision in the German Arts*, London 1924, pp. 172, 173.
69 'E.K.', in the epistle to Gabriel Harvey prefixed to Spenser's *Shepheardes Calender*, 1579.
70 *TLS*, 22 September 1927, pp. 650-51.
71 Miguel de Unamuno, *The Tragic Sense of Life in Men and Peoples*, London 1921, p. 125.

"Vast imbecile mentality of those
Who cannot tell a thistle from a rose.
This is for others. . . ."

—Sachervell Sitwell

TO
F. G. SCOTT

Can ratt-rime and ragments o' quenry
And recoll o' Gillha' requite
Your faburdoun, figuration, and gemmell,
And prick-sangs' delight?

Tho' you've cappilowed me in the reapin'
—And yours was a bursten kirn tae!—
Yet you share your advantage wi' me
In the end o' the day.

And my flytin' and sclatrie sall be
Wi' your fantice and mocage entwined
As the bauch Earth is wi' the lift
Or fate wi' mankind!

ratt-rime—*anything repeated by rote, especially of the doggerel kind; incantation for killing rats* ragment—*a collection full of variety (J); odds and ends (MacD)* quenry—*abundance of bad women (J); reminiscences of dealings with women (MacD)* recoll—*a collection, selection (J); reminiscences (MacD)* Gillha'—*a house which cannot defend its inhabitants from the weather; a house where working people live in common during some job (J); pub of all weathers, hostelry of life (MacD)* faburdoun—*faux bourdon (MacD); As Fr. 'faux bourdon' signifies the drone of a bagpipe, it may refer to bass. The Fr. term, however, is used to denote what is called 'simple counterpoint' in music. (J)* figuration—*harmony, musical structure (MacD)* gemmell—*two-part harmony* prick-sang—*written vocal music* cappilowed—*outdistanced* bursten (bursen) kirn—*harvesting accomplished with great labour and difficulty* flytin'—*railing; a poetic form of verbal abuse* sclatrie—*obscenities, scandal (MacD); cf. 'scaldrie', scolding, intemperate language (J)* fantice—*vain appearance (J); imagination, whimsicality (MacD)* mocage—*sardonic humour (MacD)* bauch—*sorry, poor in quality* lift—*sky*

The royetest ane ragment with mony ratt rime. . . .

> In modulation hard I play and sing
> Faburdoun, pricksang, discant, countering,
> Cant organe, figuratioun, and gemmell.
>
> (Gavin Douglas, as quoted in Jamieson.)

Personis convict for flyting and scaldrie adjugeit to be govit on the croce quhill four afternone.

(*Burgh Records of Edinburgh*, 13 Jan. 1502/3.)

A DRUNK MAN LOOKS AT THE THISTLE

I AMNA fou' sae muckle as tired—deid dune.
It's gey and hard wark coupin' gless for gless
Wi' Cruivie and Gilsanquhar and the like,
And I'm no' juist as bauld as aince I wes.

The elbuck fankles in the coorse o' time, 5
The sheckle's no' sae souple, and the thrapple
Grows deef and dour: nae langer up and doun
Gleg as a squirrel speils the Adam's apple.

Forbye, the stuffie's no' the real Mackay.
The sun's sel' aince, as sune as ye began it, 10
Riz in your vera saul: but what keeks in
Noo is in truth the vilest "saxpenny planet."

fou'—*drunk* sae muckle—*so much* deid dune—*dead beat* gey (and)—*very, 'pretty'* coupin'—*upending* bauld—*strong, healthy* aince—*once* elbuck—*elbow* fankles—*entangles (itself); becomes clumsy* sheckle—*wrist* thrapple—*throat* deef—*numb* gleg—*quick, eager* speils—*climbs* forbye—*besides* the stuffie—*whisky* riz—*rose* keeks—*peeps*

Sic Transit Gloria Scotiae, 1-120

1. Cf. Burns: 'I was na fou, but just had plenty' ('Death and Doctor Hornbook'); 'We are na fou, we're nae that fou, / But just a drappie in our e'e' ('Willie brew'd a peck o' maut'). By beginning his poem with this plea of mitigation on an assumed charge of drunkenness, MacD suggests to the reader that he is on familiar Scots ground before ca'in the feet frae him: see lines 21-24.

3. Cruivie and Gilsanquhar are the Drunk Man's drinking companions, 'called as was the custom not by their surnames but by the names of their farms'. (Note to MacD's English translation of the poem.)

4. *Bauld* was apparently *blate* in MS and was substituted for the latter when Pittendrigh Macgillivray queried it. 'That was a stupid and quite unaccountable use of the wrong word altogether. I can't imagine how I've passed it so long without noticing it'. (Letter to Macgillivray, 28 Sept. 1926.)

8. Cf. the Gaelic proverbial saying: *cho grad ri feòraig-Chéitein*, as quick as a May squirrel.

9. *The real Mackay*, the genuine article. Current in Scotland by 1870, but the origin of the phrase is uncertain.

10-12. 'In the footsteps of Burns he [James Hogg] did follow, faithfully, if far behind, reflecting a broad ray of his literary sun. . . . Writing of his friend and comrade, from Abbotsford on June 8, 1817, to Lord Montague, . . . Sir Walter [Scott] declared: "There is an old saying of the seaman's, 'every man is not born to be a boatswain', and I think I have heard of men born under a sixpenny planet, and doomed never to be worth a groat. I fear something of this vile sixpenny influence had gleamed in at the cottage window when poor Hogg first came squeaking into the world" '. (W.H. Spence, 'The Shepherd', *Northern Review*, I, no. 2 (June-July 1924), p.122.) John Buchan made use of the same quotation in the Introduction to his *Northern Muse* (London 1924). Note that MacD links this 'saxpenny planet' with 'the star o' Rabbie Burns' (lines 70, 77). For Burns himself, in his drinking song 'Then Guidwife count the lawin', it was the 'blude-red wine', rather than the whisky, that was 'the rysin Sun'.

And as the worth's gane doun the cost has risen.
Yin canna thow the cockles o' yin's hert
Wi'oot ha'en' cauld feet noo, jalousin' what 15
The wife'll say (I dinna blame her fur't).

It's robbin' Peter to pey Paul at least. . . .
And a' that's Scotch aboot it is the name,
Like a' thing else ca'd Scottish nooadays
—A' destitute o' speerit juist the same. 20

(To prove my saul is Scots I maun begin
Wi' what's still deemed Scots and the folk expect,
And spire up syne by visible degrees
To heichts whereo' the fules ha'e never recked.

But aince I get them there I'll whummle them 25
And souse the craturs in the nether deeps,
—For it's nae choice, and ony man su'd wish
To dree the goat's weird tae as weel's the sheep's!)

Heifetz in tartan, and Sir Harry Lauder!
Whaur's Isadora Duncan dancin' noo? 30
Is Mary Garden in Chicago still
And Duncan Grant in Paris—and me fou'?

Sic transit gloria Scotiae—a' the floo'ers
O' the Forest are wede awa'. (A blin' bird's nest
Is aiblins biggin' in the thistle tho'?. . . 35
And better blin' if'ts brood is like the rest!)

You canna gang to a Burns supper even
Wi'oot some wizened scrunt o' a knock-knee
Chinee turns roon to say, "Him Haggis—velly goot!"
And ten to wan the piper is a Cockney. 40

yin—*one* thow—*thaw* ha'en'—*having* jalousin'—*suspecting, guessing* fur't—*for it* a' thing—*everything* maun—*must* spire (Eng.)—*climb* syne—*then* heichts—*heights* whummle—*overturn* souse—*let fall heavily; put one in his place* craturs—*creatures* nae—*no* s'ud—*should* dree—*suffer, endure* weird—*fate* tae—*too* as weel's—*as well as* whaur—*where* noo—*now* a'—*all* wede awa'—*vanished away; carried off by death* aiblins—*perhaps* biggin'—*building* gang—*go* scrunt—*person whose growth is stunted or emaciated*

14. *Yin canna . . . .* A rare instance of MacD going against the grain of Scots idiom. English grammar is here imposed on Scots forms, where the native usage would be 'a body canna thow the cockles o' his hert'. (Note also the switch from 'yin' to 'wan' at ll. 40, 41, and 'ane' at l. 51.)

25-28. The sheep *and* the goats (the redeemed *and* the damned—Matthew 25.32-46) embody the first statement in the poem of its major theme of the combination of contraries or opposites.

29-32. The alleged phoneyness of art in Scotland is represented by the cosmopolitan violinist, Jascha Heifetz, camouflaged in tartan alongside Sir Harry Lauder, who in MacD's view prostituted his talents by exploiting a music-hall caricature of the Scotsman. At its annual dinner in 1922, Lauder had been guest of honour of the Vernacular Circle of the London Burns Club, satirised by MacD below. He spoke in dialect, and was described as 'the greatest exponent in the world of the vernacular'. (*The Times*, 11 April 1922, p.16.) The implication of what follows is that genuine Scottish artists such as Mary Garden the soprano and Duncan Grant the painter were to be found anywhere but in Scotland. Isadora Duncan, the American dancer, is included here because MacD believed that she was of Scots descent, though there appears to be no reliable evidence of this. (Cf. 'Isadora, oor countrywoman', *To Circumjack Cencrastus*, *Complete Poems*, p.212.)

33-34. *Sic transit gloria Scotiae*: so passes away the glory of Scotland. 'The Flowers of the Forest are a' wede away'—the traditional refrain of songs lamenting the slaughter of the Scots army at Flodden, the best-known of which was written by Jean Elliot (1727-1803) and included in Walter Scott's *Minstrelsy of the Scottish Border*.

34-35. It is presumably implied that the bird would have to be blind if it is building its nest in the thistle, i.e. Scotland. Perhaps a reference to the Scottish Renaissance MacD hoped to hatch.

38-39. 'I once heard Sir Chihchenlo-feng-luh, when he was Chinese Ambassador in London, declaring that Burns was as well understood . . . by a Chinaman as by a Scot'. (Donald A. Mackenzie, letter in *Scottish Educational Journal*, 30 Oct. 1925.) It was probably his reaction to his opponent Mackenzie which led MacD to perpetrate his own music-hall caricature of a Chinaman here. He attributed any such lapse of taste in his poem to the drunkenness of its protagonist: 'Theoretically I would defend my verse—you say it is beneath me—well, drunk men go beneath themselves; i.e. to deny representation to this element in the general "drunk" would be a species of camouflage. Practically, however, I believe you're right—that the verse goes over the score and would be better out or modified'. (Letter to P. Macgillivray, 28 Sept. 1926.)

No' wan in fifty kens a wurd Burns wrote
But misapplied is a'body's property,
And gin there was his like alive the day
They'd be the last a kennin' haund to gi'e—

Croose London Scotties wi' their braw shirt fronts 45
And a' their fancy freen's, rejoicin'
That similah gatherings in Timbuctoo,
Bagdad—and Hell, nae doot—are voicin'

Burns' sentiments o' universal love,
In pidgin English or in wild-fowl Scots, 50
And toastin' ane wha's nocht to them but an
Excuse for faitherin' Genius wi' *their* thochts.

A' *they've* to say was aften said afore
A lad was born in Kyle to blaw aboot.
What unco fate mak's *him* the dumpin'-grun' 55
For a' the sloppy rubbish they jaw oot?

Mair nonsense has been uttered in his name
Than in ony's barrin' liberty and Christ.
If this keeps spreedin' as the drink declines,
Syne turns to tea, wae's me for the *Zeitgeist*! 60

Rabbie, wad'st thou wert here—the warld hath need,
And Scotland mair sae, o' the likes o' thee!
The whisky that aince moved your lyre's become
A laxative for a' loquacity.

O gin they'd stegh their guts and haud their wheesht 65
I'd thole it, for "a man's a man," I ken,
But though the feck ha'e plenty o' the "a' that,"
They're nocht but zoologically men.

wan—*one* kens—*knows* a'body's—*everyone's* gin—*if* the day—*today* kennin'—*understanding* croose—*self-important* braw—*grand* freen's—*friends* ane—*one* wha's—*who's* nocht—*nothing* blaw—*boast* mair—*more* unco—*strange* wae's—*woe's* sae—*so* stegh—*stuff* haud their wheest—*be quiet* thole—*bear, endure* feck—*majority*

45 ff. MacD's antipathy to the 'London Scotties' was exacerbated in 1923 when he gave a lecture to the Vernacular Circle of the London Burns Club on 'Unexpressed Elements of Scottish Life'. Their disagreement with his views was not unexpressed: indeed, 'the lecture provoked greater criticism than any other lecture delivered to the Circle'. (*Burns Chronicle*, no. 33, (1924), p.123.)

54. *A lad*: Burns, who wrote the song beginning 'There was a lad was born in Kyle'.

60. *Zeitgeist*: spirit of the age.

61-62. Cf. Wordsworth, 'London, 1802': 'Milton! thou shouldst be living at this hour; / England hath need of thee'. Milton is here not only the great poet but also the champion of political liberty.

66-68. Burns, 'For a' that and a' that':

> What though on hamely fare we dine,
>   Wear hoddin grey, and a' that.
> Gie fools their silks, and knaves their wine,
>   A Man's a Man for a' that.

And Spengler, *Decline of the West*: 'Mankind is a zoological expression, or an empty word'.

I'm haverin', Rabbie, but ye understaun'
It gets my dander up to see your star 70
A bauble in Babel, banged like a saxpence
'Twixt Burbank's Baedeker and Bleistein's cigar.

There's nane sae ignorant but think they can
Expatiate on *you*, if on nae ither.
The sumphs ha'e ta'en you at your wurd, and, fegs! 75
The foziest o' them claims to be a—Brither!

Syne "Here's the cheenge"—the star o' Rabbie Burns.
Sma' cheenge, "Twinkle, Twinkle." The memory slips
As G. K. Chesterton heaves up to gi'e
"The Immortal Memory" in a huge eclipse, 80

Or somebody else as famous if less fat.
You left the like in Embro in a scunner
To booze wi' thieveless cronies sic as me.
I'se warrant you'd shy clear o' a' the hunner

Odd Burns Clubs tae, or ninety-nine o' them, 85
And haud your birthday in a different kip
Whaur your name isna ta'en in vain—as Christ
Gied a' Jerusalem's Pharisees the slip

—Christ wha'd ha'e been Chief Rabbi gin he'd lik't!—
Wi' publicans and sinners to forgether, 90
But, losh! the publicans noo are Pharisees,
And I'm no' shair o' maist the sinners either.

But that's aside the point! I've got fair waun'ert.
It's no' that I'm sae fou' as juist deid dune,
And dinna ken as muckle's whaur I am 95
Or hoo I've come to sprawl here 'neth the mune.

haverin'—*rambling* dander—*temper* nae ither—*no other* sumphs—*blockheads* fegs!—*faith!, 'strewth!* foziest—*spongiest; stupidest* cheenge—*change* sma'—*small* gi'e—*give (a toast to)* Embro—*Edinburgh* scunner—*(fit of) disgust* thieveless—*profligate* sic—*such* I'se—*I'll* haud—*hold* kip—*brothel (and cf. 'play the kip', play truant)* maist—*most (of)* fair waun'ert—*quite confused*

71. 'Bang went sixpence' is the pay-off line of a comic anecdote illustrating the parsimony of the stereotyped Scotsman in London. A version of the story is given by John Buchan in *The Scottish Tongue* (W.A. Craigie and others), London 1924, p.66.

72. The allusion to T.S. Eliot's poem, 'Burbank with a Baedeker: Bleistein with a Cigar', was very avant-garde in 1926. MacD takes these two American tourists to suggest the commercialisation of culture, of which the Burns Cult was a Scottish example.

75-76. Cf. Burns:

> It's comin yet for a' that,
> That Man to Man the warld o'er,
> Shall brothers be for a' that.

77-78. The 'cheenge' is the change from the sixpence which links Burns's star with Hogg's 'saxpenny planet' (l. 12), and this is followed by a sarcastic echo of a popular children's poem, 'Twinkle, Twinkle, Little Star'. 'The Star o' Robbie Burns', a song by James Thomson and James Booth, is often sung as part of the ritual at a Burns Supper. The words by Thomson, first president of the Hawick Burns Club, are quite banal, but the Club could claim by 1925 that the song had been 'universally adopted as a Burns anniversary hymn'. (*Burns Chronicle*, no. 34, p.126.)

79-80. Despite this sarcastic reference to G.K. Chesterton as a representative of the London literary establishment, MacD in fact endorsed several of the points made by Chesterton in proposing 'The Immortal Memory' at a London Burns Club Supper in 1923. He reported Chesterton as saying that the more narrowly national Burns was, the more universal he became. He only failed when he took himself seriously as an 'English' poet and wrote in English. (See also note to l. 397.)

That's it! It isna me that's fou' at a',
But the fu' mune, the doited jade, that's led
Me fer agley, or 'mogrified the warld.
—For a' I ken I'm safe in my ain bed. 100

Jean! Jean! Gin *she*'s no' here it's no' *oor* bed,
Or else I'm dreamin' deep and canna wauken,
But it's a fell queer dream if this is no'
A real hillside—and thae things thistles and bracken!

It's hard wark haud'n by a thocht worth ha'en' 105
And harder speakin't, and no' for ilka man;
Maist Thocht's like whisky—a thoosan' under proof,
And a sair price is pitten on't even than.

As Kirks wi' Christianity ha'e dune,
Burns Clubs wi' Burns—wi' a'thing it's the same, 110
The core o' ocht is only for the few,
Scorned by the mony, thrang wi'ts empty name.

And a' the names in History mean nocht
To maist folk but "ideas o' their ain,"
The vera opposite o' onything 115
The Deid 'ud awn gin they cam' back again.

A greater Christ, a greater Burns, may come.
The maist they'll dae is to gi'e bigger pegs
To folly and conceit to hank their rubbish on.
They'll cheenge folks' talk but no' their natures, fegs! 120

I maun feed frae the common trough ana'
Whaur a' the lees o' hope are jumbled up;
While centuries like pigs are slorpin' owre't
Sall my wee 'oor be cryin': "Let pass this cup"?

fu'—*full* doited—*confused (as in dotage)* fer agley—*far astray* ain—*own* fell—*extremely* thae—*those* ilka—*every* sair—*sore, heavy* pitten—*put* ocht—*anything* thrang—*busy* awn—*own (to)* dae—*do* hank—*fasten* ana'—*and all, as well* slorpin'—*slobbering* owre't—*over it* sall—*shall* 'oor—*hour*

109-110. For the parallel of Christ with Burns, see MacD's early poem, 'They Know Not What They Do' (*Complete Poems*, p. 693). One might also infer a parallel between his view of the Burns Supper and the lip-service paid to the Last Supper by some professed Christians.

114. 'Ideas o' their ain'—in the philosophic sense of 'ideas of their own which have no necessary counterpart in the world outside'?

117. Two allusions with which MacD was familiar are relevant here. 'He that believeth on me, the works that I do shall he do also; and greater works than these shall he do'. (John 14. 12.) And:

> . . . another Burns,
> With future rhymes, an' other times,
> To emulate his sire,
> To sing auld Coil in nobler style,
> With more poetic fire.
> (Burns, 'Nature's Law'.)

A Vision of Myself, 121-168.

121-124. 'You remember Wells's definition of the human mind as "essentially a food-seeking system and no more necessarily a truth-finding apparatus than the snout of a pig" '. (C.M. Grieve, 'Religion and the Scottish Renaissance', *Northern Review*, I, no. 4 (Sept. 1924), p. 256.)

124. 'O my Father, if it be possible, let this cup pass from me'. (Jesus at Gethsemane, Matthew 26. 39.)

In wi' your gruntle then, puir wheengin' saul, 125
Lap up the ugsome aidle wi' the lave,
What gin it's your ain vomit that you swill
And frae Life's gantin' and unfaddomed grave?

I doot I'm geylies mixed, like Life itsel',
But I was never ane that thocht to pit 130
An ocean in a mutchkin. As the haill's
Mair than the pairt sae I than reason yet.

I dinna haud the warld's end in my heid
As maist folk think they dae; nor filter truth
In fishy gills through which its tides may poor 135
For ony *animalcula* forsooth.

I lauch to see my crazy little brain
—And ither folks'—tak'n' itsel' seriously,
And in a sudden lowe o' fun my saul
Blinks dozent as the owl I ken't to be. 140

I'll ha'e nae hauf-way hoose, but aye be whaur
Extremes meet—it's the only way I ken
To dodge the curst conceit o' bein' richt
That damns the vast majority o' men.

I'll bury nae heid like an ostrich's, 145
Nor yet believe my een and naething else.
My senses may advise me, but I'll be
Mysel' nae maitter what they tell's. . . .

I ha'e nae doot some foreign philosopher
Has wrocht a system oot to justify 150
A' this: but I'm a Scot wha blin'ly follows
Auld Scottish instincts, and I winna try.

gruntle—*snout* wheengin'—*whining* ugsome—*repulsive* aidle—*foul slop; urine of cattle* the lave—*the rest* gantin'—*yawning* doot—*suspect* geylies—*pretty well* mutchkin—*pint measure* haill—*whole* dinna—*don't* poor—*pour* lowe—*blaze* dozent—*stupified* een—*eyes* wrocht—*wrought* winna—*won't*

131-132. Cf. Dostoevsky, *Notes from Underground*, I. 8: 'Reason is nothing but reason and satisfies only the rational part of man's nature, while will is a manifestation of the whole life, that is, of the whole human life including reason and all the impulses'.

141-142. *Whaur extremes meet*: the basic philosophic stance adopted by the Drunk Man. It is reminiscent of both the writers, Nietzsche and Dostoevsky, whose influence will emerge most prominently as the poem progresses. It was specifically with Nietzsche in mind that A.R. Orage declared that 'in all great natures extremes meet' (*Nietzsche in Outline and Aphorism*, Edinburgh 1907, p.12), and Leo Shestov said of him that 'at almost one and the same moment you can find him at two diametrically opposite poles of human thought' (*Dostoevsky, Tolstoy and Nietzsche*, Ohio 1969, p.294). Dostoevsky's 'method of evolving a new style by the fusion of extremes' was pointed out by D.S. Mirsky in *A History of Russian Literature*, London 1927, p.225; and the novelist himself claimed that the ability to encompass extremes was a Russian characteristic. He said of himself, 'Everywhere and in everything I go to extremes', (letter to A.N. Maykov, August 1876), and he had some of his characters declare like Alyosha Karamazov that they 'admit of no half-way house', or like Mitya, also in *The Brothers Karamazov*, Book 3, 3, that 'God makes nothing but riddles . . . [where] extremes meet and contraries lie down together'.

143-144. Quoted elsewhere by MacD (*Annals of the Five Senses*, Montrose 1923, p.14) as the 'curst conceit of being right which kills all noble feeling', opposition to which he associated with his favourite philosopher, his 'master', Shestov.

152. *Auld Scottish instincts*—which may be traced through manifestations of the Caledonian Antisyzygy, claimed to be the characteristically Scottish form of the combination of opposites or meeting of extremes.

For I've nae faith in ocht I can explain,
And stert whaur the philosophers leave aff,
Content to glimpse its loops I dinna ettle 155
To land the sea-serpent's sel' wi' ony gaff.

Like staundin' water in a pocket o'
Impervious clay I pray I'll never be,
Cut aff and self-sufficient, but let reenge
Heichts o' the lift and benmaist deeps o' sea. 160

Water! Water! There was owre muckle o't
In yonder whisky, sae I'm in deep water
(And gin I could wun hame I'd be in het,
For even Jean maun natter, natter, natter). . . .

And in the toon that I belang tae 165
—What tho'ts Montrose or Nazareth?—
Helplessly the folk continue
To lead their livin' death! . . .

***At darknin' hings abune the howff*
A weet and wild and eisenin' air. 170
Spring's spirit wi' its waesome sough
Rules owre the drucken stramash there.

And heich abune the vennel's pokiness,
Whaur a' the white-weshed cottons lie,
The Inn's sign blinters in the mochiness, 175
And lood and shrill the bairnies cry.

* From the Russian of Alexander Blok.

ettle—*aspire* reenge—*range; explore* lift—*sky* benmaist—*innermost* owre muckle—*too much* wun—*get, reach* het—*hot* natter—*nag* hings—*hangs* abune—*above* howff—*pub, tavern* weet—*wet* eisenin'—*lustful, yearning* sough—*sigh, moan* drucken—*drunken* stramash—*rumpus* vennel—*alley* cotton—*cottar house (MacD); hamlet (J)* blinters—*gleams* mochiness—*mugginess* bairnies—*small children*

153. For Shestov, much of whose thinking is based repeatedly on key-passages in Dostoevsky and Nietzsche, 'real' philosophy begins where strictly rational explanation leaves off.

155-156. See 'Sea-Serpent' (*Complete Poems*, pp. 48-51). This serpent is conceived to be the original manifestation of the life force which emanated from the divine creative power.

> Or does the serpent dern wi' a mortal wound
> Unseen in its unseen side,
> And are the surges that still come owre us
> Like the thraws o' a stricken man
> Wi' the pooer to inform undeemis lives
> Wi' the single movement o' life nae mair,
> But ebbin' fast—and ebbin' for aye—
> Tho' we skinkle ahint like pools in the san'?

165-168. This stanza seems to be a solitary survivor of editorial cutting which has come to rest here, although it would not be difficult to find a more appropriate place for it. Note the ellipses before and after it, and the metrical change.

166. MacD lived in Montrose when writing this poem.

Poet's Pub, 169-220.

The Lady Unknown

> Of evenings hangs above the restaurant
> A humid, wild and heavy air.
> The Springtide spirit, brooding, pestilent,
> Commands the drunken outcries there.
>
> Far off, above the alley's mustiness,
> Where bored gray summerhouses lie,
> The baker's sign swings gold through dustiness,
> And loud and shrill the children cry.

The hauflins 'yont the burgh boonds
Gang ilka nicht, and a' the same,
Their bonnets cocked; their bluid that stounds
Is playin' at a fine auld game. 180

And on the lochan there, hauf-herted
Wee screams and creakin' oar-locks soon',
And in the lift, heich, hauf-averted,
The mune looks owre the yirdly roon'.

And ilka evenin', derf and serious 185
(Jean ettles nocht o' this, puir lass),
In liquor, raw yet still mysterious,
A'e freend's aye mirrored in my glass.

Ahint the sheenin' coonter gruff
Thrang barmen ding the tumblers doun; 190
"In vino veritas" cry rough
And reid-een'd fules that in it droon.

But ilka evenin' fey and fremt
(Is it a dream nae wauk'nin' proves?)
As to a trystin'-place undreamt, 195
A silken leddy darkly moves.

Slow gangs she by the drunken anes,
And lanely by the winnock sits;
Frae'r robes, atour the sunken anes,
A rooky dwamin' perfume flits. 200

Her gleamin' silks, the taperin'
O' her ringed fingers, and her feathers
Move dimly like a dream wi'in,
While endless faith aboot them gethers.

hauflins—*youths* 'yont—*beyond* stounds—*throbs* lochan—*small lake* soon'—*sound* yirdly—*earthly* derf—*taciturn* ettles—*guesses; suspects (MacD)* a'e—*one* ahint—*behind* sheenin'—*shining* thrang—*busy* ding—*bang* 'in vino veritas'—*there is truth in wine* reid-een'd—*red-eyed* fey—*fated* fremt—*estranged* winnock—*window* frae'r—*from her* atour—*out over* rooky—*misty* dwamin'—*swooning*

Beyond the city stroll the exquisites,
At every dusk and all the same:
Their derbies tilted back, the pretty wits
Are playing at the ancient game.

Upon the lake but feebly furious
Soft screams and creaking oar-locks sound.
And in the sky, blasé, incurious,
The moon beholds the earthly round.

And every evening, dazed and serious,
I watch the same procession pass;
In liquor, raw and yet mysterious,
One friend is mirrored in my glass.

Beside the scattered tables, somnolent
And dreary waiters stick around.
'*In vino veritas!*' shout violent
And red-eyed fools in liquor drowned.

And every evening, strange, immutable,
(Is it a dream no waking proves?)
As to a rendezvous inscrutable
A silken lady darkly moves.

She slowly passes by the drunken ones
And lonely by the window sits;
And from her robes, above the sunken ones,
A misty fainting perfume flits.

Her silks' resilience, and the tapering
Of her ringed fingers, and her plumes,
Stir vaguely like dim incense vaporing,
Deep ancient faiths their mystery illumes.

I seek, in this captivity, 205
To pierce the veils that darklin' fa'
—See white clints slidin' to the sea,
And hear the horns o' Elfland blaw.

I ha'e dark secrets' turns and twists,
A sun is gi'en to me to haud, 210
The whisky in my bluid insists,
And spiers my benmaist history, lad.

And owre my brain the flitterin'
O' the dim feathers gangs aince mair,
And, faddomless, the dark blue glitterin' 215
O' twa een in the ocean there.

My soul stores up this wealth unspent,
The key is safe and nane's but mine.
You're richt, auld drunk impenitent,
I ken it tae—the truth's in wine! 220

clints—*cliffs* spiers—*searches out* twa—*two* een—*eyes*

I try, held in this strange captivity,
To pierce the veil that darkling falls—
I see enchanted shores' declivity,
And an enchanted distance calls.

I guard dark secrets' tortuosities.
A sun is given me to hold.
An acrid wine finds out the sinuosities
That in my soul were locked of old.

And in my brain the soft slow flittering
Of ostrich feathers waves once more;
And fathomless the azure glittering
Where two eyes blossom on the shore.

My soul holds fast its treasure renitent,
The key is safe and solely mine.
Ah, you are right, drunken impenitent!
I also know: truth lies in wine.

(Alexander Blok, trans. B. Deutsch & A. Yarmolinsky, in *Modern Russian Poetry*, London 1923.)

207-208. MacD inserts an echo of Tennyson's poem, 'The splendour falls' from *The Princess*: 'O sweet and far from cliff and scar / The horns of Elfland faintly blowing'.

210. Cf. the association of the sun with whisky, ll. 10-11.

216. The two eyes in the ocean suggest the sea-serpent of l. 156. Other symbols of major importance to MacD are already present in Blok's poem: the moon, the liquor as his 'spiritual' inspiration, and the mysterious woman. In this instance the woman was a prostitute in a resort near Petersburg—a demonic opposite of the 'Beautiful Lady' of Blok's earlier poems. A warning against taking the poem 'straight' may be seen in Blok's essay on 'Irony', where the twin extremes appear as Dante's Beatrice and Sologub's Nedotykomka, the 'Shabby Demon': 'Everything is confused as though in a tavern and in the gloom the truth of wine, 'in vino veritas', is revealed to the world . . . I shall fall on my knees before the 'Nedotykomka', I shall seduce Beatrice. . . . Or I shall prove that Beatrice and the 'Nedotykomka' are one and the same. Whatever I feel like, for I am drunk. And what can one expect of a drunk man? Drunk with irony, with laughter, as though with vodka'. Elsewhere Blok echoes Dostoevsky's view that the ability to encompass extremes and entertain contradictions is a Russian characteristic, and MacD had certainly read Mirsky's remarks about Blok's work being 'akin to Dostoevsky's world of antithesis' (*Modern Russian Literature* (1925), p. 107).

The munelicht's like a lookin'-glass,
The thistle's like mysel',
But whaur ye've gane, my bonnie lass,
Is mair than I can tell.

Were you a vision o' mysel', 225
Transmuted by the mellow liquor?
Neist time I glisk you in a glass,
I'se warrant I'll mak' siccar.

A man's a clean contrairy sicht
Turned this way in-ootside, 230
And, fegs, I feel like Dr Jekyll
Tak'n' guid tent o' Mr Hyde. . . .

Gurly thistle—hic—you canna
Daunton me wi' your shaggy mien,
I'm sair—hic—needin' a shave, 235
That's plainly to be seen.

But what aboot it—hic—aboot it?
Mony a man's been that afore.
It's no' a fact that in his lugs
A wund like this need roar! . . . 240

**I ha'e forekent ye! O I ha'e forekent.*
The years forecast your face afore they went.
A licht I canna thole is in the lift.
I bide in silence your slow-comin' pace.
The ends o' space are bricht: at last—oh swift! 245
While terror clings to me—an unkent face!

Ill-faith stirs in me as she comes at last,
The features lang forekent . . . are unforecast.
O it gangs hard wi' me, I am forspent.
Deid dreams ha'e beaten me and a face unkent, 250
And generations that I thocht unborn
Hail the strange Goddess frae my hert's-hert torn! . . .

*Freely adapted from the Russian of Alexander Blok.

nane's— *no one's* tae—*too* bonnie—*beautiful* neist—*next* glisk—*glimpse* I'se—*I'll* siccar—*sure* tak'n guid tent o'—*keeping a sharp eye on* gurly—*surly* daunton—*frighten* sair—*sorely* lugs—*ears* wund—*wind* forekent—*foreknown* thole—*endure* lift—*sky* deid—*dead*

The Looking Glass, 221-240.

225. *A vision o' mysel'*: his *anima*, in the Jungian sense, since the vision was female.

227-228. The person mirrored in the drinker's glass in Blok's poem (l.188) was actually a male figure—not the mysterious woman, as assumed by MacD.

231-232. Stevenson, with his belief in 'the thorough and primitive duality of man', is highly relevant to Gregory Smith's conception of the Caledonian Antisyzygy. It was from *Dr. Jekyll and Mr. Hyde*, that Smith took the idea of a continuous struggle of 'polar twins'—Stevenson's phrase, in the final section of that story. However, the two sides of the dualism which for Stevenson manifest themselves alternately, emerge simultaneously in Dostoevsky's psychology, as MacD was aware.

240. The wind roaring in the Drunk Man's ears will recur in other parts of the poem (ll. 372, 1244, 2159, 2222). According to Jung, this is an archetypal symbol for the advent of the numinous—that is, it is suffused with the feeling of a divinity of some sort. And in fact its occurrence here is immediately followed by the manifestation of a divinity, in the adaptation of Blok to which MacD gave the title 'The Unknown Goddess', though there is no specific reference to a goddess in the original or in the crib he used. The wind will also have particular relevance to the manifestation of the Holy Ghost at Pentecost (note to ll. 1394-5), but in typical antisyzygical fashion it is associated with the Devil at ll.372-3.

The Unknown Goddess, 241-252.

The Unknown Woman

I have foreknown Thee! Oh, I have foreknown Thee.
Going,
The years have shown me Thy premonitory face.
Intolerably clear, the farthest sky is glowing.
I wait in silence Thy withheld and worshipped grace.
The farthest sky is glowing: white for Thy appearing.
Yet terror clings to me. Thy image will be strange.

And insolent suspicion will rouse upon Thy nearing.
The features long foreknown, beheld at last, will change.
How shall I then be fallen!—low, with no defender:
Dead dreams will conquer me; the glory, glimpsed, will change.
The farthest sky is glowing! Nearer looms the splendor!
Yet terror clings to me. Thy image will be strange.

(Blok, trans. Deutsch & Yarmolinsky, in *Modern Russian Poetry*.)

Or dost thou mak' a thistle o' me, wumman? But for thee
I were as happy as the munelicht, withoot care,
But thocht o' thee—o' thy contempt and ire— 255
Turns hauf the warld into the youky thistle there,

Feedin' on the munelicht and transformin' it
To this wanrestfu' growth that winna let me be.
The munelicht is the freedom that I'd ha'e
But for this cursèd Conscience thou hast set in me. 260

It is morality, the knowledge o' Guid and Ill,
Fear, shame, pity, like a will and wilyart growth,
That kills a' else wi'in its reach and craves
Nae less at last than a' the warld to gi'e it scouth.

The need to wark, the need to think, the need to be, 265
And a'thing that twists Life into a certain shape
And interferes wi' perfect liberty—
These feed this Frankenstein that nae man can escape.

For ilka thing a man can be or think or dae
Aye leaves a million mair unbeen, unthocht, undune, 270
Till his puir warped performance is,
To a' that micht ha' been, a thistle to the mune.

It is Mortality itsel'—the mortal coil,
Mockin' Perfection, Man afore the Throne o' God
He yet has bigged himsel', Man torn in twa 275
And glorious in the lift and grisly on the sod! . . .

There's nocht sae sober as a man blin' drunk.
I maun ha'e got an unco bellyfu'
To jaw like this—and yet what I am sayin'
Is a' the apter, aiblins, to be true. 280

hauf—*half* youky—*itchy* wanrestfu'—*restless* winna—*won't* will—*straggling, spreading unchecked* wilyart—*obstinate* scouth—*scope* wark—*work* ilka—*every* bigged—*built* unco—*extraordinary; very great* aiblins—*perhaps*

My Nation's Soul, 253-308.

By supplying this title, MacD suggested that for him the Goddess was a Scottish deity, whom he suspects of trapping the Drunk Man in a particularly Scottish form of constricted religious morality. (He will actually apply the phrase 'my nation's soul' to the thistle at l. 336 in what, by these divisions, is presented as a separate section of the poem.) Similarly, Blok said of his early visionary poem adapted by MacD as 'The Unknown Goddess': 'We have . . . demanded miracles prematurely: the nation's soul met, in fact, the same fate'. ('On the Present State of Russian Symbolism', in *Symbolism*, ed. T.G. West, London 1980, p.155.)

At the same time, in MacD's context, the female figure suggests Eve, who was allegedly responsible for the eating of the forbidden fruit in Eden, resulting in human knowledge of good and evil—morality—as well as mortality.

262. Shame, pity, and fear of God (the positive form of which is piety) are the three bases for morality laid down by Vladimir Solovyov (1853-1900) in *The Justification of the Good* (London 1918, pp.25-39). There is also a link with Solovyov in the preceding poem by Blok. It was built round a phrase in a poem by Solovyov, whose vision of Sophia, the Divine Wisdom, strongly influenced Blok in the period to which that poem belongs.

273. *The mortal coil*: the bustle or turmoil of mortal life. (*Hamlet*, III. 1. 68.)

This munelicht's fell like whisky noo I see't.
—Am I a thingum mebbe that is kept
Preserved in spirits in a muckle bottle
Lang centuries efter sin' wi' Jean I slept?

—Mounted on a hillside, wi' the thistles 285
And bracken for verisimilitude,
Like a stuffed bird on metal like a brainch,
Or a seal on a stump o' rock-like wood?

Or am I juist a figure in a scene
O' Scottish life A.D. one-nine-two-five? 290
The haill thing kelters like a theatre claith
Till I micht fancy that I was alive!

I dinna ken and nae man ever can.
I micht be in my ain bed efter a'.
The haill damned thing's a dream for ocht we ken 295
—The Warld and Life and Daith, Heaven, Hell ana'.

We maun juist tak' things as we find them then,
And mak' a kirk or mill o' them as we can
—And yet I feel this muckle thistle's staun'in'
Atween me and the mune as pairt o' a Plan. 300

It isna there—nor me—by accident.
We're brocht thegither for a certain reason,
Ev'n gin it's naething mair than juist to gi'e
My jaded soul a necessary *frisson*.

I never saw afore a thistle quite 305
Sae intimately, or at sic an 'oor.
There's something in the fickle licht that gi'es
A different life to't and an unco poo'er.

fell—*extremely* thingum—*thingumajig* kelters—*undulates* claith—*cloth*
micht—*might* mak' a kirk or mill o'—*make the most of* mune—*moon*
brocht thegither—*brought together* gin—*if* 'oor—*hour* unco—*weird*

282. *Thingum*: substituted at the suggestion of P. Macgillivray for 'mummy' in the MS.

304-308. Cf. Victor Hugo congratulating Baudelaire on *Les Fleurs du Mal*: 'Vous dotez le ciel d'art d'on ne sait quel rayon macabre, vous créez un frisson nouveau' (letter of 6 Oct. 1859).

*"*Rootit on gressless peaks, whaur its erect*
And jaggy leafs, austerely cauld and dumb, 310
Haud the slow scaly serpent in respect,
The Gothic thistle, whaur the insect's hum
Soon's fer aff, lifts abune the rock it scorns
Its rigid virtue for the Heavens to see.
The too'ering boulders gaird it. And the bee 315
Mak's honey frae the roses on its thorns."

But that's a Belgian refugee, of coorse.
This Freudian complex has somehoo slunken
Frae Scotland's soul—the Scots aboulia—
Whilst a' its *terra nullius* is *betrunken.* 320

And a' the country roon' aboot it noo
Lies clapt and shrunken syne like somebody wha
Has lang o' seven devils been possessed;
Then when he turns a corner tines them a',

Or like a body that has tint its soul, 325
Perched like a monkey on its heedless kist,
Or like a sea that peacefu' fa's again
When frae its deeps an octopus is fished.

I canna feel it has to dae wi' me
Mair than a composite diagram o' 330
Cross-sections o' my forbears' organs
—And mine—'ud bring a kind o' freen'ly glow.

And yet like bindweed through my clay it's run,
And a' my folks'—it's queer to see't unroll.
My ain soul looks me in the face, as 'twere, 335
And mair than my ain soul—my nation's soul!

And sall a Belgian pit it into words
And sing a sang to't syne, and no' a Scot?
Oors is a wilder thistle, and Ramaekers
Canna bear aff the gree—avaunt the thocht! 340

*From the Belgian poet, Georges Ramaekers.

gressless—*grassless* fer aff—*far off* abune—*above* clapt—*collapsed; flat* tines—*loses* tint—*lost* kist—*chest; coffin* fa's—*falls* has to dae wi'—*has (anything) to do with* pit—*put* gree—*prize* syne—*afterwards; then*

The Gothic Thistle, 309-352.

The Thistle

Rooted on herbless peaks, where its erect
And prickly leaves, austerely cold and dumb,
Hold the slow, scaly serpent in respect,
The Gothic thistle, while the insects' hum
Sounds far off, rears above the rock it scorns
Its rigid virtue for the Heavens to see.
The towering boulders guard it. And the bee
Makes honey from the blossoms on its thorns.

(Georges Ramaekers, trans. J. Bithell, in *Contemporary Belgian Poetry*, London 1911.)

While generally content to leave well alone in stealing from Bithell's version, MacD's change of the 'blossoms' to the 'roses' of the thistle in the last line is significant because it makes his thistle-symbol more complex. The use of the word 'roses' to indicate the flowers of the thistle appears to be peculiar to MacD, and by giving it this special sense he is able at times to internalise the opposition and consequent tension between rose and thistle, which are normally opposed as separate entities—most obviously as the national emblems of England and Scotland. Note also that other images in the Belgian symbolist's poem, the serpent and the honey-bees, will reappear in quite different contexts in *A Drunk Man*: the latter in connection with the Yggdrasill myth (ll. 1348-9, 2097-8).

319. *Aboulia*: inability, usually pathological, to make or to act on decisions. A now outmoded psychological term, used e.g. by A.R. Orage, and a favourite term of the younger MacD in diagnoses of his own and Scotland's condition. An example of the latter: 'The decay of the Doric and the failure of Doric drama and prose was due to . . . a "specific aboulia" caused by the suppression imposed by the rigours of Puritanism and accentuated by Anglicisation'. (Report of MacD's lecture on 13 Feb. 1924 in *Burns Chronicle*, no. 33, p.122.)

320. *Terra nullius*: no man's land. 'Mr. McDiarmid has been tending further and further . . . into the terra nullius of Scots psychology ever since he first began to write'. (J.G. Outterstone Buglass (!), in *Northern Review*, 1, (Sept. 1924), p.276.) *Betrunken* (German): drunk.

326. Cf. Walter Scott's story 'Wandering Willie's Tale' in *Redgauntlet*, Letter the Eleventh, where the Devil is said to have been seen sitting on the dead laird's coffin (*kist*), but the non-supernatural explanation for this is provided by the laird's pet monkey.

To meddle wi' the thistle and to pluck
The figs frae't is *my* metier, I think.
Awak', my muse, and gin you're in puir fettle,
We aye can blame it on th' inferior drink.

T. S. Eliot—it's a Scottish name— 345
Afore he wrote 'The Waste Land' s'ud ha'e come
To Scotland here. He wad ha'e written
A better poem syne—like this, by gum!

Type o' the Wissenschaftsfeindlichkeit,
Begriffsmüdigkeit that has gar't 350
Men try Morphologies der Weltgeschichte,
And mad Expressionismus syne in Art.

**A shameless thing, for ilka vileness able,*
It is deid grey as dust, the dust o' a man.
I perish o' a nearness I canna win awa' frae, 355
Its deidly coils aboot my buik are thrawn.

A shaggy poulp, embracin' me and stingin',
And as a serpent cauld agen' my hert,
Its scales are poisoned shafts that jag me to the quick
—And waur than them's my scunner's fearfu' smert! 360

*Adapted from the Russian of Zinaida Hippius.

The octopus like something from the depths of the unconcious mind / or the unconcious mind itself.

win awa'—*get away* buik—*trunk (of body)* poulp (Eng.)—*octopus* agen'—*against* waur—*worse* scunner—*disgust*

341-342. 'Wha daur meddle wi' me?' is the Scots version of the Latin motto, 'Nemo me impune lacessit', inscribed on the national emblem of the thistle. 'To "meddle wi' the Thistle" and pluck the figs' is one of the principal aims of *The Scottish Chapbook*, MacD's pioneering journal of the Scottish Renaissance, as listed in its first number (August 1922). In addition to the biblical allusion (Matthew 7. 16), he may have encountered the following reference in Jamieson's Dictionary: 'May yee gather grapes of thornes, or figges of thrisles? no, no, it is contrary thare nature' (Balnave's *Confession of Faith*, Edinburgh 1584).

345-348. Eliot's 'The Waste Land' was published in 1922, and few enough of MacD's readers in 1926 would have thought it excessively ambitious to claim to have written a better poem than that. His bluster here should not obscure the acuteness with which he detected the historic importance of 'The Waste Land' (as also of Joyce's *Ulysses*, published in the same year). Another reference to contemporary Scotland as the prime example of the Waste Land occurs at l. 1650.

349-352. The German terms mean respectively: 'hostility to scientific knowledge' (as in Bergson); 'weariness with ideas'; 'morphologies of world history' (particularly Spengler's attempt at such in *The Decline of the West*); and 'Expressionism'. MacD is following up his reference to avant-garde Eliot with a display of his awareness of recent developments in Germany. The same German terms (at second hand from Carl Dyrssen's *Bergson Und Die Deutsche Romantik*) are used by him in articles in *The Scottish Nation* (8 May 1923) and *New Age* (19 June 1924). This is showing off, of course, but not just that, since his poem does reflect his awareness of the tendencies his references suggest.

The Octopus, 353-368.

Psyche

A shameless thing, of every vileness capable,
It is as drab as dust, as earthly dust.
I perish of a nearness inescapable;
Its fatal coils about my limbs are thrust.

A shaggy poulp, embracing me, and pricking me,
And as a serpent cold against my heart,
Its branching scales are poisoned arrows sticking me;
Worse than their bite: repulsion's horrid smart.

O that its prickles were a knife indeed,
But it is thowless, flabby, dowf, and numb.
Sae sluggishly it drains my benmaist life,
A dozent dragon, dreidfu', deef, and dumb.

In mum obscurity it twines its obstinate rings 365
And hings caressin'ly, its purpose whole;
And this deid thing, whale-white obscenity,
This horror that I writhe in—is my soul!

Is it the munelicht or a leprosy
That spreids aboot me; and a thistle 370
Or my ain skeleton through wha's bare banes
A fiendish wund's begood to whistle?

The devil's lauchter has a *hwyl* like this.
My face has flown open like a lid
—And gibberin' on the hillside there 375
Is a' humanity sae lang has hid! . . .

My harns are seaweed—when the tide is in
They swall like blethers and in comfort float,
But when the tide is oot they lie like gealed
And runkled auld bluid-vessels in a knot! 380

The munelicht ebbs and flows and wi't my thocht,
Noo movin' mellow and noo lourd and rough.
I ken what I am like in Life and Daith,
But Life and Daith for nae man are enough. . . .

thowless—*lethargic; impotent (MacD)* dowf—*inert* benmaist—*innermost* dozent—*stupefied* deef—*deaf (Also applied to deficiency in the other senses; hence 'unimpressionalble', MacD.)* hings—*hangs* wha's—*whose* begood—*begun* lauchter—*laughter* hwyl *(Welsh)*—*ululation (MacD)* harns—*brains* swall—*swell* blethers—*bladders* gealed—*congealed* runkled—*wrinkled* lourd—*heavy*

Oh, were its sting a veritable knife in me!
But it is flaccid, clumsy, still and numb.
Thus sluggishly sucking the very life in me,
A torpid dragon, dreadful, deaf, and dumb.

With stubborn rings it winds in mute obscurity
And clings caressingly, its purpose whole.
And this dead thing, this loathsome black impurity,
This horror that I shrink from—is my soul.

(Zinaida Hippius, trans. B. Deutsch & A. Yarmolinsky, in *Modern Russian Poetry*.)

MacD's title, 'The Octopus', comes from Deutsch and Yarmolinsky's insertion of a 'poulp' in line 5, though there is no octopus in the original, the title of which is 'Ona' ('She'). MacD brilliantly adds a suggestion of Moby Dick, the White Whale, which together with the serpent, the dragon, and the octopus, form a cluster of powerful images which will recur later in his poem. He turns black into white in the penultimate line because, as Melville said, 'It was the whiteness of the whale that above all things appalled me'. (*Moby Dick*, chpt. 42.)

Ebb and Flow, 369-400.

Printed as three separate poems in *The Glasgow Herald* 13 Feb. 1926, p. 4: 'Denouement' (ll. 369-376), 'Beyond Life and Death' (ll. 377-384), and 'The Better Part' (ll. 385-400).

369. The peculiar horror of whiteness in association with disease is now highlighted by the moonlight's suggesting leprosy, the traditional venereal associations of which link up with the guilt-ridden sexuality of Hippius's poem.

372-373. Leprosy as an emblem of sin is linked to the 'fiendish wind' and 'devil's laughter'. Cf. Blok on the modern malaise of irony: 'Its manifestations are fits of exhausting laughter which begin with a devilishly taunting, provocative smile and end up with turbulence and sacrilege'. *Hwyl* (*hwll* in previous editions) is a Welsh expression referring to emotional turbulence and the sort of intonation that accompanies it.

374. 'The faces of some Scotsmen are mere wooden lids to wooden boxes'. (Lewis Spence in *The Scottish Nation*, 12 June 1923, p. 4.)

And O! to think that there are members o' 385
St. Andrew's Societies sleepin' soon',
Wha to the papers wrote afore they bedded
On regimental buttons or buckled shoon,

Or use o' England whaur the U.K.'s meent,
Or this or that anent the Blue Saltire, 390
Recruitin', pedigrees, and Gude kens what,
Filled wi' a proper patriotic fire!

Wad I were them—they've chosen a better pairt,
The couthie craturs, than the ane I've ta'en,
Tyauvin' wi' this root-hewn Scottis soul; 395
A fer, fer better pairt—except for men.

Nae doot they're sober, as a Scot ne'er was,
Each tethered to a punctual-snorin' missus,
Whilst I, puir fule, owre continents unkent
And wine-dark oceans waunder like Ulysses. . . . 400

* *The Mune sits on my bed the nicht unsocht,*
And mak's my soul obedient to her will;
And in the dumb-deid, still as dreams are still,
Her pupils narraw to bricht threids that thrill
Aboot the sensuous windin's o' her thocht. 405

* Suggested by the German of Else Lasker-Schüler.

shoon—*shoes* meent—*meant* anent—*concerning* wad—*would* couthie—*comfortable* craturs—*creatures* tyauvin'—*struggling* root-hewn—*perverse* the nicht—*tonight* dumb-deid—*dead of night*

386. *St Andrew*: the Scottish national saint.

389. Cf. Donald A. Mackenzie's letter to the *Scottish Educational Journal* (13 Aug. 1926): 'I have always been a Scottish patriot, and I have never used 'England' for 'Britain', as did Mr. Lewis Spence in other days in certain of his sonnets'.

390. *Blue Saltire*: the Scottish national flag.

397. 'In the face of a hundred glorious examples to the contrary they [the Scots] are told that they are sober; most slanderous of all, they are accused of being law-abiding'. (G.K. Chesterton, in his speech at the London Burns Club, as reported by MacD in the *Dunfermline Press*, 3 Feb. 1923.) Chesterton's view that the popular stereotype of the 'canny Scot' was a travesty of the truth, the Scots being 'more elevated, more mystical, and more violent' than the English, 'with a passion for freedom', lent support to MacD's conception of the Scot as an embodiment of Nietzsche's 'Dionysian' type.

400. The wanderings of the Drunk Man are adventures of the mind only, but again the implication is of reversion to what MacD saw as an authentic national type, the Wandering Scot. If a passing thought of Joyce's Jewish Ulysses—recently hailed by MacD—should cross the reader's mind, so much the better from MacD's point of view.

All the Ins and Outs, 401-410.

Sphinx

She sits upon my bed at dusk, unsought,
And makes my soul obedient to her will,
And in the twilight, still as dreams are still,
Her pupils narrow to bright threads that thrill
About the sensuous windings of her thought.

404-405. Cf. Edwin Muir on MacD himself: 'He takes a delight in the subtle windings of the intellect for their own sake, and . . . that delight is in him partly sensuous'. (*The New Age*, 15 Nov. 1923, p. 32.)

But ilka windin' has its coonter-pairt
—The opposite 'thoot which it couldna be—
In some wild kink or queer perversity
O' this great thistle, green wi' jealousy,
That breenges 'twixt the munelicht and my hert. . . . 410

Plant, what are you then? Your leafs
Mind me o' the pipes' lood drone
—And a' your purple tops
Are the pirly-wirly notes
That gang staggerin' owre them as they groan. 415

Or your leafs are alligators
That ha'e gobbled owre a haill
Company o' Heilant sodgers,
And left naethin' but the toories
O' their Balmoral bonnets to tell the tale. 420

Or a muckle bellows blawin'
Wi' the sperks a' whizzin' oot;
Or green tides sweeshin'
'Neth heich-skeich stars,
Or centuries fleein' doun a water-chute. 425

Grinnin' gargoyle by a saint,
Mephistopheles in Heaven,
Skeleton at a tea-meetin',
Missin' link—or creakin'
Hinge atween the deid and livin'. . . . 430

(I kent a Terrier in a sham fecht aince,
Wha louped a dyke and landed on a thistle.
He'd naething on ava aneth his kilt.
Schönberg has nae notation for his whistle.) . . .

'thoot—*without* breenges—*plunges forward; bursts (MacD)* mind—*remind* lood—*loud* pirly- (or tirly-) wirly—*tiny and intricate (of the grace notes in piping)* Heilant—*Highland* sodgers—*soldiers* toories—*pompons* Balmoral bonnets—*flat caps* sweeshin'—*swishing* heich-skeich—*irresponsible (MacD. The only examples in SND are from him.)* water-chute—*artificial cascade down which boats slide for sport* atween—*between* Terrier—*soldier in the Territorial Army* fecht—*fight* louped—*leaped* ava—*at all* aneth—*beneath*

And on the neighbouring couch, spread crepitant,
The pointed-patterned, pale narcissus fling
Their hands toward the pillow, where yet cling
His kisses, and the dreams thence blossoming,—
On the white beds a sweet and swooning scent.

The smiling moonwoman dips in cloudy swells,
And my wan, suffering psyches know new power,
Finding their strength in conflict's tortured hour.

(Else Lasker-Schüler, trans. B. Deutsch & A. Yarmolinsky, in *Contemporary German Poetry*, London, 1923.)

MacD concentrates on the 'conflict'—the *Kampf mit Widerspruechen* or 'struggle with contradictions' of Lasker-Schüler's last line—in order to link it with his antisyzygical theme, and also to produce a much tighter poem. He dispenses with her Sphinx, and all her perfumed boudoir imagery, makes the Moon more explicit, and counterpoints it against his other key-symbol of the Thistle. This is a concentrated example of the principal method he employs in his efforts to hold his diverse materials together in the course of his long work.

406-407. For the mutual dependence of the opposites, cf. Coleridge and Yeats: 'A struggle between two opposites, two polar Forces, both of which are alike necessary . . . each to the continued existence of the other'. (*Collected Letters of S.T. Coleridge*, Oxford 1971, V, p.35.) 'In our system . . . it is a cardinal principle that anything separated from its opposite—and victory is separation—"consumes itself away". The existence of the one depends upon the existence of the other'. (*A Vision*, London 1925, p.134.)

To the Music of the Pipes, 411-434.

426. 'Scottish literature is more medieval in habit than criticism has suspected, and owes some part of its picturesque strength to this freedom in passing from one mood to another. It takes some people more time than they can spare to see the absolute propriety of a gargoyle's grinning at the elbow of a kneeling saint'. (Gregory Smith on the 'Caledonian Antisyzygy', in *Scottish Literature* (1919), p.35.)

434. The comic reference to Schoenberg contains something of an in-joke. Francis George Scott was influenced by the then little-known Schoenberg (little-known in Britain at least) in some of his settings of poems by MacD.

(Gin you're surprised a village drunk 435
Foreign references s'ud fool in,
You ha'ena the respect you s'ud
For oor guid Scottish schoolin'.

For we've the maist unlikely folk
Aye braggin' o' oor lear, 440
And, tho' I'm drunk, for Scotland's sake
I tak' my barrowsteel here!

Yet Europe's faur eneuch for me,
Puir fule, when bairns ken mair
O' th' ither warld than I o' this 445
—But that's no' here nor there!). . .

Guid sakes, I'm in a dreidfu' state.
I'll ha'e nae inklin' sune
Gin I'm the drinker or the drink,
The thistle or the mune. 450

I'm geylies feart I couldna tell
Gin I s'ud lay me doon
The difference betwixt the warld
And my ain heid gaen' roon'! . . .

Drums in the Walligate, pipes in the air, 455
Come and hear the cryin' o' the Fair.

A' as it used to be, when I was a loon
On Common-Ridin' Day in the Muckle Toon.

lear—*learning* tak' my barrowsteel—*keep my end up; co-operate* faur—*far* eneuch—*enough* bairns—*children* geylies feart—*rather afraid* heid—*head* gaen'—*going* cryin'—*proclamation* loon—*lad* the Muckle Toon—*Langholm, Dumfriesshire (see note)*

Our Educational System, 435-454.

The Crying of the Fair, 455-476.

455. 'Ra-ra-rae, the nicht afore the Fair! The drum's i' the Walligate, the pipes i' the air'. Children's chant, in procession on May Hiring-day eve. (G. Watson, *Roxburghshire Word-Book*, Cambridge 1923.)

Like other Border towns, MacD's birthplace, Langholm, has an annual Fair associated with the Common Riding, the ceremony of riding round the official boundaries of land held in common. One of his Scots prose sketches features a young man who is a heroic bearer of the thistle in the procession, and an expert on all the ritual of this great local occasion:

> Ye couldna riddle him wi' the Common Ridin'. He'd the names o' a' the Cornets aff by hert frae A to Z, and no' only the Cornets, but the dogs that wun the hound trail; the horses that wun the races; the men that wun the wrestlin' and wha cairried the Croon o' Roses and the Thistle and the Bannock and Saut Herrin', and wha cried the Fair, . . . and dod! I'm no' shair that he didna ken the name o' ilka bairn that ever toddled wi' a heather besom and got a thripp'ny bit. He was a fair miracle. And forbye, he was an authority on the rites themselves the size o' the Thistle, the bakin' o' the bannock, the twal' penny nail that hauds the saut herrin' to the bannock, the order o' precedence in the procession, the exact wordin' o' the Cryin' o' the Fair, and a' the ancient details o' the burgh boonds and the rights o' the freemen. . . .
>
> The thistle for the Common Ridin' was grown doon at the Toonfit. A plot o' grun' was set apairt for the purpose, and mebbes half a dizzen thistles were grown each year, and for weeks aforehand croods used to gang doon on Sunday efternunes to see hoo they were comin' on. The biggest and shapeliest was chosen, but it was an unwritten law—and a point o' honour wi' the gairdener—that it had to be at least aucht fit high wi' the tap aboot as muckle in diameter. Tied to the tap o' a flag pole it made a bonny sicht, wallopin' a' owre the lift, an' a hunner roses dancin' in't, a ferlie o' purple and green.

('The Common Riding', *The Glasgow Herald*, 12 March 1927, p. 4.)

It is a curious fact that this very impressive specimen is a Cotton Thistle or Onopordum acanthium, which is not native to Scotland, or for that matter Britain.

The bearer twirls the Bannock-and-Saut-Herrin',
The Croon o' Roses through the lift is farin', 460

The aucht-fit thistle wallops on hie;
In heather besoms a' the hills gang by.

But noo it's a' the fish o' the sea
Nailed on the roond o' the Earth to me;

Beauty and Love that are bobbin' there; 465
Syne the breengin' growth that alane I bear;

And Scotland followin' on ahint
For threepenny bits spleet-new frae the mint.

Drums in the Walligate, pipes in the air,
The wallopin' thistle is ill to bear. 470

But I'll dance the nicht wi' the stars o' Heaven
In the Mairket Place as shair's I'm livin'.

Easy to cairry roses or herrin',
And the lave may weel their threepenny bits earn.

Devil the star! It's Jean I'll ha'e 475
Again as she was on her weddin' day. . . .

Nerves in stounds o' delight,
Muscles in pride o' power,
Bluid as wi' roses dight
Life's toppin' pinnacles owre, 480
The thistle yet'll unite
Man and the Infinite!

Swippert and swith wi' virr
In the howes o' man's hert
Forever its muckle roots stir 485

Bannock-and-Saut-Herrin'—*a flat cake (nailed to) a salted herring* Croon—*Crown* aucht-fit—*eight-foot* wallops—*dances* hie—*high* besoms—*brooms* breengin'—*plunging* ahint—*behind* spleet-new—*brand-new* ill—*difficult* shair's—*sure as* the lave—*the rest* threepenny bits—*coins of that value* stounds—*throbs* dight—*arrayed* toppin'—*crowning* swippert—*agile* swith wi' virr—*quick with vigour* howes—*hollows*

462 and 468. All the children carried heather brooms, for which they were rewarded with newly minted threepenny coins.

465. *Beauty and Love*: MacD's interpretation of the symbolism of the floral crown carried in the procession.

471. Perhaps linking the ancient ritual of the Common Riding with dances representing the movement of the stars.

Man and the Infinite, 477-512.

The allusions to Leviathan and the Dragon may recall MacD's image of the Serpent as the original embodiment of the life force. There is also a suggestion of the cosmic tree, Yggdrasill, with the dragon gnawing at its root, which MacD will develop later. And cf. Isaiah 14. 29: 'Out of the serpent's root shall come forth a cockatrice, and his fruit shall be a fiery flying serpent'.

483. *Swith wi' virr*: a phrase MacD admired in George Beattie's 'John o' Arnha''.

Like a Leviathan astert,
Till'ts coils like a thistle's leafs
Sweep space wi' levin sheafs.

Frae laichest deeps o' the ocean
It rises in flight upon flight, 490
And 'yont its uttermaist motion
Can still set roses alight,
As else unreachable height
Fa's under its triumphin' sight.

Here is the root that feeds 495
The shank wi' the blindin' wings
Dwinin' abundheid to gleids
Like stars in their keethin' rings,
And blooms in sunrise and sunset
Inowre Eternity's yett. 500

Lay haud o' my hert and feel
Fountains ootloupin' the starns
Or see the Universe reel
Set gaen' by my eident harns,
Or test the strength o' my spauld 505
The wecht o' a' thing to hauld!

—The howes o' Man's hert are bare,
The Dragon's left them for good,
There's nocht but naethingness there,
The hole whaur the Thistle stood, 510
That rootless and radiant flies
A Phoenix in Paradise! . . .

Masoch and Sade
Turned into ane
Havoc ha'e made 515
O' my a'e brain.

astert—*on the move* levin—*lightning* laichest—*lowest* fa's—*falls* dwinin'—*dwindling* abuneheid—*overhead* gleids—*embers; sparks* keethin' rings—*circles in water caused by fish* inowre—*within* haud—*hold* ootloupin'—*outleaping* starns—*stars* reel—*whirl or spin round* eident—*busy; eager (MacD)* spauld—*shoulder* wecht—*weight* a' thing—*everything* howes—*hollows* hert—*heart* nocht—*naught* a'e—*one*

496. *Wings*: as in an emblematic design of the thistle with two wing-like leaves?

499-500. Cf. Blake: 'He who kisses the Joy as it flies / Lives in Eternity's sun-rise'. ('Eternity', from the Notebook of 1793.)

511. *Rootless*. The poet has second and very much darker thoughts about the fate of the uprooted thistle, culminating in ll. 2079-88.

Man's Cruel Plight, 513-532.

The sado-masochist theme suddenly announced here is a modern, psychological exemplar of the combination of opposites.

513. *Sade* anglicised to rhyme with *made*.

Weel, gin it's Sade
Let it be said
They've made me mad
—That'll dae instead. 520

But it's no' instead
In Scots, but insteed.
—The life they've led
In my puir heid.

But aince I've seen 525
In the thistle here
A' that they've been
I'll aiblins wun clear.

Thistleless fule,
You'll ha'e nocht left 530
But the hole frae which
Life's struggle is reft! . . .

Reason ser's nae end but pleasure,
Truth's no' an end but a means
To a wider knowledge o' life 535
And a keener interest in't.

We wha are poets and artists
Move frae inklin' to inklin',
And live for oor antrin lichtnin's
In the haingles atweenwhiles, 540

Laich as the feck o' mankind
Whence we breenge in unkennable shapes
—Crockats up, hair kaimed to the lift,
And no' to cree legs wi'! . . .

weel—*well* wun—*get* ser's—*serves* antrin—*rare* haingles—*state of ennui* atweenwhiles—*in between* laich—*low* feck—*bulk, majority* crockats up—*on one's dignity (MacD—but J has 'to set up one's crockats': to show ill-humour, or give an indiscreet answer)* kaimed—*combed* no' to cree legs wi'—*not safe to meddle with (an aberrant form of 'no' (gude) to creel eggs wi', not safe to deal with. This refers to the practice of Cadgers or Egglers, who collect eggs through the country, and pack them in their hampers—J.)*

517. *Sade* to rhyme with *mad.*

529-532. Life *is* the struggle of contraries. To evade or transcend the conflict is to lose touch with life itself.

The Challenge of the Arts, 533-544.

The philosophising here is unexpectedly reminiscent of Pragmatism, as in William James: 'The possession of truth, so far from being an end in itself, is only a preliminary means towards other vital satisfactions' (*Pragmatism*, London 1907). But what follows does not appear to accord with the principle enunciated. Presumably the 'inklings' of poets and artists are inklings of truth: in which case, should they not be condemned for living lives of boredom except for the occasional moments of revelation?

543-544. In view of the dubious nature of MacD's Scots at this point (see glossary), there is a certain irony in the fact that he was to quote these lines as an example of 'the real Mackay!—phrases of pure Scots a man can not come by unless he is thinking in Scots and has recovered for himself, and achieved a mastery of, the full canon of that magnificent tongue'. (*Lucky Poet*, London 1943, p.22.)

We're ootward boond frae Scotland. 545
Guid-bye, fare-ye-weel; guid-bye, fare-ye-weel.
—A' the Scots that ever wur
Gang ootward in a creel.

We're ootward boond frae Scotland.
Guid-bye, fare-ye-weel; guid-bye, fare-ye-weel. 550
The cross-tap is a monkey-tree
That nane o' us can spiel.

We've never seen the Captain,
But the first mate is a Jew.
We've shipped aboord Eternity. 555
Adieu, kind freends, adieu! . . .

In the creel or on the gell
O' oor coutribat and ganien,
What gin ithers see or hear
Naething but a gowkstorm? 560

Gin you stop the galliard
To teach them hoo to dance,
There comes in Corbaudie
And turns their gammons up! . . .

wur—*were* creel—*wicker basket (for fish); state of excitement* cross-tap—*mizzen-mast (MacD. From Swedish 'kryss-topp', the mizzen-top, as cited by J?)* monkey tree—*monkey puzzle? (But monkey spars are reduced masts and yards for a vessel devoted to the instruction and exercise of boys.)* spiel—*climb* in the creel—*in a state of mental excitement or confusion, or physical agony* on the gell—*on the spree* coutribat—*confused struggle* ganien—*rodomontade* gowkstorm—*storm which was believed to coincide with the appearance of the cuckoo; a passing disturbance* galliard—*a quick dance* there comes in Corbaudie—*that is where the snag comes in* gammons—*feet (of animals, e.g. pigs)*

Outward Bound, 545-556.

Cf. the following fragment of a sea-shanty:

> Good-bye, fare ye well
> Good-bye, fare ye well
> We're outward bound from Peterhead town
> Hurrah my boys, we're outward bound.
>
> (*The Greig-Duncan Folk Song Collection*, ed. Patrick Shuldham-Shaw & Emily B. Lyle, Aberdeen 1981, I, 6.)

See also the epilogue of Melville's *White-Jacket*, in which we are told that 'God was the shipwright' and the 'Lord High Admiral' of our craft. Though we 'sail with sealed orders, and our last destination remains a secret to ourselves and our officers; yet our final haven was predestinated ere we slipped from the stocks at Creation'.

548. *Creel.* Here meaning 'basket' rather than 'state of excitement' as in l. 557. Cf. the Edward Lear characters, the Jumblies, who went to sea in a sieve ('The Dong with a Luminous Nose').

551. The monkey-puzzle tree is presumably the enigmatic thistle.

The Ineducable, 557-564.

Like some of MacD's earlier lyrics, this is a little poem constructed around unusual Scots expressions found in Jamieson's Dictionary.

558. 'Oor' apparently refers back to the 'poets and artists' of l. 537.

You vegetable cat's melody! 565
Your *Concert Miaulant* is
A triumph o' discord shairly,
And suits my fancy fairly
—I'm shair that Scott'll agree
He canna vie wi' this. . . . 570

Said my body to my mind,
"I've been startled whiles to find,
When Jean has been in bed wi' me,
A kind o' Christianity!"

To my body said my mind, 575
"But your benmaist thocht you'll find
Was 'Bother what I think I feel
—Jean kens the set o' my bluid owre weel,
And lauchs to see me in the creel
O' my courage-bag confined.' " . . . 580

I wish I kent the physical basis
O' a' life's seemin' airs and graces.

It's queer the thochts a kittled cull
Can lowse or splairgin' glit annul.

Man's spreit is wi' his ingangs twined 585
In ways that he can ne'er unwind.

A wumman whiles a bawaw gi'es
That clean abaws him gin he sees.

Or wi' a movement o' a leg
Shows'm his mind is juist a geg. 590

shairly—*surely* set—*cast, disposition* bluid—*blood* creel—*basket (as used as a trap)* courage-bag—*scrotum* kittled—*tickled* cull—*testicle (of a ram)* lowse—*let loose* splairgin'—*splattering* glit—*slime* spreit—*spirit* ingangs—*entrails* bawaw—*scornful side-glance* abaws—*abashes (MacD. But see J: 'to abaw, abay', to astonish; 'to abays', to abash. MacD confused the two verbs.)* geg—*hoax*

The Psycho-Somatic Quandary, 565-594.

The title suggests another modern version of the antisyzygy, in this case combining the mental and the physical.

565-568. The vegetable being addressed is the thistle, though that may not be immediately apparent because of the placing of this passage. Melody made with the cacophonous sounds of cats is a musical illustration of the 'reconciliation of opposite or discordant qualities'. MacD may have had in mind the 'Comic Duet for Two Cats', attributed to Rossini.

569. *Scott*: Francis George Scott, the composer, to whom this work was dedicated.

581-594. 'It is impossible to say what finest elements in art, in morals, in civilisation generally, may not really be rooted in an auto-erotic impulse. . . . It is along this path, it may be claimed—as dimly glimpsed by Nietzsche, Hinton, and other earlier thinkers—that the main explanation of the dynamic process by which the arts, in the widest sense, have come into being, is now chiefly being explored. One thinks of Freud and especially of Dr. Otto Rank'. (Havelock Ellis, *The Dance of Life*, London 1923, pp. 101-2.) And cf.: 'We already know . . . that many of our spiritual faculties can only be manifested if certain glands, notably the thyroid and sex-glands, are functioning properly, and that very minute changes in such glands affect the character greatly'. (J.B.S. Haldane, *Daedalus*, London 1924, p. 70.)

I'se warrant Jean 'ud no' be lang
In findin' whence this thistle sprang.

Mebbe it's juist because I'm no'
Beddit wi' her that gars it grow! . . .

A luvin' wumman is a licht* 595
That shows a man his waefu' plicht,
Bleezin' steady on ilka bane,
Wrigglin' sinnen an' twinin' vein,
Or fleerin' quick and gane again,
And the mair scunnersome the sicht 600
The mair for love and licht he's fain
Till clear and chitterin' and nesh
Move a' the miseries o' his flesh. . . .

O lass, wha see'est me
As I daur hardly see, 605
I marvel that your bonny een
Are as they hadna seen.

Through a' my self-respect
They see the truth abject
—Gin you could pierce their blindin' licht 610
You'd see a fouler sicht! . . .

* Suggested by the French of Edmond Rocher.

beddit—*bedded* gars—*makes, compels to* bane—*bone (But the sense of English 'bane' is also relevant.)* sinnen—*sinew* fleerin'—*flaring; taunting* scunnersome—*disgusting* chittering—*quivering* nesh—*raw, sensitised (with sexual undertone)* daur—*dare* een—*eyes*

591-594. The Freudian point of this passage is that the thistle has become a phallic symbol.

Love, 595-603.

This poem appeared previously in MacD's collection *Penny Wheep* (1926). His debt to Edmond Rocher is confined to the final lines of a poem in *Le Manteau du Passé*, translated as follows by Jethro Bithell in *Contemporary French Poetry* (1912), p.lxxix: 'they are flaring torches who / Illume thee—and the miseries of thy flesh'. MacD's is in every way a subtler poem than Rocher's, the message of which, as announced by the title, is 'Love Them All': all women, physically, since their souls are mere illusions.

602. 'That peculiar word "nesh", for which there is no equivalent in English, is related to an Icelandic word which means to smell out, to inquire after; and is a figure of speech derived from the eagerness and acuteness of smell of animals in heat'. (MacD, 'Braid Scots and the Sense of Smell', *Scottish Nation*, 15 May 1923, p. 10.) This is derived from Jamieson on *eassin* via *neeshin*.

In the Last Analysis, 604-611.

610-611. The lines in italics are to be understood as spoken by the girl. This is a common ballad procedure, but has escaped the attention of some commentators on the poem, with unfortunate results. Cf. the monsters in 'Gairmscoile':

> Brides sometimes catch their wild een, scansin' reid,
> Beekin' abune the herts they thocht to lo'e
> And horror-stricken ken that i' themselves
> A like beast stan's, and lookin' love thro' and thro'
> Meets the reid een wi' een like seevun hells.
>
> (*Complete Poems*, p. 72.)

O wha's the bride that cairries the bunch
O' thistles blinterin' white?
Her cuckold bridegroom little dreids
What he sall ken this nicht. 615

For closer than gudeman can come
And closer to'r than hersel',
Wha didna need her maidenheid
Has wrocht his purpose fell.

O wha's been here afore me, lass, 620
And hoo did he get in?
—A man that deed or I was born
This evil thing has din.

And left, as it were on a corpse,
Your maidenheid to me? 625
—Nae lass, gudeman, sin' Time began
'S hed ony mair to gi'e.

But I can gi'e ye kindness, lad,
And a pair o' willin' hands,
And you sall ha'e my briests like stars, 630
My limbs like willow wands,

And on my lips ye'll heed nae mair,
And in my hair forget,
The seed o' a' the men that in
My virgin womb ha'e met. . . . 635

Millions o' wimmen bring forth in pain
Millions o' bairns that are no' worth ha'en.

Wull ever a wumman be big again
Wi's muckle's a Christ? Yech, there's nae sayin'.

Gin that's the best that you ha'e comin', 640
Fegs but I'm sorry for you, wumman!

Yet a'e thing's certain.—Your faith is great.
Whatever happens, you'll no' be blate! . . .

blinterin'—*glimmering* dreids—*suspects* gudeman—*husband* to'r—*to her* wrocht—*wrought* deed—*died* or—*ere* din—*done* 's hed—*has had* ha'en—*having* blate—*bashful, diffident*

O Wha's the Bride?, 612-635.

For the ballad tradition behind MacD's poem, cf.:

> The lady stands in her bower door,
>   As straight as willow wand;
> The blacksmith stood a little foreby,
>   Wi hammer in his hand.
>
> 'Weel may ye dress ye, lady fair,
>   Into your robes o red;
> Before the morn at this same time,
>   I'll gain your maidenhead.'

('The Twa Magicians', F.J. Child, *The English and Scottish Popular Ballads*, Boston 1857-59, I, no. 44.)

624-625. Cf. ll. 1956-7:

> Or as frae sire to son we gang
> And coontless corpses in us thrang.

634-635. Cf.: 'I but re-inform features and attributes that have long been laid aside from evil in the quiet of the grave. Is it me you love . . . or the race that made me?' (R.L. Stevenson, 'Ollala', in *The Merry Men*.) 'And through a cylinder of wombs . . . I see . . . the ripples o' Eve's moniplies'. (ll. 1545-8.)

Repetition Complex, 636-643.

Reminiscent of Nietzsche's 'Eternal Recurrence'. 'What was the purpose of human existence? Was it simply to produce here and there a great man (and him "human; all too human") amid millions and millions of the mediocre, the dull, the unhappy? Such a thought burned the brain of Nietzsche'. (A.R. Orage, *Friedrich Nietzsche* (1906), p. 77.) 'All too little the greatest!—that was my weariness of man! And eternal recurrence of the smallest too!—that was my weariness with all existence'. (Nietzsche, *Zarathustra*, III, 13.)

640-641. 'The Superman—if I may be sententious for a moment—will not be born of woman, but of man'. (Orage, *Art of Reading* (1930), p. 259.)

Mary lay in jizzen
As it were claith o' gowd, 645
But it's in orra duds
Ilka ither bairntime's row'd.

Christ had never toothick,
Christ was never seeck,
But Man's a fiky bairn 650
Wi' bellythraw, ripples, and worm-i'-the-cheek! . . .

Dae what ye wull ye canna parry
This skeleton-at-the-feast that through the starry
Maze o' the warld's intoxicatin' soiree
Claughts ye, as micht at an affrontit quean 655
A bastard wean!

Prood mune, ye needna thring your shouder there,
And at your puir get like a snawstorm stare,
It's yours—there's nae denyin't—and I'm shair
You'd no' enjoy the evenin' much the less 660
Gin you'd but openly confess!

Dod! It's an eaten and a spewed-like thing,
Fell like a little-bodies' changeling,
And it's nae credit t'ye that you s'ud bring
The like to life—yet, gi'en a mither's love, 665
—Hee, hee!—wha kens hoo't micht improve? . . .

Or is this Heaven, this yalla licht,
And I the aft'rins o' the Earth,
Or sic's in this wanchancy time
May weel fin' sudden birth? 670

jizzen—*childbed; straw (J)* claith o' gowd—*cloth of gold* orra duds—*shabby, ragged clothes* bairntime—*a woman's breeding time (MacD. But used here as if it referred, not to her child-bearing span, but to lying-in or parturition itself.)* row'd—*rolled, wrapped up* seeck—*sick* fiky—*troublesome* bellythraw—*colic* ripples—*diarrhoea (MacD); a weakness in the back and reins (J)* worm-i'-the-cheek—*toothache* claughts—*clutches* quean—*lass* wean—*child* prood—*proud* thring—*to shrug (MacD. SND notes only a sixteenth-century example of 'thring' used as a substantive meaning 'a shrug'.)* shouder—*shoulder* get—*bastard* shair—*sure* little-bodies—*fairies* mither—*mother* yalla—*yellow* aft'rins—*off-scourings (MacD); the last milk taken from the cow (J)* sic's—*such as* wanchancy—*ill-omened* hauf-—*half-*

The Problem Child, 644-651.

Cf. Dostoevsky: 'It's all very well for Christ; he was God'.

The Skeleton at the Feast, 652-706.

653. The 'skeleton at the feast' is an ominous reminder in the midst of good cheer. Cf. the thistle as 'skeleton at a tea-meeting' (l. 428).

657-661. The Moon (Diana, goddess of virginity) might seem an unlikely mother for the bastard thistle as alleged here, but as Jamieson points out she was 'also acknowledged as the goddess who presided over love. Hence, notwithstanding the great difference of character between Venus and the chaste Diana, it is asserted, that according to the heathen mythology, they were in fact the same'. Perhaps MacD had a different mythology in mind, associating the Moon with Sophia (through his interest in Blok and Solovyov), and hence with the Gnostic account of Sophia's self-generated offspring, an abortion which led eventually to the material world and Man. This suggestion is not so far-fetched as might at first appear, since it will be seen that MacD does undoubtedly regard the thistle as an abortion resulting from the unsuccessful embodiment of the spiritual in the material world.

662. Cf. his mother's description of the infant MacD, quoted in Gordon Wright, *MacDiarmid: An Illustrated Biography*, Edinburgh 1977, p.21: 'an eaten an' spewed lookin' wee thing wi' een like twa burned holes in a blanket'. Yiddy Bally, the hero of 'The Common Riding', is also 'a puir bit eaten-an-spewed-lookin' cratur, . . . juist a rickle o' banes wi' the thews o' a maggot' (see note on ll.455-476).

665-666. The diabolical laugh hints at incest. Having settled the hash of virginity, MacD aims a passing innuendo at the sacred cow of mother love.

The roots that wi' the worms compete
Hauf-publish me upon the air.
The struggle that divides me still
Is seen fu' plainly there.

The thistle's shank scarce holes the grun', 675
My grave'll spare nae mair I doot.
—The crack's fu' wide; the shank's fu' strang;
A' that I was is oot.

My knots o' nerves that struggled sair
Are weel reflected in the herb; 680
My crookit instincts were like this,
As sterile and acerb.

My self-tormented spirit took
The shape repeated in the thistle;
Sma' beauty jouked my rawny banes 685
And maze o' gristle.

I seek nae peety, Paraclete,
And, fegs, I think the joke is rich
—Pairt soul, pairt skeleton's come up;
They kentna which was which! . . . 690

Thou Daith in which my life
Sae vain a thing can seem,
Frae whatna source d'ye borrow
Your devastatin' gleam?

Nae doot that hidden sun 695
'Ud look fu' wae ana',
Gin I could see it in the licht
That frae the Earth you draw! . . .

Shudderin' thistle, gi'e owre, gi'e owre!
A'body's gi'en in to the facts o' life; 700
The impossible truth'll triumph at last,
And mock your strife.

I doot—*I'm afraid (Scots usage carries implications of probability, unlike English 'doubt'.)* fu'—*very* sair—*sorely* sma'—*small* jouked—*evaded, escaped* rawny (randy)—*coarse, disreputable (or English dialect: clumsy, awkward, thin)* peety—*pity* kentna—*didn't know* whatna—*what sort of* fu' wae—*very woeful* ana'—*as well* gi'e owre—*give up, stop*

679-680.

> 'So let us think we are the tortured nerves
> Of Being in travail with a higher type'.

(John Davidson, 'Lammas', *A Second Book of Fleet Street Eclogues*, London 1896, p. 41.)

687. *Paraclete*: the Holy Spirit as Comforter, after Christ's resurrection (John 14. 26). The poet imagines himself as resurrected in the form of the thistle.

699. This line is echoed by 1. 1442. At various points in the poem the thistle may be seen as shuddering because of the rising of the wind, the internal tensions of its 'self-tormenting spirit', or the epileptic symptoms of the disease that afflicts it.

701. The 'impossible truth' may be faith in the meaning of life, which is irrational, and so impossible for reason to understand.

Your sallow leafs can never thraw,
Wi' a' their oorie shakin',
Ae doot into the hert o' life 705
That it may be mistak'n. . . .

O Scotland is
THE barren fig.
Up, carles, up
And roond it jig. 710

Auld Moses took
A dry stick and
Instantly it
Floo'ered in his hand.

Pu' Scotland up, 715
And wha can say
It winna bud
And blossom tae.

A miracle's
Oor only chance. 720
Up, carles, up
And let us dance!

Puir Burns, wha's bouquet like a shot kail blaws
—Will this rouch sicht no' gi'e the orchids pause?
The Gairdens o' the Muses may be braw, 725
But nane like oors can breenge and eat ana'!

And owre the kailyaird-wa' Dunbar they've flung,
And a' their countrymen that e'er ha'e sung
For ither than ploomen's lugs or to enrichen
Plots on Parnassus set apairt for kitchen. 730

thraw—*throw* oorie—*chilly; sickly* carles—*men* pu'—*pull* tae—*too* wha's—*whose* shot kail—*sprouted cabbage* blaws—*blossoms* braw—*fine, impressive* breenge and eat ana'—*'flourish and be edible too' (MacD's English translation. This is what he meant to say: not what the words themselves convey.)* kailyaird-wa'—*kitchen-garden wall* ploomen—*ploughmen* lugs—*ears*

705-706. Cf. Santayana's 'primal and universal religion, the religion of will, the faith which life has in itself because it is life and in its aims, because it is pursuing them'. (Quoted by MacD in 'Poetry and Science', *Selected Essays*, London 1969, p. 244.)

The Barren Fig, 707-722.

'Now in the morning . . . [Jesus] hungered. And when he saw a fig tree in the way, he came unto it, and found nothing thereon, but leaves only, and said unto it. Let no fruit grow on thee henceforward for ever. And presently the fig tree withered away'. (Matthew 21. 18-19.)

711-714. Despite the prizes for biblical knowledge awarded to MacD in his youth, this seems a rather inaccurate allusion to Moses, who took no active part in the miracle which MacD seems to have had in mind: 'Moses went into the tabernacle of witness; and, behold, the rod of Aaron for the house of Levi was budded, and brought forth buds, and bloomed blossoms, and yielded almonds' (Numbers 17. 8). Amongst the various Old Testament traditions concerning the rods of Moses and Aaron, this is the one which is primarily concerned with the flowering of the rod as a metaphor for the rise to power of the tribe of Aaron. Moses' own stick was actually transformed into a serpent for the rather different purpose of impressing Pharaoh. Perhaps MacD also had in mind the incident concerning Wamba, who said he would only accept the crown offered to him if the olive branch he used as a stick were to bear leaves—which it did, and so he became king of the Goths.

To Be Yourselves and Make That Worth Being, 723-750.

723. The bride's bouquet of thistles (ll. 612-3) is displaced by a Burnsian bouquet of cabbage from the Kailyard. MacD saw the literary 'Kailyard' as comprising simplistic imitations of Burns in vernacular verse as well as the 'school' of Scottish novelists so called: particularly J.M. Barrie, 'Ian Maclaren', and S.R. Crockett.

727. For MacD, William Dunbar (c.1460-c.1513) represented the artistic and intellectual standards appropriate to Scottish literature when it made a genuine contribution to the literature of Europe, in painful contrast to the recent mindless maunderings of the Kailyard.

Ploomen and ploomen's wives—shades o' the Manse
May weel be at the heid o' sic a dance,
As through the polish't ha's o' Europe leads
The rout o' bagpipes, haggis, and sheep's heids!

The vandal Scot! Frae Brankstone's deidly barrow 735
I struggle yet to free a'e winsome marrow,
To show what Scotland micht ha'e hed instead
O' this preposterous Presbyterian breed.

(Gin Glesca folk are tired o' Hengler,
And still need breid and circuses, there's Spengler, 740
Or gin ye s'ud need mair than ane to teach ye,
Then learn frae Dostoevski and frae Nietzsche.

heid—*head* ha's—*halls* rout—*fashionable evening assembly* haggis—*unknown (MacD)* marrow—*mate, companion* Glesca—*Glasgow*

731. *Shades o' the Manse.* 'Maclaren', Crockett, and the leading publicist of the Kailyard, Robertson Nichol, were Free Kirk ministers, while other ministers played a prominent part in more recent Scottish literary circles—'the most painfully sub-fusc in Europe', according to MacD ('Religion and the Scottish Renaissance', *Northern Review*, I, no. 4 (September 1924), p. 255).

734. The sheep follow, and resemble, their pastors—and sheep's head broth was a traditional Scottish dish. It went with the haggis and the piping here intended to recall the ritual of a Burns Supper, as in the opening section of the poem.

735-738. Another reference to the national Scottish disaster of Flodden (cf. ll. 33-34).

> A' the lads they used to meet
> By Ettrick braes or Yarrow
> Lyin' thrammelt head and feet
> In Brankstone's deadly barrow!
> O Flodden Field!

(J.B. Selkirk, 'Selkirk After Flodden', in *Poems*, Edinburgh 1905, p. 57.)

MacD's text had 'Branksome' for 'Brankstone' till emended in 1978. The normal spelling of the name of the battlefield is in fact Branxton.

736. *A'e winsome marrow.* Glossed by MacD as 'a creditable limb'. Used as a ballad-style formula by William Hamilton of Bangour in 'The Braes of Yarrow' and echoed by Wordsworth in 'Yarrow Unvisited' and 'Yarrow Revisited'. In Hamilton's poem the unwilling bride rejects the advances of her husband and turns to the ghost of her lover, whom he has killed.

739. Albert Hengler's Circus in Glasgow, 1867-1924.

740-742. Hengler was perhaps dragged in for the sake of the rhyme with Spengler, who came to mind when MacD was struggling with the lost causes of Scotland's history, because of Spengler's view of world history as a series of fixed, predestined cycles. The significance of Dostoevsky is dealt with at length later in the poem. Nietzsche provides the 'lesson' which follows immediately.

And let the lesson be—to be yersel's,
Ye needna fash gin it's to be ocht else.
To be yersel's—and to mak' that worth bein'. 745
Nae harder job to mortals has been gi'en.

To save your souls fu' mony o' ye are fain,
But de'il a dizzen to mak' it worth the daein'.
I widna gi'e five meenits wi' Dunbar
For a' the millions o' ye as ye are). 750

I micht ha'e been contentit wi' the Rose
Gin I'd had ony reason to suppose
That what the English dae can e'er mak' guid
For what Scots dinna—and first and foremaist should.

I micht ha'e been contentit—gin the feck 755
O' my ain folk had grovelled wi' less respec',
But their obsequious devotion
Made it for me a criminal emotion.

I micht ha'e been contentit—ere I saw
That there were fields on which it couldna draw, 760
(While strang-er roots ran under't) and a'e threid
O't drew frae Scotland a' that it could need,

And left the maist o' Scotland fallow
(Save for the patch on which the kail-blades wallow),
And saw hoo ither countries' genius drew 765
Elements like mine that in a rose ne'er grew. . . .

Gin the threid haud'n us to the rose were snapt,
There's no' a'e petal o't that 'ud be clapt.
A' Scotland gi'es gangs but to jags or stalk,
The bloom is English—and 'ud ken nae lack! . . . 770

fash—*fuss* fu' mony—*a great many* de'il a dizzen—*not a dozen* feck—*most part* strang-er—*stronger* kail-blades—*cabbage-leaves* haud'n—*holding* clapt—*shrunken* gangs—*goes* jags—*thorns*

743-746. 'To become what we are—unique, incomparable, our own law-givers, our own creators'. (A.R. Orage, *Nietzsche in Outline and Aphorism* (1907), p. 118.) 'The man who would not belong in the mass . . . should follow his conscience which shouts at him: "Be yourself! You are not really all that which you do, think, and desire now" '. (Nietzsche, *Untimely Meditations.*) And cf. Thoreau as summarised by Stevenson: 'To be what we are, and to become what we are capable of becoming, is the only end of life'. (*Familiar Studies of Men and Books* (1882) p. 164.) MacD echoes this ethic of self-realisation elsewhere in the poem (ll. 955-6, 1716), but he does not merely follow Nietzsche. He applies the principle not only to the individual but (unlike Nietzsche) to the nation also.

747. The readers addressed as 'ye' are implicitly Scots.

My Quarrel with the Rose, 751-770.

A political dimension to the poem is suggested here, with MacD writing from an anti-Union, Scottish Nationalist position about the Rose not so much of England as of English colonialism. However, this theme is not picked up again until near the end of the work, at l. 2371.

764. *The patch*: the cabbage patch (the Kailyard).

O drumlie clood o' crudity and cant,
Obliteratin' as the Easter rouk
That rows up frae the howes and droons the heichs,
And turns the country to a faceless spook.

Like blurry shapes o' landmarks in the haar 775
The bonny idiosyncratic place-names loom,
Clues to the vieve and maikless life that's lain
Happit for centuries in an alien gloom. . . .

Eneuch! For noo I'm in the mood,
Scotland, responsive to my thoughts, 780
Lichts mile by mile, as my ain nerves,
Frae Maidenkirk to John o' Groats!

What are prophets and priests and kings,
What's ocht to the people o' Scotland?
Speak—and Cruivie'll goam at you, 785
Gilsanquhar jalouse you're dottlin!

And Edinburgh and Glasgow
Are like ploomen in a pub.
They want to hear o' naething
But their ain foul hubbub. . . . 790

The fules are richt; an extra thocht
Is neither here nor there.
Oor lives may differ as they like
—The self-same fate we share.

And whiles I wish I'd nae mair sense 795
Than Cruivie and Gilsanquhar,
And envy their rude health and curse
My gnawin' canker.

drumlie—*dark; troubled* rouk—*mist* rows—*rolls* howes—*hollows* heichs—*heights* haar—*mist, fog* vieve—*vivid* maikless—*matchless* happit—*covered, buried* eneuch—*enough* goam—*stare vacuously* jalouse—*suspect* dottlin—*becoming senile, crazy* whiles—*sometimes*

779-782. This and the subsequent passage in italics (ll. 805-808) seem intended to be read as coming from one voice which is challenged by the other in an internal dialogue.

782. From one end of Scotland to the other, south to north. The phrase is used by Burns in his poem 'On the Late Captain Grose's Peregrinations Thro' Scotland':

> Hear, Land o' Cakes, and brither Scots,
> Frae Maidenkirk to Johny Groats!—

(Note Burns's rhyming of 'Scots' and MacD's of 'thoughts' with 'Groats'.)

783. Cf. A.G. Gardiner, *Prophets, Priests, and Kings*, London 1908—a collection of articles on recent influential or prestigious figures.

797-798. Since the poet is presented as a thinker, the implication is that at least his kind of thought may be, like art, a product of 'the artist's diseased nervous system'. The theme of disease (associated in particular with Dostoevsky) will be given major development later in the poem.

Guid sakes, ye dinna need to pass
Ony exam. to dee 800
—Daith canna tell a common flech
Frae a performin' flea! . . .

It sets you weel to slaver
To let sic gaadies fa'
—*The mune's the muckle white whale* 805
I seek in vain to kaa!

The Earth's my mastless samyn,
The thistle my ruined sail.
—Le'e go as you maun in the end,
And droon in your plumm o' ale! . . . 810

Clear keltie aff an' fill again
Withoot corneigh bein' cryit,
The drink's aye best that follows a drink.
Clear keltie aff and try it.

Be't whisky gill or penny wheep, 815
Or ony ither lotion,
We bood to ha'e a thimblefu' first,
And syne we'll toom an ocean! . . .

"To Luna at the Craidle-and-Coffin
To sof'n her hert if owt can sof'n:— 820

Auld bag o' tricks, ye needna come
And think to stap me in your womb.

You needna fash to rax and strain.
Carline, I'll *no'* be born again

dee—*die* flech—*flea* it sets you weel—*it well becomes you (Generally used in an ironic sense—J.)* slaver—*slobber; talk fulsomely* gaadies—*beads; gems; gaffes (MacD); note also 'gawd', of saliva: to fall in slavers or thread-like streams (SND)* kaa (ca')—*drive* samyn—*deck of ship (MacD); cf. 'seyme', in ship-building, a nail driven through the overlapping portion of two planks and clenched with a rivet (J)* le'e—*leave* plumm—*deep pool* clear keltie aff—*drink off a bumper, empty one's glass* corneigh—*enough (coeur ennuyé, internally disquieted—MacD, but see note)* cryit—*cried* gill—*a Scots measure: quarter-mutchkin* penny wheep—*small beer* we bood to—*it behoves us to* toom—*empty* owt—*anything* fash—*trouble* rax—*stretch* carline—*old woman; witch*

803-804. 'It sets you well to slaver, you let such *gaadys* fall', Scots proverb, 'ironically signifying that what he is saying, or doing, is too assuming for him'. (James Kelly, *A Complete Collection of Scotish Proverbs* (1721), quoted by Jamieson.)

805. An allusion to Melville's *Moby Dick*, foreshadowed in l. 367 and taken up again at l. 1787.

The Splore, 811-860.

811-818. Printed as a separate poem, 'Calister Hall', *Glasgow Herald*, 2 Aug. 1926, p. 4.

811-812. 'It is a singular fancy that the ingenious Sir James Foulis throws out as to the origin of this custom. When describing the manners of the ancient Albanich of Scotland, he says: "A horn was twisted so as to go round the arm. This being filled with liquor, was to be applied to the lips, and drunk off at one draught. If, in withdrawing the arm, any liquor was left, it discovered itself by rattling in the windings of the horn. Then the company called out *corneigh*, i.e. the *horn cries*; and the delinquent was obliged to drink *keltie*, that is, to fill up his cup again and drink it out, according to the laws of the *Kelts*" '. (Jamieson, quoting from *Transactions of the Antiquarian Society of Scotland*, I, 23.)

815-816. Cf. Burns, 'The Holy Fair', ll. 167-171:

> Be't *whisky-gill* or *penny-wheep*,
> Or onie stronger potion,
> It never fails, on drinkin deep,
> To kittle up our *notion*,
> By night or day.

819-820. *The Craidle-and-Coffin*. Cf. the Gillha', glossed by MacD as 'the hostelry of life', in the dedication of the poem. *Sof'n* is there for the rhyme. His message to Luna, the moon goddess, has nothing to do with softening her heart, even on a comic level.

In ony brat you can produce. 825
Carline, gi'e owre—O what's the use?

You pay nae heed but plop me in,
Syne shove me oot, and winna be din

—Owre and owre, the same auld trick,
Cratur withoot climacteric! . . . 830

"Noo Cutty Sark's tint that ana',
And dances in her skin—Ha! Ha!

I canna ride awa' like Tam,
But e'en maun bide juist whaur I am.

I canna ride—and gin I could, 835
I'd sune be sorry I hedna stude,

For less than a' there is to see
'll never be owre muckle for me.

Cutty, gin you've mair to strip,
Aff wi't, lass—and let it rip!". . . 840

Ilka pleesure I can ha'e
Ends like a dram ta'en yesterday.

And tho' to ha'e it I am lorn
—What better 'ud I be the morn? . . .

My belly on the gantrees there, 845
The spigot frae my cullage,
And wow but how the fizzin' yill
In spilth increased the ullage!

gi'e owre—*desist* syne—*then* winna be din—*won't be done* cratur—*creature* tint—*lost* bide—*stay* dram—*measure of liquor; a (small) drink* lorn—*lost, destroyed, ruined (J. But used by MacD with a sense of longing.)* the morn—*tomorrow* gantrees—*support for barrels* cullage—*male genitals (formed by MacD from 'cull', testicle, when in need of a rhyme?)* yill—*ale* spilth *(English)*—*spillage, overflow* ullage *(English)*—*deficiency in contents of a vessel*

821-830. Cf. the mysteries associated with the moon goddess (Astarte, Luna, etc.) who brought the god (e.g. Adonis) to life again in her womb, so that he was reborn. Also Yeats, 'The Crazed Moon': 'Crazed through much child-bearing / The moon is staggering in the sky'.

831. *Cutty Sark*—'Short Shirt'— was the name given by Tam o' Shanter in Burns's poem to the witch who was wearing a very abbreviated shift.

841-844. This awkwardly placed piece of moralising was presumably suggested by the 'pleasures are like poppies spread' passage in 'Tam o' Shanter' (ll. 59-60).

I was an anxious barrel, lad,
When first they tapped my bung. 850
They whistled me up, yet thro' the lift
My freaths like rainbows swung.

Waesucks, a pride for ony bar,
The boast o' barleyhood,
Like Noah's Ark abune the faem 855
Maun float, a gantin' cude,

For I was thrawn fu' cock owre sune,
And wi' a single jaw
I made the pub a blindin' swelth,
And how'd the warld awa'! . . . 860

What forest worn to the back-hauf's this,
What Eden brocht doon to a bean-swaup?
The thistle's to earth as the man
In the mune's to the mune, puir chap.

The haill warld's barkin' and fleein', 865
And this is its echo and aiker,
A soond that arrears in my lug,
Herrin'-banein' back to its maker,

A swaw like a flaw in a jewel
Or *nadryv** jaloused in a man, 870
Or Creation unbiggit again
To the draucht wi' which it began. . . .

* Tragical crack (Dostoevski's term).

freath—*froth* waesucks—*alas* barleyhood—*a state of drunkenness or violent temper* faem—*foam* gantin'—*gaping* cude—*tub; barrel (MacD)* fu' cock—*(of a tap:) full open* jaw—*splash* swelth—*gulf; whirlpool* how'd—*shorn down (MacD, who also offers 'hosed' in his English translation. J has 'howd', to float away, as on a flooded river.)* worn to the back-hauf—*nearly worn out* bean-swaup—*hull of a bean; anything of no value or strength* barkin' and fleein'—*on the verge of ruin, bankruptcy* aiker—*the break or movement made in water by fish swimming rapidly* arrears—*goes backward (Obsolete English. J has adverb 'arreir', backward.)* herrin'-banein'—*herring-boning; zig-zagging (as in weaving, carpentry, architecture, or skiing)* swaw—*ripple* jaloused—*divined, suspected* unbiggit—*unbuilt* draucht—*draught*

845-860. 'A piece of mystification. I haven't an idea of what I was after—or rather of what the words mean—what matters is the sound—shout it out loud and don't bother about the sense and I think you'll find it fairly comes off'. (MacD to P. Macgillivray, 28 Sept. 1926.) One might doubt if Macgillivray swallowed this protestation of innocence.

The Mortal Flaw, 861-900.

861. *What forest?* The Caledonian Forest.

863-864. A possible link between the Man in the Moon and the thistle here is the tradition that he carries a thorn-bush—the worthless produce of the land—on his back.

868. *Herrin'-banein' back to its maker.* In addition to MacD's celebration of the verb 'to herring-bone', there is a tradition that the herring preserves the mark of its Maker's thumb in it, the primitive mark of creation.

870. 'The theory of Imaginism was that the principal thing in poetry is "imagery", and their poetry (as well as much of Esenin's) is an agglomeration of "images" of the most far-fetched and exaggerated description. A principal point of their practice was not to distinguish between "pure" and "impure", and to introduce the coarsest and crudest images in the immediate neighbourhood of the pathetic and sublime. Some of the Imaginists were merely "hooligans", but in others a tragical "crack" (*nadryv*, to use Dostoevsky's word) is clearly present. They had a morbid craving for dirt, humiliation, and suffering, like the Man from Underground'. (D.S. Mirsky, *Contemporary Russian Literature 1881-1925* (1926), p. 266.) 'Blok successfully expresses [in the poem MacD's version of which is called 'Poet's Pub', ll. 169-220] . . . that psychological state which Dostoevskij calls *nadryv*, that feeling of "laceration" experienced by the human heart when torn between opposite forces, good and evil, foul and fair'. (R. Poggioli, *The Poets of Russia 1890-1930*, Cambridge, Mass. 1960, p. 200.)

Abordage o' this toom houk's nae mowse.
It munks and's ill to lay haud o',
As gin a man ettled to ride 875
On the shouders o' his ain shadow.

I canna biel't; tho' steekin' an e'e,
Tither's munkie wi' munebeam for knool in't,
For there's nae sta'-tree and the brute's awa'
Wi' me kinkin' like foudrie ahint. . . . 880

Sae Eternity'll buff nor stye
For Time, and shies at a touch, man;
Yet aye in a belth o' Thocht
Comes alist like the Fleein' Dutchman. . . .

As the worms'll breed in my corpse until 885
It's like a rice-puddin', the thistle
Has made an eel-ark o' the lift
Whaur elvers like skirl-in-the-pan sizzle,

Like a thunder-plump on the sunlicht,
Or the slounge o' daith on my dreams, 890
Or as to a fair forfochen man
A breedin' wife's beddiness seems,

abordage—*boarding a ship* toom—*empty* houk—*hulk* nae mowse—*no joke* munks—*diminishes below the proper size (J); swings away (MacD)* ettled—*aimed* biel—*shelter (MacD. But note J: 'beiled', moored, secured.)* steekin' an e'e—*shutting an eye* tither—*the other* munkie—*a small rope, with a loop or eye at one end, for receiving a bit of wood called a 'knool' at the other; used for binding up cattle to the 'sta'-tree', or stake in a cow-house (J)* kinkin'—*twisting* foudrie—*lightning (MacD. Cf. French, and obsolete English, 'foudre'.)* ahint—*behind* buff nor stye—*(say or do) neither one thing nor another* belth—*whirlpool or rushing of waters (J); sudden swirl (MacD)* comes alist—*comes to; recovers from faintness or decay (J)* eel-ark—*box used for catching eels (J); breeding ground for eels (MacD)* elvers *(English)*—*young eels* skirl-in-the-pan—*oatmeal fried in fat* thunder-plump—*heavy shower following thunder* slounge—*splash made by a heavy body falling into water; heavy fall of rain* fair forfochen—*very exhausted* beddiness—*silly importunacy (MacD—formed from 'beddie' as in 'breeding wives are aye beddie'—covetous of some silly things; Kelly's* Proverbs, *quoted by J.)*

873-892. A passage of thick Dictionary Scots: note the outlandish expressions beginning with the letter 'm' or 'b'. The imagery suggested to MacD by his newly discovered vocabulary seems overstrained here, but perhaps we would not have been given the splendid rice puddin' (l. 886) without it.

884. *The Fleein' Dutchman.* An allusion to the disappearing and reappearing of the phantom ship in which the blasphemous captain was doomed to sail till the Day of Judgment. He could 'change at will the appearance of his ship, so as not to be recognised'. (J.G. Lockhart, *Northern Review*, I, no. 2, (June-July 1924), p.89.) In Washington Irving's version (*Chronicles of Woolfert's Roost*, mentioned by Lockhart) the Dutchman is another Drunk Man, lost on his way homeward.

Saragossa Sea, St. Vitus' Dance,
A *cafard* in a brain's despite,
Or lunacy that thinks a' else 895
Is loony—and is dootless richt! . . .

Gin my thochts that circle like hobby-horses
'Udna loosen to nightmares I'd sleep;
For nocht but a chowed core's left whaur Jerusalem lay
Like aipples in a heap! . . . 900

It's a queer thing to tryst wi' a wumman
When the boss o' her body's gane,
And her banes in the wund as she comes
Dirl like a raff o' rain.

It's a queer thing to tryst wi' a wumman 905
When her ghaist frae abuneheid keeks,
And you see in the licht o't that a'
You ha'e o'r's the cleiks. . . .

What forest worn to the back-hauf's this,
What Eden brocht doon to a bean-swaup? 910
—A' the ferlies o' natur' spring frae the earth,
And into't again maun drap.

Animals, vegetables, what are they a'
But as thochts that a man has ha'en?
And Earth sall be like a toom skull syne. 915
—Whaur'll its thochts be then? . . .

The munelicht is my knowledge o' mysel',
Mysel' the thistle in the munelicht seen,
And hauf my shape has fund itsel' in thee
And hauf my knowledge in your piercin' een. 920

cafard *(French)—fit of depression (lit. 'cockroach')* chowed—*chewed* boss o' her body—*front of her torso* dirl—*rattle* raff—*flying shower* abuneheid—*overhead* keeks—*peers* o'r's—*of her is* the cleiks—*the merest adumbration (MacD. For J 'the cleiks' is 'a cramp in the legs, to which horses are subject'; but cf. 'cleek', an inclination to trick, a trick. David Murison suggests association with 'the glaiks', which can mean 'deception, especially applied to a person or thing that suddenly eludes one's grasp or sight', and 'the act of jilting'—J.)* worn to the back-hauf—*nearly worn out* bean-swaup—*bean-husk* ferlies—*wonders* toom—*empty* een—*eyes*

893. *Saragossa Sea.* The references to eels in lines 887-88 suggest that what was intended by this was the *Sargasso* Sea, where all European and North American eels are known to have been spawned.

The Tragic Tryst, 901-908.

A miniature exercise in the macabre of the ballads.

Reductio ad Absurdum, 909-916.

Latin phrase in traditional formal logic meaning 'reduction to absurdity'.

The Spur of Love, 917-932.

Addressed presumably to Jean, the Drunk Man's wife. No presumption would be needed if it were more strategically placed.

E'en as the munelicht's borrowed frae the sun
I ha'e my knowledge o' mysel' frae thee,
And much that nane but thee can e'er mak' clear,
Save my licht's frae the source, is dark to me.

Your acid tongue, vieve lauchter, and hawk's een, 925
And bluid that drobs like hail to quicken me,
Can turn the mid-day black or midnicht bricht,
Lowse me frae licht or eke frae darkness free.

Bite into me forever mair and lift
Me clear o' chaos in a great relief 930
Till, like this thistle in the munelicht growin',
I brak in roses owre a hedge o' grief. . . .

I am like Burns, and ony wench
Can ser' me for a time.
Licht's in them a'—in some a sun, 935
In some the merest skime.

I'm no' like Burns, and weel I ken,
Tho' ony wench can ser',
It's no' through mony but through yin
That ony man wuns fer. . . . 940

I weddit thee frae fause love, lass,
To free thee and to free mysel';
But man and wumman tied for life
True can be and truth can tell.

Pit ony couple in a knot 945
They canna lowse and needna try,
And mair o' love at last they'll ken
—If ocht!—than joy'll alane descry.

For them as for the beasts, my wife,
A's fer frae dune when pleesure's owre, 950
And coontless difficulties gar
Ilk hert discover a' its power.

vieve—*vigorous* drobs—*pricks, stings* lowse—*free* brak—*break* ser'—*serve*
skime—*gleam* wuns fer—*gets far* fause—*false* ocht—*any* gar—*compel*

The Feminine Principle, 933-976

933-940. *Like / no' like Burns.* In actual fact he is probably like Burns in both respects. MacD may have had in mind Edmond Rocher's poem, noted at l. 595, which begins: 'Desire no single woman: love them all'.

I dinna say that bairns alane
Are true love's task—a sairer task
Is aiblins to create oorsels 955
As we can be—it's that I ask.

Create oorsels, syne bairns, syne race.
Sae on the cod I see't in you
Wi' Maidenkirk to John o' Groats
The bosom that you draw me to. 960

And nae Scot wi' a wumman lies,
But I am he and ken as 'twere
A stage I've passed as he maun pass't,
Gin he grows up, his way wi' her! . . .

A'thing wi' which a man 965
Can intromit's a wumman,
And can, and s'ud, become
As intimate and human.

And Jean's nae mair my wife
Than whisky is at times, 970
Or munelicht or a thistle
Or kittle thochts or rhymes.

He's no' a man ava',
And lacks a proper pride,
Gin less than a' the warld 975
Can ser' him for a bride! . . .

Use, then, my lust for whisky and for thee,
Your function but to be and let me be
And see and let me see.

If in a lesser licht I grope my way, 980
Or use't for ends that need your different ray,
Whelm't in superior day.

sairer—*sorer, more difficult* aiblins—*perhaps* cod—*pillow* intromit—*intermeddle with someone's goods or property (Scots law); insert, esp. in copulation (zoology)* kittle—*tricky, ticklish* ava'—*at all*

958. *I see't*: 'it' seems to be the task of creating the race.

959. *Maidenkirk to John o' Groats*: see note to l. 782.

964. *His way wi' her*: 'the way of a man with a maid' (Proverbs 30. 19). If our 'physical basis' (l. 581) is sexual, we must outgrow it?

Then aye increase and ne'er withdraw your licht.
—Gin it shows either o's in hideous plicht,
What gain to turn't to nicht? 985

Whisky mak's Heaven or Hell and whiles mells baith,
Disease is but the privy torch o' Daith
—But sex reveals life, faith!

I need them a' and maun be aye at strife.
Daith and ayont are nocht but pairts o' life. 990
—Then be life's licht, my wife! . . .

Love often wuns free
In lust to be strangled,
Or love, o' lust free,
In law's sairly tangled. 995

And it's ill to tell whether
Law or lust is to blame
When love's chokit up
—It comes a' to the same.

In this sorry growth 1000
Whatna beauty is tint
That freed o't micht find
A waur fate than is in't? . . .

Yank oot your orra boughs, my hert!

God gied man speech and speech created thocht, 1005
He gied man speech but to the Scots gied nocht
Barrin' this clytach that they've never brocht
To onything but sic a Blottie O
As some bairn's copybook micht show,

whiles—*sometimes* mells—*mixes* baith—*both* ayont—*beyond* wuns—*wins, succeeds in getting* ill—*difficult* whatna—*what (kind of)* tint—*lost* waur—*worse* orra—*not up to much* clytach—*inarticulate or childish chatter* sic—*such* Blottie O—*a schoolboy's slate-game*

The Light of Life, 977-991.

986-991. This passage links up with ll. 2024-2031. *Life's licht*: in contrast to disease, the privy torch of death.

Love Often Wuns Free, 992-1003.

1000. *This sorry growth.* It is likely that MacD intends this to refer back to the thistle, though that was last mentioned at l. 931.

Yank Oot Your Orra Boughs, 1004-1070.

The phrase of the title is repeated like a mantra aimed at effecting a spiritual 'pruning' on the biblical model: 'I am the true vine, and my Father is the husbandman. Every branch in me that beareth not fruit he taketh away: and every branch that beareth fruit he purgeth it, that it may bring forth more fruit. Now ye are clean through the word which I have spoken unto you.' (John 15. 1-3.)

1005. Cf. Shelley, of Prometheus: 'He gave man speech, and speech created thought, / Which is the measure of the Universe'. (*Prometheus Unbound*, II. 4. 72.)

1008. SND gives plural form, *Blotty O's:* A schoolboys' game, played on slates or with pencil and paper. A certain number of 'O's are drawn and one boy, at the direction of another, joins up one to the other by lines, each 'O' being 'blotted' out as soon as it is touched. The object of the game is to join up every 'O' as directed without intersecting any of the lines.

A spook o' soond that frae the unkent grave 1010
In which oor nation lies loups up to wave
Sic leprous chuns as tatties have
That cellar-boond send spindles gropin'
Towards ony hole that's open,

Like waesome fingers in the dark that think 1015
They still may widen the ane and only chink
That e'er has gi'en mankind a blink
O' Hope—tho' ev'n in that puir licht
They s'ud ha'e seen their hopeless plicht.

This puir relation o' my topplin' mood, 1020
This country cousin, streak o' churl-bluid,
This hopeless airgh 'twixt a' we can and should,
This Past that like Astarte's sting I feel,
This arrow in Achilles' heel.

Yank oot your orra boughs, my hert! 1025

Mebbe we're in a vicious circle cast,
Mebbe there's limits we can ne'er get past,
Mebbe we're sentrices that at the last
Are flung aside, and no' the pillars and props
O' Heaven foraye as in oor hopes. 1030

Oor growth at least nae steady progress shows,
Genius in mankind like an antrin rose
Abune a jungly waste o' effort grows,
But to Man's purpose it mak's little odds,
And seems irrelevant to God's. . . . 1035

Eneuch? Then here you are. Here's the haill story.
Life's connached shapes too'er up in croons o' glory,
Perpetuatin', natheless, in their gory
Colour the endless sacrifice and pain
That to their makin's gane. 1040

loups—*leaps* chuns—*sprouts* tatties—*potatoes* blink—*glimpse* -bluid—*-blood* airgh—*lack, or what anything requires to bring it up to the level (MacD, from adjective which J cites in that sense.)* sentrice(s)—*scaffolding ('Sentrice'—a plural—is the normal form)* foraye—*forever* antrin—*rare* abune—*above* eneuch—*enough* connached—*abused, spoiled* natheless—*nevertheless*

1023. Cf. D.S. Mirsky on Ivanov: 'the sting of a refined and ecstatic sensuality—the sting of Astarte—rather than that of Dionysos'. (*Contemporary Russian Literature* (1926), p. 208.) Astarte was the Phoenician sex-goddess of the moon. Her 'sting' is perhaps the equivalent of 'the thorn in the flesh'. Blok gave her name to the doll, the 'sex object', that took the place of the 'Beautiful Lady' of his vision.

1028-1030. The image of mankind as 'sentrices' is developed later: ll. 1512-15. *Sentrice* was a term applied to 'cooms' or wooden frames used in the construction of bridge-arches. Hence MacD's speculation is on similar lines to Nietzsche's idea that man is only a bridge, not a goal.

The roses like the saints in Heaven treid
Triumphant owre the agonies o' their breed,
And wag fu' mony a celestial heid
Abune the thorter-ills o' leaf and prick
In which they ken the feck maun stick. 1045

Yank oot your orra boughs, my hert!

A mongrel growth, jumble o' disproportions,
Whirlin' in its incredible contortions,
Or wad-be client that an auld whore shuns,
Wardin' her wizened orange o' a bosom 1050
Frae importunities sae gruesome,

Or new diversion o' the hormones
Mair fond o' procreation than the Mormons,
And fetchin' like a devastatin' storm on's
A' the uncouth dilemmas o' oor natur' 1055
Objectified in vegetable maitter.

Yank oot your orra boughs, my hert!

And heed nae mair the foolish cries that beg
You slice nae mair to aff or pu' to leg,
You skitin' duffer that gars a'body fleg, 1060
—What tho' you ding the haill warld oot o' joint
Wi' a skier to cover-point!

Yank oot your orra boughs, my hert!

thorter-ill—*a kind of palsy to which sheep are subject (J); paralytic seizure (MacD)* feck—*majority* skitin'—*wild-hitting; flying off at a tangent* gars a'body fleg—*makes everybody take fright* ding—*strike*

1041. Cf. the face among the heavenly roses glimpsed by Blok and Solovyov.

1055-1056. Note that, behind the proliferation of the poet's imagery, it is the Thistle that stands for the human condition, embodying 'a' the uncouth dilemmas o' oor natur''.

1058-1062. Cricketing terms.

There *was* a danger—and it's weel I see't—
Had brocht ye like Mallarmé to defeat:— 1065
"Mon doute, amas de nuit ancienne, s'achève
En maint rameau subtil, qui, demeuré les vrais
Bois mêmes, prouve, hélas! que bien seul je m'offrais
Pour triomphe la faute idéale de roses."*

Yank oot your orra boughs, my hert! . . . 1070

I love to muse upon the skill that gangs
To mak' the simplest thing that Earth displays,
The eident life that ilka atom thrangs,
And uses it in the appointit ways,
And a' the endless brain that nocht escapes 1075
That myriad moves them to inimitable shapes.

Nor to their customed form nor ony ither
New to Creation, by man's cleverest mind,
A' needfu' particles first brocht thegither,
Could they wi' timeless labour be combined. 1080
There's nocht that Science yet's begood to see
In hauf its deemless detail or its destiny.

Oor een gi'e answers based on pairt-seen facts
That beg a' questions, to ebb minds' content,
But hoo a'e feature or the neist attracts, 1085
Wi' millions mair unseen, wha kens what's meant
By human brains and to what ends may tell
—For naething's seen or kent that's near a thing itsel'!

*The line which precedes these in Mallarmé's poem is "Aime-je un rêve?" and Wilfred Thorley translates the passage thus:—

"Loved I Love's counterfeit?
My doubts, begotten of the long night's heat,
Dislimn the woodland till my triumph shows
As the flawed shadow of a frustrate rose."

eident—*busy* thrangs—*throngs, crowds* thegither—*together* begood—*begun*
deemless—*countless (McD)* neist—*next* near—*nearly*

1064-1069. The quotation is from Mallarmé's 'L'après-midi d'un faune'. The translation supplied (from *A Bouquet from France* (1926), p. 173) unfortunately ignores the word *rameau*, which would provide a link with MacD's orra boughs. There is perhaps not much more to the allusion than the attraction for MacD of the phrase 'la faute idéale de roses', which might have appeared to more effect if he had found a contextually more suitable place for it.

The Form and Purpose of the Thistle, 1071-1118.

1084. *To ebb minds' content.* MacD's intention is perhaps clearer in his English version: 'to shallow minds' content'.

Let whasae vaunts his knowledge then and syne
Sets up a God and kens *His* purpose tae 1090
Tell me what's gart a'e strain o' maitter twine
In sic an extraordinary way,
And what God's purpose wi' the Thistle is
—I'll aiblins ken what he and his God's worth by this.

I've watched it lang and hard until I ha'e 1095
A certain symp'thy wi' its orra ways
And pride in its success, as weel I may,
In growin' exactly as its instinct says,
Save in sae fer as thwarts o' weather or grun'
Or man or ither foes ha'e'ts aims perchance fordone. 1100

But I can form nae notion o' the spirit
That gars it tak' the difficult shape it does,
Nor judge the merit yet or the demerit
O' this detail or that sae fer as it goes
T' advance the cause that gied it sic a guise 1105
As maun ha'e pleased its Maker wi' a gey surprise.

The craft that hit upon the reishlin' stalk,
Wi'ts gausty leafs and a' its datchie jags,
And spired it syne in seely flooers to brak
Like sudden lauchter owre its fousome rags 1110
Jouks me, sardonic lover, in the routh
O' contrairies that jostle in this dumfoondrin' growth.

What strength 't'ud need to pit its roses oot,
Or double them in number or in size,
He canna tell wha canna plumb the root, 1115
And learn what's gar't its present state arise,
And what the limits are that ha'e been put
To change in thistles, and why—and what a change
'ud boot. . . .

whasae—*who(so)ever* gart—*made, compelled to* aiblins—*maybe* orra—*odd* thwarts—*frustrations* grun'—*ground* ha'e'ts—*have its* fordone—*exhausted, destroyed* gey—*notable* reishlin'—*rustling* gausty (gousty)—*ghastly; emaciated* datchie—*secret, hidden (J. But 'this word is of dubious authenticity'—SND.)* spired it—*made it soar (McD's coinage?)* seely—*happy, pleasant* fousome—*disgusting* jouks—*evades* routh—*profusion* boot—*avail*

1106. For MacD, the deity who created this world is not all-knowing. Cf. the God who, 'gin e'er He saw a man, 'ud be / E'en mair dumfooner'd at the sicht than he' (ll. 2678-9).

1112. Cf. Gregory Smith on the Caledonian antisyzygy: 'The sudden jostling of contraries seems to preclude any relationship by literary suggestion'. (*Scottish Literature* (1919), p. 20.)

1117-1118. Cf. Shestov: 'But from our own minds and our own experience we can deduce nothing that would serve us as a ground for setting even the smallest limit to nature's own arbitrary behaviour'. (*All Things Are Possible*, London 1920, p. 24.)

I saw a rose come loupin' oot*
Frae a camsteerie plant. 1120
O wha'd ha'e thocht yon puir stock had
Sic an inhabitant?

For centuries it ran to waste,
Wi' pin-heid flooers at times.
O'ts hidden hert o' beauty they 1125
Were but the merest skimes.

Yet while it ran to wud and thorns,
The feckless growth was seekin'
Some airt to cheenge its life until
A' in a rose was beekin'. 1130

"Is there nae way in which my life
Can mair to flooerin' come,
And bring its waste on shank and jags
Doon to a minimum?

"It's hard to struggle as I maun 1135
For scrunts o' blooms like mine,
While blossom covers ither plants
As by a knack divine.

"What hinders me unless I lack
Some needfu' discipline? 1140
—I wis I'll bring my orra life
To beauty or I'm din!"

Sae ran the thocht that hid ahint
The thistle's ugsome guise,
"I'll brak' the habit o' my life 1145
A worthier to devise.

* The General Strike (May 1926).

loupin'—*leaping* camsteerie—*perverse, unmanageable* stock—*stem* skimes—*gleams* wud—*wood* airt—*direction; way* beekin'—*shining brightly; basking* maun—*must* scrunts—*stunted growths* wis—*believe; know* orra—*nondescript, not up to much* din—*done* ahint—*behind* ugsome—*repulsive*

Ballad of the Crucified Rose, 1119-1218.

'I was in the thick of the General Strike too. I was the only Socialist Town Councillor in Montrose and a Justice of the Peace for the county, and we had the whole area sewn up. One of my most poignant memories is of how, when the news of the great betrayal came through, I was in the act of addressing a packed meeting mainly of railwaymen. When I told them the terrible news most of them burst into tears—and I am not ashamed to say I did too'. (MacD, *The Company I've Kept*, London 1966, p. 158.)

'Nothing ever so shook me to my foundations as this Strike—and the hellish Betrayal of its Collapse. I have been unable to think of anything else. Inter alia I have incorporated in my 'Drunk Man' a long 'Ballad of the General Strike' which I think will rank as one of the most passionate cris-de-coeur in contemporary literature'. (Letter of 25 May 1926 to J.K. Annand.) Nevertheless, without the footnote, or the earlier title as given in the above letter, the reader would not know that the poem had anything to do with the General Strike. Interpretations of it in specifically political terms do not take account of certain things in the poem: most notably the idea that the rose which the thistle aspires to produce will bring its life to *beauty*, and the later imagery with the rose becoming a ball of fire in the sky and Earth resuming its original place in the mind of God. All this seems somewhat remote from the political aims of the Strike. And it is rash to give priority to MacD's politics. He himself declared: 'As a Socialist, of course, I am, it should be obvious, interested only in a very subordinate way in the politics of Socialism as a political theory; my real concern with Socialism is as an artist's organized approach to the interdependencies of life' (*Lucky Poet*, p. 241). And that, as it happens, is an unacknowledged quotation from Lincoln Kirstein, writing about Gaudier-Brzeska.

"My nobler instincts sall nae mair
This contrair shape be gi'en.
I sall nae mair consent to live
A life no' fit to be seen." 1150

Sae ran the thocht that hid ahint
The thistle's ugsome guise,
Till a' at aince a rose loupt out
—I watched it wi' surprise.

A rose loupt oot and grew, until 1155
It was ten times the size
O' ony rose the thistle afore
Had heistit to the skies.

And still it grew till a' the buss
Was hidden in its flame. 1160
I never saw sae braw a floo'er
As yon thrawn stock became.

And still it grew until it seemed
The haill braid earth had turned
A reid reid rose that in the lift 1165
Like a ball o' fire burned.

The waefu' clay was fire aince mair,
As Earth had been resumed
Into God's mind, frae which sae lang
To grugous state 'twas doomed. 1170

Syne the rose shrivelled suddenly
As a balloon is burst;
The thistle was a ghaistly stick,
As gin it had been curst.

Was it the ancient vicious sway 1175
Imposed itsel' again,
Or nerve owre weak for new emprise
That made the effort vain,

heisted—*hoisted* buss—*bush* braw—*handsome* thrawn—*stubborn* braid—*broad* lift—*sky* grugous—*grim* owre—*too* emprise *(English)—enterprise*

1165. *A reid reid rose.* An echo of Burns—but not the *political* Burns.

A coward strain in that lorn growth
That wrocht the sorry trick? 1180
—The thistle like a rocket soared
And cam' doon like the stick.

Like grieshuckle the roses glint,
The leafs like farles hing,
As roond a hopeless sacrifice 1185
Earth draws its barren ring.

The dream o' beauty's dernin' yet
Ahint the ugsome shape.
—Vain dream that in a pinheid here
And there can e'er escape! 1190

The vices that defeat the dream
Are in the plant itsel',
And till they're purged its virtues maun
In pain and misery dwell.

Let Deils rejoice to see the waste, 1195
The fond hope brocht to nocht.
The thistle in their een is as
A favourite lust they've wrocht.

The orderin' o' the thistle means
Nae richtin' o't to them. 1200
Its loss they ca' a law, its thorns
A fule's fit diadem.

And still the idiot nails itsel'
To its ain crucifix,
While here a rose and there a rose 1205
Jaups oot abune the pricks.

Like connoisseurs the Deils gang roond
And praise its attitude,
Till on the Cross the silly Christ
To fidge fu' fain's begood! 1210

lorn—*ruined* wrocht—*wraught* grieshuckle—*embers* farles—*curly flakes (of ash)* hing—*hang* dernin'—*hiding* Deils—*Devils* een—*eyes* jaups—*splashes; flies like sparks from metal* gang—*go* fidge fu' fain—*twitch excitedly or anxiously* begood—*begun*

1181-1182. Perhaps recalling Bergson, for whom the *élan vital* is like a rocket whose extinguished remains fall to the ground as matter.

1210. Another echo of Burns: 'Ev'n Satan glowr'd, and fidg'd fu' fain' ('Tam o' Shanter', l. 185).

Like connoisseurs the Deils gang roond
Wi' ready platitude.
It's no' sae dear as vinegar,
And every bit as good!

The bitter taste is on my tongue, 1215
I chowl my chafts, and pray
"Let God forsake me noo and no'
Staund connoisseur-like tae!". . .

The language that but sparely flooers
And maistly gangs to weed; 1220
The thocht o' Christ and Calvary
Aye liddenin' in my heid;
And a' the dour provincial thocht
That merks the Scottish breed
—These are the thistle's characters, 1225
To argie there's nae need.
Hoo weel my verse embodies
The thistle you can read!
—But will a Scotsman never
Frae this vile growth be freed? . . . 1230

O ilka man alive is like
A quart that's squeezed into a pint
(A maist unScottish-like affair!)
Or like the little maid that showed
Me into a still sma'er room. 1235

What use to let a sunrise fade
To ha'e anither like't the morn,
Or let a generation pass
That ane nae better may succeed,
Or wi' a' Time's machinery 1240
Keep naething new aneth the sun,
Or change things oot o' kennin' that
They may be a' the mair the same?

to chowl one's chafts—*to distort one's mouth, often for the purpose of provoking another; to emit a mournful cry (J)* liddenin'—*resounding; going backwards and forwards (MacD)* argie—*argue* the morn—*tomorrow (morning)* aneth—*beneath* kennin'—*recognition; knowledge*

1213. Cf. Mark 15. 36, of Christ on the Cross: 'And one ran and filled a spunge full of vinegar, and put it on a reed, and gave him to drink'.

1217. Cf. Christ on the Cross: 'My God, my God, why hast thou forsaken me?' (Matthew 27. 46.)

1218. Cf. John Davidson on the gods as 'connoisseurs of Hell' ('The Testament of John Davidson', l. 1950).

The Thistle's Characteristics, 1219-1441.

Note the curious coming and going and final eclipse of rhyme in this section. The specifically Scottish characteristics of the thistle are followed immediately by the thistle as symbol of the universal predicament of mankind in the face of the mystery of life. This is in effect the basis of the symbolism of the entire work.

1221-1222. Cf. Orage's complaint about some of Nietzsche's disciples: 'For them he is what Jesus is for many Christians—nothing without the cross and passion'. (*Art of Reading* (1930), p. 211.)

1234-1235. 'By what secret mechanism did she and all other human beings so dwarf and confine themselves, and why? It made her think of the author who wrote that "he followed a small maid into an even smaller room" '. (MacD, *Annals of the Five Senses* (1923), p. 168.) The author referred to is (I think) Sir Walter Raleigh, and the implication was originally sexual. In a version used by Stevenson, however, the 'smaller room' is the grave: 'He went out of a small cell into a smaller, that he might come forth again to freedom' ('The Suicide Club').

The thistle in the wund dissolves
In lichtnin's as shook foil gi'es way 1245
In sudden splendours, or the flesh
At Daith lets slip the infinite soul;
And syne it's like a sunrise tint
In grey o' day, or love and life
That in a cloody blash o' sperm 1250
Undae the warld to big't again,
Or like a pickled foetus that
Nae man feels ocht in common wi'
—But micht as easily ha' been!
Or like a corpse a soul set free 1255
Scunners to think it tenanted
—And little recks that but for it
It never micht ha' been at a',
Like love frae lust and God frae man!

The wasted seam that dries like stairch 1260
And pooders aff, that micht ha' been
A warld o' men and syne o' Gods;
The grey that haunts the vievest green;
The wrang side o' the noblest scene
We ne'er can whummle to oor een, 1265
As 'twere the hinderpairts o' God,
His face aye turned the opposite road,
Or's neth the flooers the drumlie clods
Frae which they come at sicna odds,
As a' Earth's magic frae a spirt, 1270
In shame and secrecy, o' dirt!

Then shak' nae mair in silly life,
Nor stand impossible as Daith,
Incredible as a'thing is
Inside or oot owre closely scanned. 1275
As mithers aften think the warld
O' bairns that ha'e nae end or object,
Or lovers think their sweethearts made

wund—*wind* tint—*lost* blash—*splash, downpour* undae—*undo* big't—*build it* scunners—*shudders with disgust* seam—*semen (MacD); lard, grease* vievest—*most vivid* whummle—*turn over; overcome* road—*direction, way* drumlie—*muddy; dark* sicna (siccan)—*such*

1245-1246. Cf. G.M. Hopkins, 'God's Grandeur':

> The world is charged with the grandeur of God.
> It will flame out, like shining from shook foil.

1250-1251. Implied by the image of orgasm are seeds of thistledown in the wind.

1266-1267. Cf. the words of God when he appeared to Moses: 'I . . . will cover thee with my hand while I pass by: And I will take away mine hand, and thou shalt see my back parts: but my face shall not be seen'. (Exodus 33. 22-23.)

1272. *Shak'*: in the wind.

1273. *Impossible as Daith.* Perhaps this is poetic shorthand for the following line of thought. It is impossible to comprehend the reality of death, since when you know it you are dead, and there is no other way of experiencing it so as to understand its nature.

Yince-yirn—wha ha'ena waled the lave,
Maikless—when they are naebody, 1280
Or men o' ilka sort and kind
Are prood o' thochts they ca' their ain,
That nameless millions had afore
And nameless millions yet'll ha'e,
And that were never worth the ha'en, 1285
Or Cruivie's "latest" story or
Gilsanquhar's vows to sign the pledge,
Or's if I thocht maist whisky *was*,
Or failed to coont the cheenge I got,
Sae wad I be gin I rejoiced, 1290
Or didna ken my place, in thee.

O stranglin' rictus, sterile spasm,
Thou stricture in the groins o' licht,
Thou ootrie gangrel frae the wilds
O' chaos fenced frae Eden yet 1295
By the unsplinterable wa'
O' munebeams like a bleeze o' swords!

Nae chance lunge cuts the Gordian knot,
Nor sall the belly find relief
In wha's entangled moniplies 1300
Creation like a stoppage jams,
Or in whose loins the mapamound
Runkles in strawns o' bubos whaur
The generations gravel.
The soond o' water winnin' free, 1305
The sicht o' licht that braks the rouk,
The thocht o' every thwart owrecome
Are in my ears and een and brain,
In whom the bluid is spilt in stour,

yince-yirn (-yirrand)—*on special purpose* waled the lave—*sorted out the rest* maikless—*matchless* ilka—*every* ca'—*call* ootrie—*outré (MacD. Cf. 'ootrel', strange, foreign.)* gangrel—*vagrant* bleeze—*blaze* moniplies—*that part of the tripe of a beast which consists of many folds; sometimes coarsely and vulgarly applied, in a ludicrous sense, to the intestines of a man (J.)* mapamound—*(map of) the world* runkles—*wrinkles, crumples* strawns—*strings (of beads)* bubos *(English)*—*swellings of glands, especially in groin or armpit* gravel—*(form) deposits of stones in kidney or bladder; come to a standstill* rouk—*mist, fog* thwart—*obstacle* stour—*spray; strife*

1294-1297. After the Fall of Adam and Eve resulting in their expulsion from Eden, the earth brought forth thorns and thistles. (See ll. 1739-1742.) Note that here the Moon is outside the fallen world, with the moonbeams fencing Eden like swords.

1299-1304. Cf. Ahab in *Moby Dick*, addressing the heavens: 'What a hoorosh aloft there! I would e'en take it for sublime, did I not know that the colic is a noisy malady. Oh, take medicine, take medicine!'. (Standard edition, London 1922-3, II, 285.) MacD here regards the thistle (mortal life on earth) as the result of a malfunction of the original creative power, or an obstruction in the creative process.

In whom a' licht in darkness fails, 1310
In whom the mystery o' life
Is to a wretched weed bewrayed.

But let my soul increase in me,
God dwarfed to enter my puir thocht
Expand to his true size again, 1315
And protoplasm's look befit
The nature o' its destiny,
And seed and sequence be nae mair
Incongruous to ane anither,
And liquor packed impossibly 1320
Mak' pint-pot an eternal well,
And art be relevant to life,
And poets mair than dominies yet,
And ends nae langer tint in means,
Nor forests hidden by their trees, 1325
Nor men be sacrificed alive
In foonds o' fates designed for them,
Nor mansions o' the soul stand toom
Their owners in their cellars trapped,
Nor a' a people's genius be 1330
A rumple-fyke in Heaven's doup,
While Calvinism uses her
To breed a minister or twa!

A black leaf owre a white leaf twirls,
A grey leaf flauchters in atween, 1335
Sae ply my thochts aboot the stem
O' loppert slime frae which they spring.
The thistle like a snawstorm drives,
Or like a flicht o' swallows lifts,
Or like a swarm o' midges hings, 1340
A plague o' moths, a starry sky,
But's naething but a thistle yet,
And still the puzzle stands unsolved.

bewrayed *(English)—betrayed; exposed* dominies—*schoolmasters; ministers* foonds—*foundations* toom—*empty* rumple-fyke—*itch in the anus* doup—*backside* flauchters—*flutters* loppert—*coagulated* hings—*hangs*

1311-1312. Here, and at ll. 1343-1350, it is made explicit that the thistle symbolises 'the mystery of life'.

1334-1335. (Echoed by l. 1557.) The black and white leaves are reminiscent of the Taoist *yin-yang* symbol. Perhaps the grey leaf of thought fluttering between them is a sort of dull compromise: all that the human mind can produce because it cannot arrive at a synthesis of the opposites. Cf. the 'grey deluded brain' of l. 1685, and the initial attitude in MacD's poem 'Milk-Wort and Bog-Cotton': 'Wad that nae leaf upon anither wheeled / A shadow either' (*Complete Poems*, p. 331).

1338-1342. The imagery here is the result of the poet having thistle *and thistledown* in mind (as in Gregory Smith).

Beauty and ugliness alike,
And life and daith and God and man, 1345
Are aspects o't but nane can tell
The secret that I'd fain find oot
O' this bricht hive, this sorry weed,
The tree that fills the universe,
Or like a reistit herrin' crines. 1350

Gin I was sober I micht think
It was like something drunk men see!

The necromancy in my bluid
Through a' the gamut cheenges me
O' dwarf and giant, foul and fair, 1355
But winna let me be mysel'
—My mither's womb that reins me still
Until I tae can prick the witch
And "Wumman" cry wi' Christ at last,
"Then what hast thou to do wi' me?" 1360

The tug-o'-war is in me still,
The dog-hank o' the flesh and soul—
Faither in Heaven, what gar'd ye tak'
A village slut to mither me,
Your mongrel o' the fire and clay? 1365
The trollop and the Deity share
My writhen form as tho' I were
A picture o' the time they had
When Licht rejoiced to file itsel'
And Earth upshuddered like a star. 1370

A drucken hizzie gane to bed
Wi' three-in-ane and ane-in-three.

nane—*no one* reistit herrin'—*dried herring* crines—*shrinks* gin—*if* winna—*won't* tae—*too* prick the witch—*cf. 'prickit-witch', a tested and proven witch (Suspected witches were tested by pricking; for a real witch was believed to bear on her body the witch-mark which was insensible. J.)* dog-hank—*pair of dogs stuck together during mating (MacD); baiting of the animals at dog-fight* gar'd—*made* writhen—*twisted* file—*defile* drucken—*drunken* hizzie—*hussy*

1348-1349. As 'the tree that fills the universe', the thistle is now associated with Yggdrasill. The 'hive' of the previous line may be associated with the bees which feed on the honeydew dripping from that cosmic tree. (Cf. ll. 2097-8.)

1350. Cf. 'Reistit and crynd, as hangit man on hill' (Dunbar, quoted by Jamieson).

1353. *Necromancy*: sorcery by calling up the spirits of the dead.

1359-1360. Jesus's response to his mother when she said there was no wine at the wedding feast in Cana (John 2. 4). Cf. Blake, 'To Tirzah':

> Whate'er is Born of Mortal Birth
> Must be consumed with the Earth,
> To rise from Generation free:
> Then what have I to do with thee?

O fain I'd drink until I saw
Scotland a ferlie o' delicht,
And fain bide drunk nor ha'e't recede 1375
Into a shrivelled thistle syne,
As when a sperklin' tide rins oot,
And leaves a wreath o' rubbish there!

Wull a' the seas gang dry at last
(As dry as I am gettin' noo), 1380
Or wull they aye come back again,
Seilfu' as my neist drink to me,
Or as the sunlicht to the mune,
Or as the bonny sangs o' men,
Wha're but puir craturs in themsels, 1385
And save when genius mak's them drunk,
As donnert as their audiences,
—As dreams that mak' a tramp a king,
A madman sane to his ain mind,
Or what a Scotsman thinks himsel', 1390
Tho' naethin' but a thistle kyths.

The mair I drink the thirstier yet,
And whiles when I'm alowe wi' booze,
I'm like God's sel' and clad in fire,
And ha'e a Pentecost like this. 1395
O wad that I could aye be fou',
And no' come back as aye I maun
To naething but a fule that nane
'Ud credit wi' sic thochts as thae,
A fule that kens they're empty dreams! 1400

Yet but fer drink and drink's effects,
The yeast o' God that barms in us,
We micht as weel no' be alive.
It maitters not what drink is ta'en,
The barley bree, ambition, love, 1405
Or Guid or Evil workin' in's,

ferlie—*marvel* bide—*remain* syne—*then* gang—*go* seilfu'—*blissful* neist—*next* craturs—*creatures* donnert—*stupified* kyths—*appears* whiles—*sometimes* alowe—*ablaze* thae—*those* fou'—*drunk* barms—*ferments* barley bree—*whisky (lit. brew)*

1379. Another echo of Burns's song, 'A red red Rose':

> And I will love thee still, my Dear,
> Till a' the seas gang dry.

1394-1395. Of the apostles at Pentecost it is recorded that 'there appeared unto them cloven tongues like as of fire, and it sat upon each of them'. There were people of all nations present, and each of them heard the tongue of the apostles as their own native tongue. This was preceded by 'a sound from heaven as of a rushing mighty wind', and followed by Peter's assurance that the apostles were 'not drunken, as ye suppose, seeing it is but the third hour of the day'. (Acts 2. 2-15.)

Sae lang's we feel like souls set free
Frae mortal coils and speak in tongues
We dinna ken and never wull,
And find a merit in oorsels, 1410
In Cruivies and Gilsanquhars tae,
And see the thistle as ocht but that!

For wha o's ha'e the thistle's poo'er
To see we're worthless and believe 't?

A'thing that ony man can be's 1415
A mockery o' his soul at last.
The mair it shows't the better, and
I'd suner be a tramp than king,
Lest in the pride o' place and poo'er
I e'er forgot my waesomeness. 1420
Sae to debauchery and dirt,
And to disease and daith I turn,
Sin' otherwise my seemin' worth
'Ud block my view o' what is what,
And blin' me to the irony 1425
O' bein' a grocer 'neth the sun,
A lawyer gin Justice ope'd her een,
A pedant like an ant promoted,
A parson buttonholin' God,
Or ony cratur o' the Earth 1430
Sma'-bookt to John Smith, High Street, Perth,
Or sic like vulgar gaffe o' life
Sub specie aeternitatis—
Nae void can fleg me hauf as much
As bein' mysel', whate'er I am, 1435
Or, waur, bein' onybody else.

The nervous thistle's shiverin' like
A horse's skin aneth a cleg,
Or Northern Lichts or lustres o'
A soul that Daith has fastened on, 1440
Or mornin' efter the nicht afore.

ocht—*anything* cratur—*creature* sma'-bookt—*shrunken; scaled down* sic-like—*similar* gaffe *(French)*—*blunder* fleg—*frighten* waur—*worse* aneth—*beneath* cleg—*gadfly*

1408-1409. *Speak in tongues*: glossolalia. In addition to the allusion to Pentecost, MacD was aware of Kruchenykh's belief that the glossolalia of the religious dissenters was a forecast of the new language of the Futurists.

1421-1424. This passage is reminiscent of Dostoevsky (the connection with whom is made explicit at ll. 1821-1828); the Imaginists who 'had a morbid craving for dirt, humiliation, and suffering, like the Man from Underground' (see note on l. 870); and the Blok of such poems as 'Yes. This is the Call of Inspiration' (*Selected Poems: Alexander Blok*, trans. J. Stallworthy & P. France, Harmondsworth 1970, p.92):

> My daydreams constantly revert
> to places of humiliation,
> darkness, poverty, and dirt.

1433. *Sub specie aeternitatis*: 'under the aspect of Eternity'; viewed in relation to the one eternal Substance.

1434-1435. Cf. Robert Frost, 'Desert Places':

> They cannot scare me with their empty spaces
> Between stars—on stars where no human race is.
> I have it in me so much nearer home
> To scare myself with my own desert places.

And Melville's *Pierre*: 'Appalling is the soul of man! Better might one be pushed off in the material spaces beyond the uttermost orbit of our sun, than once feel himself fairly afloat in himself'.

Shudderin' thistle, gi'e owre, gi'e owre. . . .

Grey sand is churnin' in my lugs,
The munelicht flets, and gantin' there
The grave o' a' mankind's laid bare 1445
—On Hell itsel' the drawback rugs!

Nae man can ken his hert until
The tide o' life uncovers it,
And horror-struck he sees a pit
Returnin' life can never fill! . . . 1450

Thou art the facts in ilka airt
That breenge into infinity,
Criss-crossed wi' coontless ither facts
Nae man can follow, and o' which
He is himsel' a helpless pairt, 1455
Held in their tangle as he were
A stick-nest in Ygdrasil!

The less man sees the mair he is
Content wi't, but the mair he sees
The mair he kens hoo little o' 1460
A' that there is he'll ever see,
And hoo it mak's confusion aye
The waur confoondit till at last
His brain inside his heid is like
Ariadne wi' an empty pirn, 1465
Or like a birlin' reel frae which
A whale has rived the line awa'.

What better's a forhooied nest
Than shasloch scattered owre the grun'?

gi'e owre—*give up, stop* lugs—*ears* flets—*flits* gantin'—*gaping* drawback—*undertow (MacD)* rugs—*pulls* ken—*know* ilka—*every* airt—*direction* breenge—*dash, plunge* waur—*worse* pirn—*bobbin* birlin'—*whirling* rived—*wrenched* forhooied—*forsaken* shasloch—*loose straw, litter (MacD)*

The Grave of All Mankind, 1442-1450.

1442. This line, which might seem a rather extraneous link between the poem which follows and the preceding section, is an exact echo of l. 699; and what follows is an extension of the imagery in the passage beginning 'My harns are seaweed', ll. 377-384. This illustrates the difficulty caused by related elements in the work being placed so far apart.

1446. 'Drawback' here has been glossed by some editors as meaning 'obstruction', which Jamieson regarded as a specifically Scots usage. But its meaning with reference to the tide in this context is quite different, as is confirmed by MacD's use of 'undertow' in his English version.

1447-1450. Cf. MacD's short story, 'Andy': 'His face like that was like seein' the flair o' the sea—a'e meenit a' jobblin' waves, and the next—naething but dour black glaur. He felt he could gang richt through the bottom o' Andy's mind noo to the promised land like the Jews gaen through the Reid Sea; but it was a fell clarty road. If it 'ud only bide like that it micht dry; but nae doot in a meenit or twa the muckle treacherous flood that generally hid it 'ud sweep owre't again and naebody that hadna seen't for themsel's 'ud ken the horror it covered' (*Glasgow Herald*, 22 Oct. 1927, p. 4).

A Stick-Nest in Ygdrasil, 1451-1631.

In Scandinavian mythology, Yggdrasill is the cosmic ash-tree which supports all the nine worlds. It is subject to both malevolent and benevolent forces (e.g., the dragon and serpents at its roots, the Norns who sprinkle it with holy water), and it has been associated by many occultists with the Tree of Life and the Tree of Knowledge. MacD seems to have the latter in mind at the beginning of this section.

1457. *Stick-nest* is presumably one of the most recondite terms in MacD's vocabulary, since I have been unable to find it in any dictionary. The same applies to *shasloch* (*skasloch* in 1926), l. 1469.

1465. *Ariadne*—who provided Theseus with the clue of thread with which to find his way out of the Labyrinth.

1467. The whale / sea-serpent as embodying the original mystery of creation.

O hard it is for man to ken 1470
He's no' creation's goal nor yet
A benefitter by't at last—
A means to ends he'll never ken,
And as to michtier elements
The slauchtered brutes he eats to him 1475
Or forms o' life owre sma' to see
Wi' which his heedless body swarms,
And a' man's thocht nae mair to them
Than ony moosewob to a man,
His Heaven to them the blinterin' o' 1480
A snail-trail on their closet wa'!

For what's an atom o' a twig
That tak's a billion to an inch
To a' the routh o' shoots that mak'
The bygrowth o' the Earth aboot 1485
The michty trunk o' Space that spreids
Ramel o' licht that ha'e nae end,
—The trunk wi' centuries for rings,
Comets for fruit, November shooers
For leafs that in its Autumns fa' 1490
—And Man at maist o' sic a twig
Ane o' the coontless atoms is!

My sinnens and my veins are but
As muckle o' a single shoot
Wha's fibre I can ne'er unwaft 1495
O' my wife's flesh and mither's flesh
And a' the flesh o' humankind,
And revelled thrums o' beasts and plants
As gangs to mak' twixt birth and daith
A'e sliver for a microscope; 1500
And a' the life o' Earth to be
Can never lift frae underneath

michtier—*mightier* moosewob—*spider's web* blinterin'—*glimmering* closet—*lavatory* wa'—*wall* routh—*abundance* ramel—*branches* sinnens—*sinews* muckle—*much* unwaft—*unweave* revelled—*ravelled* thrums—*odds and ends of threads* a'e—*one* heich—*high*

1470-1473. What was raised as a speculative question at ll. 1026-1030 now appears to be presented as fact. Cf. Orage's digest of Nietzsche: 'Man is . . . not an end in himself, nor is the universe designed for his happiness or perfection. . . . That he as individual is generally incapable of appreciating the spectacle of himself, or, again, that he should believe himself the end and crown of existence are errors natural enough in the early stages of self-consciousness'. (*Nietzsche in Outline and Aphorism* (1907), p. 42.)

The shank o' which oor destiny's pairt
As heich's to stand forenenst the trunk
Stupendous as a windlestrae! 1505

I'm under nae delusions, fegs!
The whuppin' sooker at wha's tip
Oor little point o' view appears,
A midget coom o' continents
Wi' blebs o' oceans set, sends up 1510
The braith o' daith as weel as life,
And we maun braird anither tip
Oot owre us ere we wither tae,
And join the sentrice skeleton
As coral insects big their reefs. 1515

What is the tree? As fer as Man's
Concerned it disna maitter
Gin but a giant thistle 'tis
That spreids eternal mischief there,
As I'm inclined to think. 1520
Ruthless it sends its solid growth
Through mair than he can e'er conceive,
And braks his warlds abreid and rives
His Heavens to tatters on its horns.

The nature or the purpose o't 1525
He needna fash to spier, for he
Is destined to be sune owre grown
And hidden wi' the parent wud
The spreidin' boughs in darkness hap,
And a' its future life'll be 1530
Ootwith'm as he's ootwith his banes.

forenen(s)t—*over against* windlestrae—*withered stalk of grass; something of no account* whuppin'—*whopping* sooker—*sucker* coom—*honeycomb (MacD. But J also has: 'the wooden frame used in building the arch of a bridge'.)* blebs—*blobs, drops* braith—*breath* maun—*must* braird—*sprout* tae—*too* sentrice—*scaffolding* big—*build* abreid—*asunder* rives—*rends* fash—*trouble* spier—*ask* wud—*wood* hap—*cover*

1507. *The whuppin' sooker.* Perhaps a reminiscence of the 'sappy sucker' in Charles Murray's poem, 'The Whistle'. MacD renders *whuppin'* as 'sappy' in his English version.

1512-1515. 'Nature goes on building life upon dead bones—for ever, but in vain'. (J.N. Duddington on Solovyov, *Hibbert Journal*, April 1917, p. 442.)

1523-1524. Even as conceived by man, Yggdrasill extends its branches beyond the heavens.

Juist as man's skeleton has left
Its ancient ape-like shape ahint,
Sae states o' mind in turn gi'e way
To different states, and quickly seem 1535
Impossible to later men,
And Man's mind in its final shape
Or lang'll seem a monkey's spook,
And, strewth, to me the vera thocht
O' Thocht already's fell like that! 1540
Yet still the cracklin' thorns persist
In fitba' match and peepy show;
To antic hay a dog-fecht's mair
Than Jacob *v.* the Angel;
And through a cylinder o' wombs, 1545
A star reflected in a dub,
I see as 'twere my ain wild harns
The ripple o' Eve's moniplies.

And faith! yestreen in Cruivie's een
Life rocked at midnicht in a tree, 1550
And in Gilsanquhar's glower I saw
The taps o' waves 'neth which the warld
Ga'ed rowin' like a jeelyfish,
And whiles I canna look at Jean
For fear I'd see the sunlicht turn 1555
Worm-like into the glaur again!

A black leaf owre a white leaf twirls,
My liver's shadow on my soul,
And clots o' bluid loup oot frae stems
That back into the jungle rin, 1560
Or in the waters underneath
Kelter like seaweed, while I hear
Abune the thunder o' the flood,
The voice that aince commanded licht
Sing 'Scots Wha Ha'e' and hyne awa' 1565

ahint—*behind* or lang—*ere long* vera—*very* fell—*extremely* fitba'—*football* peepy show—*cinema* antic hay *(English)*—*a dance of grotesques (e.g. mixed human and other forms)* dub—*puddle; gutter* harns—*brains* moniplies—*intestines* yestreen—*yesterday evening* een—*eyes* glower—*stare* rowin'—*rolling, lurching* glaur—*mire* loup—*leap* kelter—*undulate* abune—*above* hyne awa'—*(go) far away*

1532-1540. Cf. Nietzsche, *Zarathustra*, Prologue, 3: 'What is the ape to man? A laughing-stock or a painful embarrassment. And just so shall man be to the Superman: a laughing-stock or a painful embarrassment'.

1541. *Crackling thorns*: cf. l. 2236. 'For as the crackling of thorns under a pot, so is the laughter of the fool: this also is vanity'. (Ecclesiastes 7. 6.)

1543. *Antic hay*: 'My men, like satyrs gazing on the lawns, / Shall with their goat feet dance an antic hay'. (Marlowe, *Edward II*, I. 1. 59.) Evidently MacD had in mind Aldous Huxley's novel with that title (1923), applying the phrase to modern life.

1544. *Jacob v. the Angel.* Jacob's wrestling match with the angel, after which he declared: 'I have seen God face to face, and my life is preserved'. (Genesis 32. 24-32.) Cf. Melville, 'Art':

> What unlike things must meet and mate . . .
> And fuse with Jacob's mystic heart,
> To wrestle with the angel—Art.

1550. *In a tree*—like an ape. Cf. Stevenson on his grandfather: 'There was an aboriginal frisking of the blood that was not his; tree-top memories, like undeveloped negatives, lay dormant in his mind'. ('The Manse', in *Memories and Portraits*.)

1557. Note the echo of l. 1334.

1565. '*Scots Wha Ha'e*'. Burns's song, written to the supposed tune of Robert the Bruce's march to Bannockburn where the invading English army was defeated.

Like Cruivie up a different glen,
And leave me like a mixture o'
A wee Scotch nicht and Judgment Day,
The bile, the Bible, and the *Scotsman*,
Poetry and pigs—Infernal Thistle, 1570
Damnition haggis I've spewed up,
And syne return to like twa dogs!
Blin' Proteus wi' leafs or hands
Or flippers ditherin' in the lift
—Thou Samson in a warld that has 1575
Nae pillars but your cheengin' shapes
That dung doon, rise in ither airts
Like windblawn reek frae smoo'drin' ess!
—Hoo lang maun I gi'e aff your forms
O' plants and beasts and men and Gods 1580
And like a doited Atlas bear
This steeple o' fish, this eemis warld,
Or, maniac heid wi' snakes for hair,
A Maenad, ape Aphrodite,
And scunner the Eternal sea? 1585

Man needna fash and even noo
The cells that mak' a'e sliver wi'm,
The threidy knit he's woven wi',
'Ud fain destroy what sicht he has
O' this puir transitory stage, 1590
Yet tho' he kens the fragment is
O' little worth he e'er can view,
Jalousin' it's a cheatrie weed,
He tyauves wi' a' his micht and main
To keep his sicht despite his kind 1595
Conspirin' as their nature is
'Gainst ocht wi' better sicht than theirs.

What gars him strive? He canna tell—
It may be nocht but cussedness.

haggis—*unknown (MacD)* lift—*sky* dung doon—*dashed down* airts—*directions* reek—*smoke* ess—*ash (Shetland)* maun—*must* doited—*deranged* steeple—*stack of partially dried fish (Shetland)* emmis—*wobbly* heid—*head* scunner—*disgust* fash—*trouble* threidy knit—*thready texture* jalousin'—*suspecting* cheatrie—*delusive* tyauves—*strives* gars—*makes, compels to*

1568. *A wee Scotch nicht.* An evening entertainment including Scots songs, etc. To the Drunk Man, as emetic as a London Scottish Burns Supper.

1571. *Haggis.* Featured in the ritual of a Burns Supper.

1572. *Two* dogs—because of Burns's poem, 'The Twa Dogs'.

1576-1580. Cf. Orage on Nietzsche: 'Life, as it thus appears to the eye of the imaginative mind, is the spectacle of the eternal play and conflict of two mutually opposing principles: Dionysos ever escaping from the forms that Apollo is ever creating for him'. (*Friedrich Nietzsche* (1906), p. 35.)

1581-1582. Cf. Ahab in *Moby Dick*, who feels as though he were 'Adam, staggering underneath the piled centuries since Paradise'.

1583. *Maniac heid wi' snakes for hair.* The context suggests that MacD is remembering Medusa (a Gorgon rather than a Maenad), whose severed head, shown by Perseus to Atlas, turned him into a mountain seemingly supporting the heavens.

1586. *Man needna fash*: reiterating the assertion made in l. 1526.

1594-1597. Though 'he' refers syntactically to 'Man', its real reference is to the poet, whose function is seen as visionary.

—At best he hopes for little mair 1600
Than his suspicions to confirm,
To mock the sicht he hains sae weel
At last wi' a' he sees wi' it,
Yet, thistle or no' whate'er its end,
Aiblins the force that mak's it grow 1605
And lets him see a kennin' mair
Than ither folk and fend his sicht
Agen their jealous plots awhile
'll use the poo'ers it seems to waste,
This purpose ser'd, in ither ways, 1610
That may be better worth the bein'
—Or sae he dreams, syne mocks his dream
Till Life grows sheer awa' frae him,
And bratts o' darkness plug his een.

It may be nocht but cussedness, 1615
But I'm content gin a' my thocht
Can dae nae mair than let me see,
Free frae desire o' happiness,
The foolish faiths o' ither men
In breedin', industry, and War, 1620
Religion, Science, or ocht else
Gang smash—when I ha'e nane mysel',
Or better gin I share them tae,
Or mind at least a time I did!

Aye, this is Calvary—to bear 1625
Your Cross wi'in you frae the seed,
And feel it grow by slow degrees
Until it rends your flesh apairt,
And turn, and see your fellow-men
In similar case but sufferin' less 1630
Thro' bein' mair wudden frae the stert! . . .

I'm fu' o' a stickit God.
THAT'S *what's the maitter wi' me.*
Jean has stuck sic a fork in the wa'
That I row in agonie. 1635

hains—*guards* aiblins—*perhaps* a kennin' mair—*a trifle more* fend—*defend* ser'd—*served* bratt(s)—*scum* mind—*remember* wudden—*wooden* stickit—*thwarted; aborted (MacD)* to stick a fork in the wa'—*to transfer, by doing this, the pains of a woman in labour to her husband (J)* row—*roll about*

The Fork in the Wall, 1632-1639.

1632. A well-known product of the Kailyard was S.R. Crockett's novel, *The Stickit Minister* (1893). Mindful that he also came of 'a God-bearing People' (l. 1640), MacD was perhaps going one better than Crockett with his 'stickit God'.

1634-1635. The couvade had particular historical associations on MacD's home ground. 'Near where the tower of Langholm stood is a piece of ground on which a number of witches were burned so lately as the eighteenth century. It is recounted of the witches of Eskdale that they were sufficiently potent to be able to transfer the labours of child-birth from the mother to the father. As several of them were able midwives, the belief in their powers was much emphasized'. (H.D. Gauld, *Brave Borderland*, London 1935, pp. 349-350.)

Mary never let dab.
SHE *was a canny wumman.*
She hedna a gaw in Joseph at a'
But, wow, this seecund comin'! . . .

*Narodbogonosets** are my folk tae, 1640
But in a sma' way nooadays—
A faitherly God wi' a lang white beard,
Or painted Jesus in a haze
O' blue and gowd, a gird aboot his heid
Or some sic thing. It's been a sair come-doon, 1645
And the trade's nocht to what it was.
Unnatural practices are the cause.
Baith bairns and Gods'll be obsolete soon
(The twaesome gang thegither), and forsooth
Scotland turn Eliot's waste—the Land o' Drouth. 1650

But even as the stane the builders rejec'
Becomes the corner-stane, the time may be
When Scotland sall find oot its destiny,
And yield the *vse-chelovek*.†
—At a' events, owre Europe flaught atween, 1655
My whim (and mair than whim) it pleases
To seek the haund o' Russia as a freen'
In workin' oot mankind's great synthesis. . . .

* God-bearers. † The All-Man or Pan-Human.

let dab—*let on, disclose information (But note also 'dab', to strike with a pointed weapon.)* canny—*cautious, gentle* to ha'e a gaw in (the back of another)—*to have the power of giving him pain (J)* seecund—*second* sma'—*small* gowd—*gold* gird—*hoop* baith—*both* twaesome—*twosome* gang thegither—*go together* Drouth—*Drought* flaught—*stretched out; abased (MacD)* atween—*between*

The Goal of Scottish History, 1640-1744.

1640-1658. 'His [Dostoevsky's] doctrine was . . . a democratic Slavophilism, a profound belief that the Russian People (with a big P, and mainly meaning the peasants) was a *narodbogonosets*—"a God-bearing People". . . . Dostoevsky's greatest triumph during his lifetime, and at the same time the fullest and most brilliant assertion of his national doctrine, was the Address he delivered in 1880 on the unveiling of the Pushkin memorial in Moscow. Pushkin, said Dostoevsky, was Russia's all-in-all (*nashe vse*), for the very reason that he was a cosmopolitan, or, as Dostoevsky put it, an All-man (*vse-chelovek*). This pan-Humanity is the national characteristic of Russia, and Russia's mission is to effect the final synthesis of all mankind'. (D.S. Mirsky, *Modern Russian Literature* (1925), p. 48.) MacD was not of course alone in claiming that it is not only in Russia that such a synthesis is the mission. Cf. Mazzini, who saw united Humanity as a synthesis of all the nations, with each one pursuing its divinely allotted task, its 'historic mission'.

1651-1652. 'The stone which the builders refused is become the head stone of the corner'. (Psalm 118. 22.) In Dostoevsky's *The Brothers Karamazov*, Zosima, who has called the Russians 'a God-bearing People', goes on to declare: 'Our people will shine forth in the world, and all men will say: "The stone which the builders refused, the same is become the head stone of the corner" '. (Harmondsworth 1958, I, p. 374.)

Melville‡ (a Scot) kent weel hoo Christ's
Corrupted into creeds malign, 1660
Begotten strife's pernicious brood
That claims for patron Him Divine.
(The Kirk in Scotland still I cry
Crooks whaur it canna crucify!)

Christ, bleedin' like the thistle's roses, 1665
He saw—as I in similar case—
Maistly, in beauty and in fear,
'Ud "paralyse the nobler race,
Smite or suspend, perplex, deter,
And, tortured, prove the torturer." 1670

And never mair a Scot sall tryst,
Abies on Calvary, wi' Christ,
Unless, mebbe, a poem like this'll
Exteriorise things in a thistle,
And gi'e him in this form forlorn 1675
What Melville socht in vain frae Hawthorne. . . .

‡ Herman Melville.

abies—*except (MacD—who provides SND with earliest instance of this usage. Normal meanings: in comparison with; in addition to. MacD seems to have transferred the meaning of 'beis', except, to 'abies'.)* socht—*sought*

1695-1696. (Cf. l. 2069.) MacD seems to have envisaged something like Rilke's *Umschlag* (reversal): the idea that if his torments of mind were allowed to intensify unimpeded they would suddenly swing round into their opposite, a divine euphoria.

1700. *Coil and recoil.* Reminiscent of another of Bergson's analogies: the flow of the *élan vital* is interrupted and, like the recoil of a spring, turns back upon itself. This inverse movement is matter.

Be like the thistle, O my soul,
Heedless o' praise and quick to tak' affront, 1710
And growin' like a mockery o' a'
Maist life can want or thole,
And manifest forevermair
Contempt o' ilka goal.

O' ilka goal—save ane alane; 1715
To be yoursel', whatever that may be,
And as contemptuous o' that,
Kennin' nocht's worth the ha'en,
But certainty that nocht can be,
And hoo that certainty to gain. 1720

For this you still maun grow and grope
In the abyss wi' ever-deepenin' roots
That croon your scunner wi' the grue
O' hopeless hope
—And gin the abyss is bottomless, 1725
Your growth'll never stop! . . .

What earthquake chitters oot
In the Thistle's oorie shape,
What gleids o' central fire
In its reid heids escape, 1730
And whatna coonter forces
In growth and ingrowth graip
In an eternal clinch
In this ootcuissen form
That winna be outcast, 1735
But triumphs at the last
(Owre a' abies itsel'
As fer as we can tell,
Sin' frae the Eden o' the world
Ilka man in turn is hurled, 1740
And ilka gairden rins to waste
That was ever to his taste)?

thole—*endure* ilka—*every* croon—*crown* grue—*shudder* chitters—*trembles* oorie—*bleak; weird* gleids—*sparks* whatna—*what kind of* coonter—*counter* ingrowth—*increase* graip—*grope* ootcuissen—*cast out, rejected (Past participle of verb 'to ootcast'.)* abies—*except (MacD's usage in this sense is the earliest cited by SND.)*

1715-1716. Cf. Nietzsche: 'What does your conscience say?—"You shall become what you are" '. (*The Joyful Science*, III, 270.) But note what follows.

1718-1720. 'Knowing nothing is worth the having but certainty that nothing can be (worth the having), and how to gain that certainty'. This applies even to 'being yourself': even that is not worth having.

1721-1726. For MacD 'the abyss' is usually a sign-post to his 'master' Shestov. Cf. Mirsky: 'Shestov . . . is in tune with those thinkers who saw the irrational roots of the moral universe and fearlessly looked down into the abyss with . . . Dostoevsky, Nietzsche'. . . . (*Modern Russian Literature* (1925), p. 104.) And cf. MacD's 'Miguel de Unamuno':

> Only upon the floor of the abyss
> Is rooting ground to rear through seas of schism
> A soul of living adamant like his.

1739-1742. After Adam has eaten the forbidden fruit in Eden, God says to him: 'Cursed is the ground for thy sake. . . .Thorns also and thistles shall it bring forth to thee'. (Genesis 3. 17-18.)

O keep the Thistle 'yont the wa'
Owre which your skeletons you'll thraw.

I, in the Thistle's land, 1745
As you* in Russia where
Struggle in giant form
Proceeds for evermair,
In my sma' measure bood
Address a similar task, 1750
And for a share o' your
Appallin' genius ask.

Wha built in revelations
What maist men in reserves
(And only men confound!) 1755
A better gift deserves
Frae ane wha like hissel
(As ant-heap unto mountain)
Needs big his life upon
The everloupin' fountain 1760
That frae the Dark ascends
Whaur Life begins, Thocht ends
—A better gift deserves
Than thae wheen yatterin' nerves!

For mine's the clearest insicht 1765
O' man's facility
For constant self-deception,
And hoo his mind can be
But as a floatin' iceberg
That hides aneth the sea 1770
Its bulk: and hoo frae depths
O' an unfaddomed flood

* Dostoevski.

'yont—*beyond* wa'—*wall* thraw—*throw* bood—*must; ought to* hissel—*himself* big—*build* everloupin'—*everleaping* thae—*those* wheen—*few* yatterin'—*fretful; jarring* aneth—*beneath*

1743-1744. The wall of the graveyard which 'the deid come loupin' owre' at the Resurrection, in MacD's poem 'Crowdieknowe'. Or the wall of Heaven, which they then hope to scale, and thus regain paradise.

Letter to Dostoevsky, 1745-2023.

1760-1762. The fountain from the Dark is a major theme which emerges for development at l. 2086.

Tensions o' nerves arise
And humours o' the blood
—Keethin's nane can trace 1775
To their original place.

Hoo mony men to mak' a man
It tak's he kens wha kens Life's plan.

But there are flegsome deeps
Whaur the soul o' Scotland sleeps 1780
That I to bottom need
To wauk Guid kens what deid,
Play at stertle-a-stobie,
Wi' nation's dust for hobby,
Or wi' God's sel' commerce 1785
For the makin' o' a verse.

"Melville, sea-compelling man,
Before whose wand Leviathan
*Rose hoary-white upon the Deep,"**
What thou hast sown I fain 'ud reap 1790
O' knowledge 'yont the human mind
In keepin' wi' oor Scottish kind,
And, thanks to thee, may aiblins reach
To what this Russian has to teach,
Closer than ony ither Scot, 1795
Closer to me than my ain thocht,
Closer than my ain braith to me,
As close as to the Deity
Approachable in whom appears
This Christ o' the neist thoosand years. 1800

* Quoted from Robert Buchanan.

keethin's—*manifestations; disturbances in water which betray the movements of fish* kens—*knows* flegsome—*frightening* wauk—*wake* deid—*dead* stertle-a-stobie (Jock-startle-a-stobie)—*exhalations rising from the ground on a hot day* braith—*breath* neist—*next*

1785-1786. Cf. Stevenson on Whitman, 'commercing with God and the universe'. (*Familiar Studies of Men and Books* (1882), p. 110.)

1787-1789. Robert Buchanan's tribute to Melville occurs in the course of a poem in homage to Walt Whitman, 'Socrates in Camden', *The Academy*, 15 August 1885, pp. 102-103. Buchanan (whose spelling of Melville's name as 'Hermann' was followed by MacD) provided the following note: 'I sought everywhere for this Triton, who is still living somewhere in New York. No one seemed to know anything of the one great imaginative writer fit to stand shoulder to shoulder with Whitman in that continent'. The 25 lines of this poem devoted to praise for Melville were silently omitted from Buchanan's *Complete Poetical Works*,(London 1901), but he had cannibalised them in *The Outcast*, London 1891, pp. 77-78.

1800. 'To Dostoyevski's Christianity the next thousand years will belong'. (Spengler, *Decline of the West*, London 1926, II, 196.) Spengler's view of Dostoevsky as harbinger of the new civilisation destined to replace that of the declining West is featured in the first work to appear under the name of Hugh MacDiarmid, 'Nisbet, An Interlude in Post-War Glasgow'. In it, the poet Nisbet declares that we must wait for 'the new beginning which will come from a civilisation other than ours'. He is told by Young, a Communist, that 'the renewal is coming, has begun to come, from Russia. . . . In Dostoevsky . . . is to be found the first delineation of that new world'. (*Scottish Chapbook*, I, no. 2, (Sept. 1922), pp. 48-49.) The same second-hand summary of Spengler is used more fully in 'A Theory of Scots Letters: II', *Scottish Chapbook*, I, no. 8 (March 1923), pp. 213-14.

As frae your baggit wife
You turned whenever able,
And often when you werena,
Unto the gamin' table,
And opened wide to ruin 1805
Your benmaist hert, aye brewin'
A horror o' whatever
Seemed likely to deliver
You frae the senseless strife
In which alane is life, 1810
—As Burns in Edinburgh
Breenged arse-owre-heid thoro'
A' *it* could be the spur o'
To pleuch his sauted furrow,
And turned frae a' men honour 1815
To what could only scunner
Wha thinks that common-sense
Can e'er be but a fence
To keep a soul worth ha'en
Frae what it s'ud be daein' 1820
—Sae I in turn maun gi'e
My soul to misery,
Daidle disease
Upon my knees,
And welcome madness 1825
Wi' exceedin' gladness
—Aye, open wide my hert
To a' the thistle's smert.

And a' the hopes o' men
Sall be like wiles then 1830
To gar my soul betray
Its only richtfu' way,
Or as a couthie wife
That seeks nae mair frae life
Than domesticity 1835
E'en wi' the likes o' me—

baggit—*pregnant* benmaist—*innermost* breenged—*plunged* pleuch (plew)—*to plough (Normally 'pleuch' would be the substantive, 'plew' the verbal form.)* sauted—*salted* scunner—*disgust* daidle—*dandle* aye—*yes* gar—*make* couthie—*cosy; decent (MacD)*

1801-1806. As recounted in his second wife's diary, in *Dostoevsky: Portrayed by His Wife* (London) and *Dostoiewsky à la Roulette* (Paris), both of which appeared in 1926.

1815-1820. A confused piece of writing in which the point of view attributed to Burns becomes entangled with that of the opposition, the advocates of 'common-sense'.

1821-1828. In addition to the reference to Dostoevsky, cf. Nietzsche, who held that suffering and even disease are almost indispensable to the philosopher and noted that only by virtue of what seemed to be the 'Divine' turbulence of insanity and epilepsy could any new moral law make progress. Also Melville in *Moby Dick*: 'Man's insanity is heaven's sense; and wandering from all mortal reason, man comes at last to that celestial thought, which, to reason, is absurd and frantic; and weal or woe, feels them uncompromised, indifferent as his God'. (II, 170.)

As gin I could be carin'
For her or for her bairn
When on my road I'm farin'
—O I can spend a nicht 1840
In ony man's Delicht
Or wi' ony wumman born
—But aye be aff the morn!

In a' the inklin's cryptic,
Then, o' an epileptic, 1845
I ha'e been stood in you
And droukit in their grue
Till I can see richt through
Ilk weakness o' my frame
And ilka dernin' shame, 1850
And can employ the same
To jouk the curse o' fame,
Lowsed frae the dominion
O' popular opinion,
And risen at last abune 1855
The thistle like a mune
That looks serenely doon
On what queer things there are
In an inferior star
That couldna be, or see, 1860
Themsel's, except in me.

Wi' burnt-oot hert and poxy face
I sall illumine a' the place,
And there is ne'er a fount o' grace
That isna in a similar case. 1865

Let a' the thistle's growth
Be as a process, then,
My spirit's gane richt through,
And needna threid again,
Tho' in it sall be haud'n 1870
For aye the feck o' men
Wha's queer contortions there

gin—*if* bairn—*child* aff—*off* the morn—*tomorrow* droukit—*drenched* grue—*feeling of revulsion* ilk—*every* dernin'—*hiding* jouk—*dodge* lowsed—*freed* abune—*above* haud'n—*held* for aye—*forever* feck—*most*

1844-1845. *Inklin's cryptic . . . o' an epileptic.* Not just psychological insights but also the moments of mystical revelation associated with Dostoevsky's epileptic attacks.

1862-1865. Speaking as the Moon—and perhaps also as one of those Dostoevskian characters who are not on the face of it among the likeliest-looking founts of grace. Cf. Eliot, 'Rhapsody on a Windy Night':

> The moon has lost her memory.
> A washed-out smallpox cracks her face.

As memories I ken,
As memories o' my ain
O' mony an ancient pain. 1875
But sin' wha'll e'er wun free
Maun tak' like coorse to me,
A fillip I wad gi'e
Their eccentricity,
And leave the lave to dree 1880
Their weirdless destiny.

It's no' withoot regret
That I maun follow yet
The road that led me past
Humanity sae fast, 1885
Yet scarce can gi'e a fate
That is at last mair fit
To them wha tak' that gait
Than theirs wha winna ha'e't,
Seein' that nae man can get 1890
By ony airt or wile,
A destiny quite worth while
As fer as he can tell
—Or even you yoursel'!

And O! I canna thole 1895
Aye yabblin' o' my soul,
And fain I wad be free
O' my eternal me,
Nor fare mysel' alane
—Withoot that tae be gane, 1900
And this, I ha'e nae doot,
This road'll bring aboot.

The munelicht that owre clear defines
The thistle's shrill cantankerous lines
E'en noo whiles insubstantialises 1905
Its grisly form and 'stead devises

maun—*must* coorse—*course* the lave—*the rest* dree—*endure* weirdless—*futile* gait—*road, way* ha'e't—*have it* airt—*art* thole—*endure* yabblin'—*gabbling* withoot—*unless* tae—*also* gane—*gone* doot—*doubt* road—*way of proceeding* owre clear—*too clearly* whiles—*sometimes* 'stead—*instead*

1884-1885. Cf. Shestov's insistence on Dostoevsky's total rejection of the values of 'humanity' on which his earlier work had been based, and Mirsky on Dostoevsky's characters: 'But are they human beings? At any rate they do not belong to the humanity we belong to'. (*Modern Russian Literature*, p. 51.)

1899-1902. MacD's hope seems to be that freedom from personality and from concern with his individual immortal soul will lead to the pan-human.

A maze o' licht, a siller-frame,
As 'twere God's dream frae which it came,
Ne'er into bein' coorsened yet,
The essence lowin' pure in it, 1910
As tho' the fire owrecam' the clay,
And left its wraith in endless day.

These are the moments when a' sense
Like mist is vanished and intense
Magic emerges frae the dense 1915
Body o' bein' and beeks immense
As, like a ghinn oot o' a bottle,
Daith rises frae's when oor lives crottle.

These are the moments when my sang
Clears its white feet frae oot amang 1920
My broken thocht, and moves as free
As souls frae bodies when they dee.
There's naething left o' me ava'
Save a' I'd hoped micht whiles befa'.

Sic sang to men is little worth. 1925
It has nae message for the earth.
Men see their warld turned tapsalteerie,
Drookit in a licht owre eerie,
Or sent birlin' like a peerie—
Syne it turns a' they've kent till then 1930
To shapes they can nae langer ken.

Men canna look on nakit licht.
It flings them back wi' darkened sicht,
And een that canna look at it
Maun draw earth closer roond them yet 1935
Or, their sicht tint, find nocht insteed
That answers to their waefu' need.

siller-—*silver-* coorsened—*coarsened* lowin'—*glowing* beeks—*shines* crottle—*crumble away (MacD: unique usage as verb in SND)* frae oot amang—*away from* dee—*die* ava—*at all* befa'—*befall* sic—*such* tapsalteerie—*topsy-turvy* drookit—*drenched* birlin'—*spinning* peerie—*top* syne—*then* een—*eyes* maun—*must* tint—*lost*

1907-1912. Cf. 'Sea-Serpent' (*Complete Poems*, pp. 48-51).

1913-1916. Cf. Orage: 'Those strange and rare moments when, as by magic, the world of sense grows suddenly small and insignificant, and the feeling of the power of the [transcendent] self . . . becomes overwhelmingly great'. (*Consciousness*, London 1907, p. 19.)

1924. The sense seems to require that 'whiles' should modify 'hoped' rather than 'befa''.

1927-1931. This is in effect a description by MacD of his own poetic method.

And yet this essence frae the clay
In dooble form aye braks away,
For, in addition to the licht, 1940
There is an e'er-increasin' nicht,
A nicht that is the bigger and
Gangs roond licht like an airn band
That noo and then mair tichtly grips
And snuffs it in a black eclipse, 1945
But rings it maistly as a brough
The mune, till it's juist bricht enough—
O wull I never lowse a licht
I canna dowse again in spite,
Or dull to haud within my sicht? 1950

The thistle canna vanish quite.
Inside a' licht its shape maun glint,
A spirit wi' a skeleton in't.

The world, the flesh, 'll bide in us
As in the fire the unburnt buss, 1955
Or as frae sire to son we gang
And coontless corpses in us thrang.

And e'en the glory that descends
I kenna whence on *me* depends,
And shapes itsel' to what is left 1960
Whaur I o' me ha'e me bereft,
And still the form is mine, altho'
A force to which I ne'er could grow
Is movin' in't as 'twere a sea
That lang syne drooned the last o' me 1965
—That drooned afore the warld began
A' that could ever come frae Man.

airn—*iron* brough—*halo* lowse—*set free* haud—*hold* bide—*remain* buss—*bush* thrang—*throng* kenna—*don't know* lang syne—*long ago*

1938-1939. Essence itself is held to have a dual nature.

1951-1955. Cf. Rilke on Christ: 'I believe that the core of light in him which made him shine so brightly, day and night, has long been dispersed and distributed differently. But if he were so great . . . he should somehow have been burnt up, leaving no remains behind, no remains at all—not a trace'. ('The Letter of the Young Worker' in *Symbolism*, ed. T.G. West, p. 89.) For the unburnt bush, see Exodus 3. 2.

1956-1957. Reminiscent of 'germ-plasm', that part of the nuclear protoplasmic material which, according to early theories of inheritance, is the vehicle of heredity, and maintains its continuity from generation to generation.

1963-1967. Cf. ll. 2557-2559. MacD's 'sea' is reminiscent of Bergson's conception of the Life Force in his theory of 'Creative Evolution'. Cf. J.M. Murry, commenting on Claudel's religious conversion, when he found 'quelquechose en moi qui soit plus moi-même que moi': 'It is the ocean wherein we drown and the fount whence our life springs'. (*To the Unknown God*, London 1924, p. 163.) And Orage: 'Is it possible for the human to transcend the human? Can man become more than man? May he enter the one ocean of consciousness from which the myriad streams of particular modes of consciousness flow?' (*Consciousness*, p.22.)

And as at sicna times am I,
I wad ha'e Scotland to my eye
Until I saw a timeless flame 1970
Tak' Auchtermuchty for a name,
And kent that Ecclefechan stood
As pairt o' an eternal mood.

Ahint the glory comes the nicht
As Maori to London's ruins, 1975
And I'm amused to see the plicht
O' Licht as't in the black tide droons,
Yet even in the brain o' Chaos
For Scotland I wad hain a place,
And let Tighnabruaich still 1980
Be pairt and paircel o' its will,
And Culloden, black as Hell,
A knowledge it has o' itsel'.

Thou, Dostoevski, understood,
Wha had your ain land in your bluid, 1985
And into it as in a mould
The passion o' your bein' rolled,
Inherited in turn frae Heaven
Or sources fer abune it even.

Sae God retracts in endless stage 1990
Through angel, devil, age on age,
Until at last his infinite natur'
Walks on earth a human cratur

sicna—*such* hain—*keep, preserve* ain—*own* fer abune—*far above* cratur—*creature*

1968-1973. 'The veriest tyro in literary attitudinisation knows that it is *de rigeur* to regard all things Scottish as "povré" [pauvret] English. Can any good thing come out of Auchtermuchty? Is not Ecclefechan an extinct volcano?' (MacD in *Scottish Chapbook*, I, no. 2 (Sept. 1922), p. 51.)

1974-1975. 'Some traveller from New Zealand shall, in the midst of a vast solitude, take his stand on a broken arch of London Bridge to sketch the ruins of St. Paul's'. (T.B. Macaulay, 'Von Ranke' in *Critical and Historical Essays* (1843), 3, 209.) By a curious coincidence, W.H. Dugdale suggested in *The Spectator* of 11 Sept. 1926 that Macaulay's image had been excavated from Volney's *Ruins of Empires*, 'although one would not for a moment suggest plagiarism'.

1978-1983. Note that Chaos is said to have a brain, a will, and a knowledge of itself. As in Bergson and Shestov, Chaos is not just disorder but another sort of order.

1982. *Culloden*: scene of the butchering of the Scottish Jacobites in 1746.

1988-1989. Far above Heaven, that is, as conceived by orthodox religion.

1990-1993. 'The Creation is really a Fall, a limitation, a contraction of the true God: an idea which is partly found in gnosticism and fully expressed in the Cabala. . . . Urizen is this contracting power of the Intellect. In cabalistic terms, he is the *retraction of God*'. (Denis Saurat, *Blake and Modern Thought*, London 1929, pp. 15, 40.) 'As God filled the immensity of space, there could only be room for the separated creatures if God withdrew from one part of himself. . . . It is this part of God from which God has withdrawn his direct will which forms the divine raw material of which everything is made. . . . This is the famous theory of the withdrawal, the most characteristic of the cabalistic theories. Whenever we come across it we shall be able with certainty to diagnose the influence of the Cabala'. (Saurat, *Literature and Occult Tradition*, London 1930, pp. 82-3.)

(Or less than human as to my een
The people are in Aiberdeen); 1995
Sae man returns in endless growth
Till God in him again has scouth.

For sic a loup towards wisdom's croon
Hoo fer a man maun base him doon,
Hoo plunge aboot in Chaos ere 2000
He finds his needfu' fittin' there,
The matrix oot o' which sublime
Serenity sall soar in time!

Ha'e I the cruelty I need,
Contempt and syne contempt o' that, 2005
And still contempt in endless meed
That I may never yet be caught
In ony satisfaction, or
Bird-lime that winna let me soar?

Is Scotland big enough to be 2010
A symbol o' that force in me,
In wha's divine inebriety
A sicht abune contempt I'll see?

For a' that's Scottish is in me,
As a' things Russian were in thee, 2015
And I in turn 'ud be an action
To pit in a concrete abstraction
My country's contrair qualities,
And mak' a unity o' these
Till my love owre its history dwells, 2020
As owretone to a peal o' bells.

And in this heicher stratosphere
As bairn at giant at thee I peer. . . .

scouth—*scope* loup—*leap* maun—*must* fittin'—*footing* ony—*any* heicher—*higher* bairn—*child*

1994-1995. *Aiberdeen.* One might question whether the amusing intrusion here of MacD's personal animus against the Aberdonians is worth the risk to the status of what comes before and after it. C.M. Grieve advertised his first book by announcing that he had been 'subjected to a venomous and violently deflamatory [sic] attack' in an Aberdeen newspaper. Several of his adversaries in the Vernacular Circle of the London Burns Club hailed from Aberdeen, and the first two collections of poems by Hugh MacDiarmid had a very hostile reception in the *Aberdeen Press and Journal*, where he was advised that, if he aspired to become the Dictator of modern Scottish letters, 'he must first of all prove himself not to be a literary imbecile'. In his insult to the Aberdonians here, MacD is turning to his own purposes Edward Dowden's remark about the value to an author of every book review 'by either a human being or a Scotsman'.

1996-1997. *Man returns* towards the Godhead. Cf. the theology of 'God-manhood', involving Christ's kenosis 'in which the Godhead is, as it were, contracted to the measure of His humanity, and the humanity exalted to the measure of His divinity'. (E. Lampert, *The Apocalypse of History*, London 1948, p. 130.)

1998-2022. 'Our immediate thought is, "With such an aim, such a dangerous leap towards the crown of wisdom, how far back must the preliminary run be before the jump; what plunging about in the horrors of chaotic Earth-substance, seeking for foothold in the densest mass?" We look, in a spirit of worship and horror, from the work to the man, trying to discover the matrix in which this sublime serenity was moulded.

It is impossible to know what Russia meant to [Dostoevsky]; but it must have been the symbol of that abnormal self within him which gave him the power, transcending intellect, to find a direction and a meaning for that spiritual inebriation which is a habit of the Slav character.

Dostoevsky . . . was aware of all these qualities [of the Slav character]; he *was* these qualities; but with an intense faith—translated for his purpose into a mystical Slav nationalism—he subtly gathered all these inconsequentialities into what we must paradoxically call a concrete abstraction. This unity is vivid through all his work. It is an additional character creeping into each novel, just as the overtone creeps into, and dominates, the clash and strife of the drama of a peal of bells.

. . .The spiritual giants. . . .A being who breathes . . . that higher stratosphere which is the life-stuff of the sublime few'. (Richard Church, 'Dostoevsky', *New Age*, 20 May 1926, pp. 25-26.)

O Jean, in whom my spirit sees,
Clearer than through whisky or disease, 2025
Its dernin' nature, wad the searchin' licht
Oor union raises poor'd owre me the nicht.

I'm faced wi' aspects o' mysel'
At last wha's portent nocht can tell,
Save that sheer licht o' life that when we're joint 2030
Loups through me like a fire a' else t' aroint.

Clear my lourd flesh, and let me move
In the peculiar licht o' love,
As aiblins in Eternity men may
When their swack souls nae mair are clogged wi' clay. 2035

Be thou the licht in which I stand
Entire, in thistle-shape, as planned,
And no' hauf-hidden and hauf-seen as here
In munelicht, whisky, and in fleshly fear,

In fear to look owre closely at 2040
The grisly form in which I'm caught,
In sic a reelin' and imperfect licht
Sprung frae incongruous elements the nicht!

But were't by thou they were shone on,
Then wad I ha'e nae dreid to con 2045
The ugsome problems shapin' in my soul,
Or gin I hed—certes, nae fear you'd thole!

Be in this fibre like an eye,
And ilka turn and twist descry,
Hoo here a leaf, a spine, a rose—or as 2050
The purpose o' the poo'er that brings 't to pass.

dernin'—*lurking* wad—*would (that)* poor'd—*poured* nocht—*naught*
t' aroint *(English)—to drive away* lourd—*dull; gross* aiblins—*maybe*
swack—*supple* owre—*too* the nicht—*tonight* wer't—*were it* dreid—*dread*
ugsome—*repulsive* certes—*for sure* thole—*tolerate* ilka—*every*

In the Peculiar Light of Love, 2024-2055.

This section links up with 'The Light of Life' (ll. 977-991).

2033. *Peculiar licht o' love.* Perhaps a faint echo of Yeats's *Vision*, which MacD read at this time: 'A man becomes passionate and this passion makes the *Daimonic* thought luminous with its peculiar light—this is the object of the Daimon—and she so creates a very personal form of heroism or of poetry' (p.28).

2043. *Form . . . sprung frae incongruous elements*: another variation on the antisyzygy theme.

Syne liberate me frae this tree,
As wha had there imprisoned me,
The end achieved—or show me at the least
Mair meanin' in't, and hope o' bein' released. 2055

I tae ha'e heard Eternity drip water
(Aye water, water!), drap by drap
On the a'e nerve, like lichtnin', I've become,
And heard God passin' wi' a bobby's feet
Ootby in the lang coffin o' the street 2060
—Seen stang by chitterin' knottit stang loup oot
Uncrushed by th' echoes o' the thunderin' boot,
Till a' the dizzy lint-white lines o' torture made
A monstrous thistle in the space aboot me,
A symbol o' the puzzle o' man's soul 2065
—And in my agony been pridefu' I could still
Tine nae least quiver or twist, watch ilka point
Like a white-het bodkin ripe my inmaist hert,
And aye wi' clearer pain that brocht nae anodyne,
But rose for ever to a fer crescendo 2070
Like eagles that ootsoar wi' skinklan' wings
The thieveless sun they blin'
—And pridefu' still
That 'yont the sherp wings o' the eagles fleein'
Aboot the dowless pole o' Space, 2075
Like leafs aboot a thistle-shank, my bluid
Could still thraw roses up
—And up!

O rootless thistle through the warld that's pairt o' you,
Gin you'd withstand the agonies still to come, 2080
You maun send roots doon to the deeps unkent,
Fer deeper than it's possible for ocht to gang,
Savin' the human soul,
Deeper than God himsel' has knowledge o',
Whaur lichtnin's canna probe that cleave the warld, 2085
Whaur only in the entire dark there's founts o' strength

syne—*then* tae—*too* ootby—*outside* stang—*spasm* chitterin'—*trembling* loup—*leap* tine—*lose* ripe—*probe* brocht—*brought* fer—*far* skinklan'—*shining* thieveless—*impotent* blin'—*blind* dowless—*feeble, powerless* thraw—*throw* unkent—*unknown* ocht—*anything* gang—*go* savin'—*except*

Metaphysical Pictures of the Thistle, 2056-2183.

It is curious that although MacD described this passage as 'vers libre', it gravitates into rhymed couplets at ll.2059-2062.

2056-2060. John Weston has suggested a reference to the water dripping from the coffin-lid in Dostoevsky's 'Dream of a Ridiculous Man'. The lightning is perhaps reminiscent of Dostoevsky's description of the 'moments like prolonged lightning' on the threshold of an epileptic attack. Note also the Scots expression *dede-drap*: a drop of water falling intermittently and heavily on a floor, viewed by the superstitious as a premonition of death (Jamieson). MacD seems to combine the idea of mortal life emerging like a disease from 'Eternity's poisoned draps' (l. 2087) with the image of the water-torture.

God as the eternal policeman or 'high-constable' (Melville) is featured by Nietzsche and by Blake, for whom he is a false god of vengeance, 'the Accuser who is the God of this World', as opposed to the true God of occult tradition, whose nature is entirely unknown—'the Deity of whom no one has any knowledge', as the Gnostics said. It is the latter Deity, much researched by his friend Denis Saurat in the cabbalistic writings, who is MacD's 'Unkent God' (l. 2094).

2065. The fourth and most explicit statement by the poet of what his thistle symbolises. (Cf. ll. 1055-6, 1311-12, 1343-50.)

2066-2078. Cf. Nietzsche: 'I test the *power of will* according to the amount of resistance it can offer and the amount of pain and torture it can endure and know how to turn to its own advantage'. And: 'Do you have courage, O my brothers? . . . *Not* the courage before witnesses, but anchorite and eagle courage, which not even the gods behold? . . . Whoever looks into the abyss, but with the eyes of an eagle, whoever *grasps* the abyss with the talons of an eagle—that man has courage'. (*Zarathustra*, IV, 'Of the Higher Man', section 4.)

2084. God, or at any rate *this* God, is not omniscient.

2086. Linked with Dostoevsky and 'The everloupin' fountain / That frae the Dark ascends' (ll. 1760-61).

Eternity's poisoned draps can never file,
And muckle roots thicken, deef to bobbies' feet.

A mony-brainchin' candelabra fills
The lift and's lowin' wi' the stars; 2090
The Octopus Creation is wallopin'
In coontless faddoms o' a nameless sea.
I am the candelabra, and burn
My endless candles to an Unkent God.
I am the mind and meanin' o' the octopus 2095
That thraws its empty airms through a' th' Inane.

And a' the bizzin' suns ha'e bigged
Their kaims upon the surface o' the sea.
My lips may feast for ever, but my guts
Ken naething o' the Food o' Gods. 2100

"Let there be Licht," said God, and there was
A little: but He lacked the poo'er
To licht up mair than pairt o' space at aince,
And there is lots o' darkness that's the same
As gin He'd never spoken 2105
—Mair darkness than there's licht,
And dwarfin't to a candle-flame,
A spalin' candle that'll sune gang oot.
—Darkness comes closer to us than the licht,
And is oor natural element. We peer oot frae't 2110
Like cats' een bleezin' in a goustrous nicht
(Whaur there is nocht to find but stars
That look like ither cats' een),
Like cats' een, and there is nocht to find
Savin' we turn them in upon oorsels; 2115
Cats canna.
Darkness is wi' us a' the time, and Licht
But veesits pairt o' us, the wee-est pairt,
Frae time to time on a short day atween twa nichts.

draps—*drops* file—*defile* muckle—*massive* deef—*deaf; unimpressionable* mony-brainchin'—*many-branching* lift—*sky* lowin'—*blazing* wallopin'—*thrashing about* bizzin'—*buzzing* bigged—*built* kaims—*(honey) combs* spalin'—*melting, guttering* een—*eyes* goustrous—*stormy* savin'—*unless* canna—*can't* veesits—*visits* wee-est—*smallest*

2093-2094. Cf. *Cencrastus* (*Complete Poems*, p. 241), where MacD talks of fencing the tables for 'my unkent God's communion'. Even in Christian contexts, the principle that God is essentially unknown is affirmed by 'apophatic' as opposed to 'cataphatic' theology. MacD was aware of the altar to the Unknown God which Paul found in Athens (Acts 27, 23; *Annals of the Five Senses*, p. 13), and he probably knew the following passage from William Hamilton's essay in the *Edinburgh Review* (1829), 'Philosophy of the Unconditioned', taken up by Herbert Spencer in *First Principles* (London 1862, I, 'The Unknowable'): 'But the last and highest consecration of all true religion must be an altar—*To the unknown and unknowable God*'.

2101-2110. God for Rilke is 'that depth whom light has never spoiled'. Darkness surrounds the Unknown God, and the light of the Creation is just a flash in the pan, appropriate to the minor deity concerned with that event.

Cf. A.E. (George Russell)'s waking dream in which 'one of the Host of Darkness' told him: ' "We of the Darkness are more ancient than you of the Light. . . . When most you rebel against the known God, the lips of the unknown God are tenderest upon your forehead" '. (*The Interpreters*, London 1922, pp. 115-16.)

2109-2110. Cf. Tyutchev, 'Holy night ascended': 'And in the alien unresponsive night / [Man] recognises his native legacy' (*Poems and Political Letters of F.I. Tyutchev*, trans. J. Zeldin, Knoxville 1973, p.74.) MacD shares with Tyutchev the positive discrimination in favour of the Dark which follows.

2119. *Twa nichts*: before birth and after death.

Nae licht is thrawn on *them* by ony licht. 2120
Licht thraws nae licht upon itsel';
But in the darkness them wha's een
Nae fleetin' lichts ha'e dazzled and deceived
Find qualities o' licht, keener than ony licht,
Keen and abidin', 2125
That show the nicht unto itsel',
And syne the licht,
That queer extension o' the dark,
That seems a separate and a different thing,
And, seemin' sae, has lang confused the dark, 2130
And set it at cross-purposes wi' itsel'.

O little Life
In which Daith guises and deceives itsel',
Joy that mak's Grief a Janus,
Hope that is Despair's fause-face, 2135
And Guid and Ill that are the same,
Save as the chance licht fa's!

And yet the licht is there,
Whether frae within or frae withoot.
The conscious Dark can use it, dazzled nor deceived. 2140
The licht is there, and th' instinct for it,
Pairt o' the Dark and o' the need to guise,
To deceive and be deceived;
But let us then be undeceived
When we deceive, 2145
When we deceive oorsels.
Let us enjoy deceit, this instinct in us.
Licht cheenges naething,
And gin there is a God wha made the licht
We are adapted to receive, 2150
He cheenged naething,
And hesna kythed Hissel!
Save in this licht that fa's whaur the Auld Nicht was,
Showin' naething that the Darkness didna hide,
And gin it shows a pairt o' that 2155
Confoondin' mair than it confides
Ev'n in that.

syne—*then* guises—*masquerades* fause-—*false-* fa's—*falls* hesna—*hasn't* kythed—*revealed* Hissel—*Himself* Auld—*Old*

2120-2121. Cf. Susan Glaspell, *Berenice*: 'Lights which only light themselves keep us from having light, from knowing what the darkness is'. (Quoted by MacD in *New Age*, 12 June 1924, p. 79.)

2122-2126. There is an occult tradition of a sun with rays of darkness as well as a sun with rays of light. And Cf. Yeats: 'There is another mind, or another part of our mind in this darkness, that is yet to its own perceptions in the light; and we in our turn are dark to that mind'. (*A Vision* (1925), p. 27.)

2132-2133. Cf. Valéry's 'Ebauche d'un Serpent', in which the sun, the source of life, is said to be a mask for death. And Melville in *Moby Dick*: 'All visible objects . . . are but as pasteboard masks' (chapt. 36).

2149-2157. 'After being separated from unimaginable primordial confusion, as light and darkness were on the first day differentiated, all forms have been forced and subordinated to the condition of being seen' (Valéry, 'Introduction to the Method of Leonardo da Vinci').

2153. *Auld Nicht*: 'The Reign of Chaos and old Night' (Milton, *Paradise Lost*, I, 543).

The epileptic thistle twitches
(A trick o' wund or mune or een—or whisky).
A brain laid bare, 2160
A nervous system,
The skeleton wi' which men labour
And bring to life in Daith
—I, risen frae the deid, ha'e seen
My deid man's eunuch offspring. 2165
—The licht frae bare banes whitening evermair,
Frae twitchin' nerves thrawn aff,
Frae nakit thocht,
Works in the Darkness like a fell disease,
A hungry acid and a cancer, 2170
Disease o' Daith-in-Life and Life-in-Daith.

O for a root in some untroubled soil,
Some cauld soil 'yont this fevered warld,
That 'ud draw darkness frae a virgin source,
And send it slow and easefu' through my veins, 2175
Release the tension o' my grisly leafs,
Withdraw my endless spikes,
Move coonter to the force in me that hauds
Me raxed and rigid and ridiculous
—And let my roses drap 2180
Like punctured ba's that at a Fair
Fa' frae the loupin' jet!
—Water again!. . .

Omsk and the Calton turn again to dust,
The suns and stars fizz out with little fuss, 2185

wund—*wind* banes—*bones* fell—*dire* cauld—*cold* 'yont—*beyond* coonter—*counter* hauds—*holds* raxed—*stretched* ba's—*balls* loupin'—*leaping*

2158. Perhaps MacD thinks of his thistle as being 'epileptic', like Dostoevsky, because it is a product of 'the artist's diseased nervous system'.

2162-2165. *Labour*—as in childbirth. Cf. the skeleton in MacD's sketch of the dead prostitute, 'In the Fulness of Time': 'Complexity has laboured and brought forth the most signal of all the simplicities. The last gaunt midwife has delivered this travailling creature of the final issue of her ravelled womb—this naked and incorruptible offspring, builded in ivory, the heir of Time!

Wanderers eastward, wanderers west
Know you why you cannot rest?
'Tis that every mother's son
Travails with a skeleton.'

(*Scottish Nation*, 18 Dec. 1923, p. 8.)

2172-2183. This passage begins like a parody of Keatsian yearning for 'easeful death'—a far cry from the expectations that have been aroused by what Solovyov called 'the dark root of being' in Chaos and Old Night. A context highly appropriate to *A Drunk Man* is however supplied for it by Havelock Ellis, writing about movements such as 'occultism, theosophy, spiritualism, all those vague forms on the border-land of the known which call to tired men weary of too much living, or never strong enough to live at all, to hide their faces from the sun of nature and grope into cool, delicious darkness, soothing the fever of life. . . . At the best one should know that this is part of the vital process by which the spiritual world moves on its axis, alternating between darkness and light. Therefore soak yourself in mysticism, follow every intoxicating path to every impossible Beyond, be drunken with mediaevalism, occultism, spiritualism, theosophy, and even, if you will, protestantism—the cup that cheers, possibly, but surely not inebriates—for the satisfaction that comes of all these is good while it lasts'. (*Affirmations*, London 1898, pp. 210-211. A new edition appeared in 1926.)

The Thistle as a Spider's Web, 2184-2215.

This section consists of a series of parodies in English, apparently intended as comic relief, with two stanzas in Scots tacked on to the end. It appears that MacD (and / or F.G. Scott) did not find an effective place for the latter, but was reluctant to throw away the fresh thistle-imagery which they contain.

2184. *Omsk and the Calton*: the city in Siberia where Dostoevsky was condemned to penal servitude, and the old gaol on Calton Hill in Edinburgh.

The bobby booms away and seems to bust,
And leaves the world to darkness and to us.

The circles of our hungry thought
Swing savagely from pole to pole.
Death and the Raven drift above 2190
The graves of Sweeney's body and soul.

My name is Norval. On the Grampian Hills
It is forgotten, and deserves to be.
So are the Grampian Hills and all the people
Who ever heard of either them or me. 2195

What's in a name? From pole to pole
Our interlinked mentality spins.
I know that you are Deosil, and suppose
That therefore I am Widdershins.

Do you reverse? Shall us? Then let's. 2200
Cyclone and Anti? —how absurd!
She should know better at her age.
Auntie's an ass, upon my word.

This is the sort of thing they teach
The Scottish children in the school. 2205
Poetry, patriotism, manners—
No wonder I am such a fool. . . .

Hoo can I graipple wi' the thistle syne,
Be intricate as it and up to a' its moves?
A' airts its sheenin' points are loupin' 'yont me, 2210
Quhile still the firmament it proves.

And syne it's like a wab in which the warld
Squats like a spider, quhile the mune and me
Are taigled in an endless corner o't
Tyauvin' fecklessly. . . . 2215

Deosil– *Sunwise* Widdershins—*Contrary to the sun* graipple—*grapple* airts—*ways, directions* sheenin'—*shining* quhile—*while (Old Scots spelling, indicating the voiceless fricative* [ʍ].*)* wab—*web* taigled—*tangled* tyauvin'—*struggling* fecklessly—*futilely*

2186-2187. Cf. Gray's 'Elegy':

The ploughman homeward plods his weary way,
And leaves the world to darkness and to me.

2188-2191. Cf. T.S. Eliot, 'Sweeney Among the Nightingales':

The circles of the stormy moon
Slide westward toward the River Plate,
Death and the Raven drift above
And Sweeney guards the hornèd gate.

Note MacD's insertion of the 'polar opposites' theme, which is itself parodied in ll. 2196-2203.

2192-2193. Cf. John Home, *Douglas*:

My name is Norval: on the Grampian hills
My father feeds his flocks; a frugal swain. . . .

'The notorious speech beginning "My name is Norval", which for some reason has acquired fame as great as much of Burns, is almost the best example possible of how not to write dramatic blank verse. It is worse than either Thomson's or Mallet's, and that is saying much'. (A.R. Williams, 'John Home', *Scottish Nation*, 12 June 1923, p. 3.)

2198-2199. *You*: Dostoevsky?

Jamieson in his Dictionary supplies information about various ancient magical rites associated with *Deasil* (Gaelic *deiseil*, sunwise) and Widdershins (the contrary direction).

2200. This invitation to the dance sounds like the talk of 'Bright Young Things' in the Twenties.

2210-2211. The thistle is said to combine the fixity of the firmament (the solid sphere in which the stars were thought to be fixed) with the fluctuating, elusive light of the stars themselves.

2212-2215. MacD perhaps remembered Svidrigailov in *Crime and Punishment* (IV, 1.), seeing eternity as a country bath-house with spiders in the corners. Cf. also *Zarathustra*: 'And this slow spider which crawls in the moonlight, and this moonlight itself, and I and you in the gateway, whispering together, whispering of eternal things—must we not all have been here before?'. (III, 2.)

The wan leafs shak' atour us like the snaw.
Here is the cavaburd in which Earth's tint.
There's naebody but Oblivion and us,
Puir gangrel buddies, waunderin' hameless in't.

The stars are larochs o' auld cottages, 2220
And a' Time's glen is fu' o' blinnin' stew.
Nae freen'ly lozen skimmers: and the wund
*Rises and separates even me and you.**

I ken nae Russian and you ken nae Scots.
We canna tell oor voices frae the wund. 2225
The snaw is seekin' everywhere: oor herts
At last like roofless ingles it has f'und,

And gethers there in drift on endless drift,
Oor broken herts that it can never fill;
And still—its leafs like snaw, its growth like wund— 2230
The thistle rises and forever will! . . .

The thistle rises and forever will,
Getherin' the generations under't.
This is the monument o' a' they were,
And a' they hoped and wondered. 2235

The barren tree, dry leafs, and cracklin' thorns,
This is the mind o' a' humanity
—The empty intellect that left to grow
'll let nocht ither be.

Lo! It has choked the sunlicht's gowden grain, 2240
And strangled syne the white hairst o' the mune.
Thocht that mak's a' the food o' nocht but Thocht
Is reishlin' grey abune. . . .

* Dostoevski.

atour—*out over* cavaburd—*heavy snowfall* tint—*lost* gangrel buddies—*'travelling folk'; tramps* larochs—*ruined foundations* blinnin'—*blinding* stew—*vapour; snowdrift* freen'ly—*friendly* lozen—*window-pane* skimmers—*glimmers* wund—*wind* ingles—*hearths* f'und—*found* nocht ither—*nothing else* gowden—*golden* syne—*next* hairst—*harvest* reishlin'—*rustling*

Farewell to Dostoevski, 2216-2235.

2216-2231. Printed as a separate poem, 'Hurricane', in *Glasgow Herald*, 13 Feb. 1926, p. 4.

2219. *Gangrel buddies*: Burns's term for the characters (including the Poet) in his cantata 'Love and Liberty'. Cf. the *skitalets*, the homeless intellectual wanderer of Dostoevsky's Pushkin speech, and the beggar-poet wandering in the blizzard, a favourite image of Blok's.

2220-2223. Cf. Blok, 'Timelessness': 'The homely fireside is gone. . . . All are caught in the spider-web, and time itself has stopped. Joy has gone cold and the hearth fires are out. Time is no more. The doors are open on the blizzard in the square'. (Trans. P. McCarey.)

2225. Cf. Middleton Murry reading Dostoevsky and hearing 'the echo of voices calling without sound across the waste and frozen universe'. (*Fyodor Dostoevsky*, London 1916, p. 33.)

2231. The thistle which 'rises and forever will' has just been likened to the wind that separates the poet from his one remaining soul-mate, Dostoevsky, and to the snow that drifts in their broken hearts. There is no indication in the text that 'rising forever' implies a *volte-face* at this point to bold phallic optimism of the sort assumed in the subsequent reduction of MacD's phrase to the status of an advertising slogan.

2232-2235. The thistle is a monument on 'the grave o' a' mankind' (l. 1445), 'life's gantin' and unfaddomed grave', 'whaur a' the lees o' hope are jumbled up' (ll. 128, 122). It is a monument to human *frustration*, like Shelley's 'painted veil' which 'mimicked . . . all men believed or hoped', or James Montgomery's 'statue in this temple of oblivion'. Note that in Scots the word 'monument' itself has the well established meaning, 'an object of ridicule or distaste'.

The Barren Tree, 2236-2303.

2236. *Cracklin' thorns*. See l. 1541 and note.

O fitly frae oor cancerous soil
May this heraldic horror rise! 2245
The Presbyterian thistle flourishes,
And its ain roses crucifies. . . .

No' Edinburgh Castle or the fields
O' Bannockburn or Flodden
Are dernin' wi' the miskent soul 2250
Scotland sae lang has hod'n.

It hauds nae pew in ony kirk,
The soul Christ cam' to save;
Nae R.S.A.'s ha'e pentit it,
F.S.A.'s fund its grave. 2255

Is it alive or deid? I show
My hert—wha will can see.
The secret clyre in Scotland's life
Has brust and reams through me,

A whummlin' sea in which is heard 2260
The clunk o' nameless banes;
A grisly thistle dirlin' shrill
Abune the broken stanes.

Westminster Abbey nor the Fleet,
Nor England's Constitution, but 2265
In a' the michty city there,
You mind a'e fleggit slut,

As Tolstoi o' Lucerne alane
Minded a'e beggar minstrel seen!
The woundit side draws a' the warld. 2270
Barbarians ha'e lizards' een.

dernin' wi'—*lit. hiding with (Misused?)* miskent—*unrecognised; misunderstood* hod'n—*hidden* hauds—*holds* pentit—*painted* clyre—*(diseased) gland; tumour* brust—*burst* reams—*froths; overflows* whummlin'—*tumbling* clunk—*hollow sound of object falling into deep water (And note 'clunker', a tumour, by association with l. 2258.)* dirlin'—*vibrating* abune—*above* michty—*mighty* mind—*remember* a'e—*one* fleggit—*frightened*

2249. *Bannockburn, Flodden*: the scene respectively of the most famous victory and defeat of the Scots in battles against their traditional enemies, the English.

2250. In MacD's English version this line reads: 'Are the hiding place of the misknown soul'.

2254. *R.S.A.'s*: Royal Scottish Academicians.

2255. *F.S.A.'s*: Fellows of the Society of Antiquaries.

2258. *The secret clyre in Scotland's life.* Associated by MacD with the contemporary situation in the Glasgow slums, which was described by William Bolitho as 'a cancerous condition which, starting from the lack of space and light in the homes of the workers, festers and complicates itself in numberless vicious circles'. (*Cancer of Empire*, London 1924, p. 14.)

2264-2271. 'What . . . remained rooted in his [Dostoevsky's] memory out of the whole gigantic city (London)? The image of the little ragged damsel to whom he gave in charity a silver coin and who thereupon fled like a wild animal before him and men in general to put her treasure in safety; not Westminster Abbey, nor the Fleet, nor England's Constitution impressed him so much. Even so it had fared shortly before with Tolstoy, on whom out of the whole life of the West only that well-known scene in Lucerne with the beggar-musician to whom nobody gave anything made an indelible impression; ay, the barbarians have lizard's eyes!' (A. Brückner, *A Literary History of Russia*, London 1908, p. 392.) ' "The barbarians have lizards' eyes", said even Herodotus, for in comparison with the West—the Romans—we are the barbarians, the Teutons'. (Brückner, summarising Herzen, p. 304.)

Glesca's a gless whaur Magdalene's
Discovered in a million crimes.
Christ comes again—wheesht, whatna bairn
In backlands cries betimes? 2275

Hard faces prate o' their success,
And pickle-makers awn the hills.
There is nae life in a' the land
But this infernal Thistle kills. . . .

Nae mair I see 2280
As aince I saw
Mysel' in the thistle
Harth and haw!

Nel suo profondo vidi che s'interna
Legato con amore in un volume 2285
(Or else by Hate, fu' aft the better Love)
Ciò che per l'universo si squaderna.

Sustanzia ed accidenti, e lor costume,
Quasi conflati insieme per tal modo,
(The michty thistle in wha's boonds I rove) 2290
Che ciò ch'io dico è un semplice lume.*

And kent and was creation
In a' its coontless forms,
Or glitterin' in raw sunlicht,
Or dark wi' hurrying storms. 2295

* Wicksteed's translation of Dante's Italian (Paradiso, canto xxxiii.85-90) is as follows: "Within its depths I saw ingathered, bound by love in one volume, the scattered leaves of all the universe; substance and accidents and their relations, as though together fused, after such fashion that what I tell of is one simple flame."

Glesca—*Glasgow* gless—*(looking-)glass* wheest—*hush* whatna—*what sort of* backlands—*dark, crowded tenements built on the back greens of existing tenements* harth and haw—*lean and hollow (MacD via J. But DOST cannot define 'harth' and gives 'haw' as meaning 'of a bluish, leaden, livid or dull colour'.)* fu' aft—*very often* boonds—*bounds*

2272-2275. Glasgow is here intended to suggest the Scottish equivalent of Dostoevsky's experience of London, referred to above. The setting for his encounter with the little girl of about six years old was the Haymarket, where child prostitutes were brought by their mothers. (*Summer Impressions*, trans. K. Fitzlyon, London 1955, pp. 65-66.)

2275. *Backlands*. 'My companions point out to me the "back-to-back" construction of all these dens, each of them ending in a dead wall, without possibility of a free current of air, any more than there is in a deep hole of the rocks'. (Bolitho on Glasgow slum backlands, *Cancer of Empire*, p. 27.)

2277. *Pickle-makers*—or sauce-manufacturers like the millionaire C.W. Dyson-Perrins of Ardross Castle, who employed MacD briefly in 1920/21 to catalogue his book collection.

2283. Cf. 'Thy hanchis hirklis with hukebanis harth and haw'. (William Dunbar, 'The Flyting of Dunbar and Kennedie', l. 181.)

2284-2291. In his essay on 'The Nature of Metaphysical Poetry', Herbert Read observes that 'the exposition of a philosophy to which are attached no considerations of personal pride or vanity makes for the exclusion of all kinds of subjective impurities—makes, in fact, for that very objective clarity that is so distinctive of Dante's poem'. He then quotes the Italian and the translation by Wicksteed used by MacD here. (*Reason and Romanticism*, London 1926, pp. 48-49.)

2286. *Hate*: opposed to Dante's divine and all-pervading 'love which moves the sun and the other stars'. The polar opposite of Dante is Ahab in *Moby Dick*, who sees (Chapter 41) 'inscrutable malice' at the heart of the universe: 'that intangible malignity which has been from the beginning'.

But what's the voice
That sings in me noo?
—A'e hauf o' me tellin'
The tither it's fou!

It's the voice o' the Sooth 2300
That's held owre lang
My Viking North
Wi' its siren sang. . . .

Fier comme un Ecossais.

If a' that I can be's nae mair 2305
Than what mankind's been yet, I'll no'
Begink the instincts thistlewise
That dern—and canna show.

Damned threids and thrums and skinny shapes
O' a' that micht, and s'ud, ha' been 2310
—Life onyhow at ony price!—
In sic I'll no' be seen!

Fier comme un Ecossais.

The wee reliefs we ha'e in booze,
Or wun at times in carnal states, 2315
May hide frae us but canna cheenge
The silly horrors o' oor fates.

Fier—comme un Ecossais!

hauf—*half* tither—*other* fou—*drunk* begink—*trick; evade* dern—*hide*
thrums—*odds and ends (of threads)* s'ud—*should* sic—*such* wun—*attain, reach*

Fier Comme un Ecossais, 2304-2318

2304. The French is a proverbial medieval phrase meaning 'as touchy as a Scot'. It was applied to Sir Thomas Urquhart by J.H. Millar in *A Literary History of Scotland*, London 1903, p. 254, and *Scottish Prose of the Seventeenth & Eighteenth Centuries*, Glasgow 1912, p. 72. MacD rendered 'fier' as 'high-spirited' in a radio programme, 'The Raucle Tongue'.

2311-2312. Cf. George Santayana: 'Nothing can be meaner than the anxiety to live on, to live on any how and in any shape: a spirit with any honour is not willing to live except in its own way, and a spirit with any wisdom is not over-eager to live at all'.

There's muckle in the root
That never can wun oot, 2320
Or't owre what is 'ud sweep
Like a thunderstorm owre sheep.

But shadows whiles upcreep,
And heavy tremors leap. . .
C'wa', Daith, again, sned Life's vain shoot, 2325
And your ain coonsel keep! . . .

Time like a bien wife,
Truth like a dog's gane—
The bien wife's gane to the aumrie
To get the puir dog a bane. 2330

Opens the aumrie door,
And lo! the skeleton's there,
And the gude dog, Truth, has gotten
Banes for evermair. . . .

Maun I tae perish in the keel o' Heaven, 2335
And is this fratt upon the air the ply
O' cross-brath'd cordage that in gloffs and gowls
Brak's up the vision o' the warld's bricht gy?

Ship's tackle and an eemis cairn o' fraucht
Darker than clamourin' veins are roond me yet, 2340
A plait o' shadows thicker than the flesh,
A fank o' tows that binds me hand and fit.

What gin the gorded fullyery on hie
And a' the fanerals o' the michty ship
Gi'e back mair licht than fa's upon them ev'n 2345
Gin sic black ingangs haud us in their grip?

muckle—*much* wun oot—*get out* or't—*or it* owre—*over* whiles—*at times* c'wa'—*come on* sned—*snip off* coonsel—*counsel* bien—*well off* aumrie—*cupboard* keel—*a lighter, a small barque (J)* fratt—*fretwork* cross-brath'd—*cross-braided* gloffs—*patches of darkness appearing denser than other parts of the atmosphere* gowls—*hollows: opposite of gloffs (MacD); hollows between hills (J)* gy—*scene; show* eemis—*unsteady* cairn—*pile of stones* fraucht—*freight* fank o' tows—*coil of ropes* fit—*foot* gorded—*frosted* fullyery—*leaved art-work (J); foliage (MacD)* fanerels—*what is loose and flapping (J); accessories (MacD)* ingangs—*intestines* haud—*hold*

The Emptiness at the End, 2319-2334.

2321. *What is*: what does exist.

2327-2334. Printed as a separate poem, 'The Skeleton in the Cupboard', in *Glasgow Herald*, 13 Feb. 1926, p. 4.

In the Keel of Heaven, 2335-2346.

An exercise in Dictionary Scots.

Grugous thistle, to my een
Your widdifow ramel evince
Sibness to snakes wha's coils
Rin coonter airts at yince, 2350
And fain I'd follow each
Gin you the trick'll teach.

Blin' root to bleezin' rose,
Through a' the whirligig
O' shanks and leafs and jags 2355
What sends ye sic a rig?
Bramble yokin' earth and heaven,
Till they're baith stramulyert driven!

Roses to lure the lift
And roots to wile the clay 2360
And wuppit brainches syne
To claught them 'midyards tae
Till you've the precious pair
Like hang'd men dancin' there,

Wi' mony a seely prickle 2365
You'll fleg a sunburst oot,
Or kittle earthquakes up
Wi' an amusin' root,
While, kilted in your tippet,
They still can mak' their rippit. . . . 2370

And let me pit in guid set terms
My quarrel wi' th' owre sonsy rose,
That roond aboot its devotees
A fair fat cast o' aureole throws
That blinds them, in its mirlygoes, 2375
To the necessity o' foes.

grugous—*grim, grisly* widdifow—*deserving to be hung (J); perverse (MacD)* ramel—*small branches* sibness—*kinship* coonter—*counter* airts—*directions* yince—*once* jags—*thorns* stramulyert—*panic-stricken* lift—*sky* wuppit—*bound round* claught—*clutch* 'midyards—*amidward, towards the middle* seely—*happy* fleg—*scare* kittle—*tickle* kilted—*hoisted* tippet—*noose* rippit—*rumpus* pit—*put* owre sonsy—*too contented, complacent; too plump* cast o' aureole—*light cast by a halo* mirlygoes—*hallucinations; effects of dazzling*

Creation's Whirligig, 2347-2370.

Holograph version with title 'The Hanging Judge (From "Twenty-Four Ways of Looking at the Thistle")' sent to J.K. Annand on 13 April 1926. Printed as 'The Hanging Judge' in *Glasgow Herald*, 19 May 1926, p. 4.

2348. The holograph version has 'souple boughs' for 'widdifow ramel'. *Widdifow* is an antiquated term which MacD apparently found in Jamieson along with *rippat* (l. 2370) in David Lindsay's usage:
Allace! this is ane fallone rippat!
The widdifow wardannis tuik my geir.

2363. *The precious pair*: i.e., earth and heaven.

2365. *Seely*. *Cunning* in holograph and in MacD's English version.

2368. *Amusin'*. The word is so weak one wonders if this could be a mistake for *amuvin'* (vexing, arousing to anger, exciting). MacD has *mischievous* in his English version.

2369. A *tippet* is a length of twisted horse-hair, straw, etc. MacD's usage here is associated with a traditional name for the hangman's noose or rope: *St. Johnston's tippet.*

My Quarrel with England, 2371-2394.

The title underlines the awkwardness of placing this section at this particular point in the work. It appears an arbitrary decision to return at this juncture to a theme last heard of more than 1600 lines before (ll. 751-770).

2376. *The necessity of foes*: a requirement of Nietzsche's 'noble morality'. This may be seen as another aspect of the principle of antisyzygy, since as Blake said: 'Without Contraries is no progression'. And 'might not Dionysos, the eternal foe, be also the eternal saviour of Apollo?' (Orage, *Friedrich Nietzsche*, p. 32.)

Upon their King and System I
Glower as on things that whiles in pairt
I may admire (at least for them),
But wi' nae claim upon my hert, 2380
While a' their pleasure and their pride
Ootside me lies—and there maun bide.

Ootside me lies—and mair than that,
For I stand still for forces which
Were subjugated to mak' way 2385
For England's poo'er, and to enrich
The kinds o' English, and o' Scots,
The least congenial to my thoughts.

Hauf his soul a Scot maun use
Indulgin' in illusions, 2390
And half in gettin' rid o' them
And comin' to conclusions
Wi' the demoralisin' dearth
O' onything worth while on Earth. . . .

I'm weary o' the rose as o' my brain, 2395
And for a deeper knowledge I am fain
Than frae this noddin' object I can gain.

Beauty is a'e thing, but it tines anither
(For, fegs, they never can be f'und thegither),
And 'twixt the twa it's no' for me to swither. 2400

As frae the grun' sae thocht frae men springs oot,
A ferlie that tells little o' its source, I doot,
And has nae vera fundamental root.

glower—*stare* bide—*remain* a'e—*one* tines—*loses* fegs—*faith!* swither—*hesitate* grun'—*ground* ferlie—*wonder* doot—*suspect* vera—*very*

2384-2388. MacD frequently developed this line of thought in terms of Oswald Spengler's historical cycles. Forces suppressed by the dominant power in one cycle remain dormant and may yet emerge in the next cycle.

2389-2394. Cf. John Freeman: 'During the first half of his life Herman Melville was investing himself with illusions and discovering them to be but illusions, and during the second half he was trying to make terms with the bareness that remained and avoid an exhausting, cynical conclusion'. (*Herman Melville*, London 1926, p.16.)

The Great Wheel, 2395-2658

The triplet form used for this section, though not terza rima, is reminiscent of Dante, and a link is no doubt intended with the passage from the *Paradiso* quoted via Herbert Read at ll. 2284-2291.

The Great Wheel is the first symbolic figure of Yeats's 'geometry' in *A Vision* (1925), representing a continuous movement of life in time from the *primary* to its opposite, the *antithetical*, and back again. He associated it with the Great Year or Platonic Year, in which the heavenly bodies were supposed to return to their original relative positions. Four months before *A Drunk Man* was published, MacD commented on Yeats's use of 'such properties as the Great Year of the Ancients, and so on', as follows: 'How grotesque, how far-fetched, how insanely ingenious all these esoteric properties, these paraphernalia of *romanticism*, these endless Chinese puzzle-boxes are . . . .' (*New Age*, 15 July 1926, pp. 119-120.)

2395. The awkwardness of the placing of the previous section affects one's reading of this one, as there is nothing to indicate that 'the rose' is *not* now to be understood as symbolising England.

2398. *Anither*: i.e., truth? (Cf. l. 2410.) Beauty and truth are opposing gyres in Yeats's *Vision*.

And cauld agen my hert are laid
The words o' Plato when he said, 2405
"God o' geometry is made."

Frae my ain mind I fa' away,
That never yet was feared to say
What turned the souls o' men to clay,

Nor cared gin truth frae me ootsprung 2410
In ne'er a leed o' ony tongue
That ever in a heid was hung.

I ken hoo much oor life is fated
Aince its first cell is animated,
The fount frae which the flesh is jetted. 2415

I ken hoo lourd the body lies
Upon the spirit when it flies
And fain abune its stars 'ud rise.

And see I noo a great wheel move,
And a' the notions that I love 2420
Drap into stented groove and groove?

It maitters not my mind the day,
Nocht maitters that I strive to dae
—For the wheel moves on in its ain way.

I sall be moved as it decides 2425
To look at Life frae ither sides;
Rejoice, rebel, its turn abides.

And as I see the great wheel spin
There flees a licht frae't lang and thin
That Earth is like a snaw-ba' in. 2430

(To the uncanny thocht I clutch
—The nature o' man's soul is such
That it can ne'er wi' life tine touch.

agen'—*against* fa'—*fall* feared—*afraid* leed—*(strain of) language* aince—*once* lourd—*heavy, gross* abune—*above* drap—*drop* stented—*allotted* dae—*do* flees—*flies* snaw-ba'—*snow-ball*

2404-2421. 'He measures and divides the cycles as if he had at heart . . . that profundity of Plato, 'God Geometrises'. . . . Here I fall away from a mind I have followed, I think with understanding, since I was a boy, and as he becomes remote in his thought I wonder whether he has forgotten his own early wisdom, the fear lest he should learn 'to speak a tongue men do not know'. I allow myself to drift apart because I feel to follow in the wake of Mr. Yeats' mind is to surrender oneself to the idea of Fate and to part from the idea of Free Will. I know how much our life is fated once life animates the original cell, the fountain from which the body is jetted; how much bodily conditions affect or even determine our thought; but I still believe in Free Will and that, to use the language of the astrologers, it is always possible for a man to rise above his stars. Now Mr. Yeats would have me believe that a great wheel turns ceaselessly, and that I and all others drop into inevitable groove after groove'. (A.E., Review of *A Vision* by W.B. Yeats, *Irish Statesman*, 13 Feb. 1926, pp. 714-715.)

2410-2412. 'In "Sangschaw" Hugh McDiarmid adopted the synthetic method, choosing any dialect word he could discover in Jamieson to express the thought in his head. His aim is frankly to form a new Scottish national language, but as the kelpie said in "John o' Arnha'":

That's nae the leid o' ony tongue
That ever in a heid was hung'.
(A.K., Review of *Penny Wheep*, *Aberdeen Press and Journal*, 19 June 1926, p. 3.)

But seek alone to hear the strange things said
By God to the bright hearts of those long dead,
And learn to chaunt a tongue men do not know.
(Yeats, 'To the Rose upon the Rood of Time'.)

2422-2436. 'It matters not my virtue to-day, my talent which I burnish, the wheel will move me to another groove where I am predestined to look on life as that new spiritual circumstance determines, and my will is only free to accept or rebel, but not to alter what is fated. . . . I encouraged myself to explore by remembering what Neander wrote in his *Church History* when he was confronted by the task of elucidating the bewildering mythology of the Gnostics. We must remember, he said, that the mind of man is made in the image of God, and therefore even in its wildest speculations it follows an image of truth. That is, there is something in the very anatomy of the soul which prohibits its adventure into that which is utterly baseless and unrelated to life'. (A.E., Review of *A Vision*, p. 715.)

Man's mind is in God's image made,
And in its wildest dreams arrayed 2435
In pairt o' Truth is still displayed.)

Then suddenly I see as weel
As me spun roon' within the wheel,
The helpless forms o' God and Deil.

And on a birlin' edge I see 2440
Wee Scotland squattin' like a flea,
And dizzy wi' the speed, and me!

I've often thrawn the warld frae me,
Into the Pool o' Space, to see
The Circles o' Infinity, 2445

Or like a flat stane gar'd it skite,
A Morse code message writ in licht
That yet I couldna read aricht.

The skippin' sparks, the ripples, rit
Like skritches o' a grain o' grit 2450
'Neth Juggernaut in which I sit.

Twenty-six thoosand years it tak's
Afore a'e single roond it mak's,
And syne it melts as it were wax.

The Phoenix guise 't'll rise in syne 2455
Is mair than Euclid or Einstein
Can dream o' or's in dreams o' mine.

Upon the huge circumference are
As neebor points the Heavenly War
That dung doun Lucifer sae far, 2460

Deil—*Devil* birlin'—*spinning* thrawn—*thrown* gar'd—*made, compelled to* skite—*skim, skip* rit—*scrape* skritches—*scratches (MacD. A nonce variant of the English word—SND.)* or's—*or is* neebor—*neighbour* dung doon—*beat down; overcame*

2441. 'He is nothing but a fly on a wheel'. (Edwin Muir on Marinetti, *New Age*, 19 Aug. 1920, p. 249.)

2451. *Juggernaut*: an incarnation of Vishnu whose image was hauled along in a car, beneath the wheels of which devotees were supposed to immolate themselves.

> – God whirlin' in Juggernaut while under its wheels
> The generations are drawn and vanish
> Like rouk in the sun!
> (*To Circumjack Cencrastus*, *Complete Poems*, p. 245.)

2452-2453. 'Our figure is based on the Great Year of some twenty-six thousand years'. (*A Vision*, p. 144.) Behind this is the 'precession of the equinoxes': the change in direction of the earth's axis as it turns round the axis of the ecliptic describes a complete cone approximately every 26,000 years.

2454. *Melts as it were wax.* This is not in Yeats, but Heraclitus saw the cycle of the world-process as 'the sport of Zeus who builds up the world times without number, ever dissolving it again in his primeval fire'. (*New Age*, 11 Feb. 1926, p. 176.)

2456. *Euclid or Einstein*: the mathematicians are brought in since 'God o' geometry is made'.

2458-2472. As if by way of an illustration of relativity, history is viewed on the time-scale appropriate to the Great Wheel.

And that upheaval in which I
Sodgered 'neth the Grecian sky
And in Italy and Marseilles,

And there isna room for men
Wha the haill o' history ken 2465
To pit a pin twixt then and then.

Whaur are Bannockburn and Flodden?
—O' a'e grain like facets hod'n,
Little wars (twixt that which God in

Focht and won, and that which He 2470
Took baith sides in hopelessly),
Less than God or I can see.

By whatna cry o' mine oot-topped
Sall be a' men ha'e sung and hoped
When to a'e note they're telescoped? 2475

And Jesus and a nameless ape
Collide and share the selfsame shape
That nocht terrestial can escape?

But less than this nae man need try.
He'd better be content to eye 2480
The wheel in silence whirlin' by.

Nae verse is worth a ha'et until
It can join issue wi' the Will
That raised the Wheel and spins it still,

But a' the music that mankind 2485
'S made yet is to the Earth confined,
Poo'erless to reach the general mind,

Poo'erless to reach the neist star e'en,
That as a pairt o'ts sel' is seen,
And only men can tell between. 2490

sodgered—*soldiered* pit—*put* hod'n—*hidden* whatna—*what sort of* ha'et—*whit* neist—*next*

2461-2463. A reference to MacD's war service with the Royal Army Medical Corps in World War I.

2469-2471. The War in Heaven and the First World War, in which both sides claimed divine support.

2476-2477. Cf. Orage: 'the unholy union of god and ape that we have set ourselves to annul'. (*New Age*, 10 June 1915, p. 133.)

2483-2484. 'If the wheel of life were itself the will to live, the will to power was its motive force. . . . The Will to Power . . . by means of which the wheel of Becoming is kept rolling'. (Orage, *Nietzsche in Outline & Aphorism*, pp. 32, 43.)

2488-2490. To the 'general mind' of the cosmos, there is no significant distance between Earth and the next star: only men register it as such on their human scale.

Yet I exult oor sang has yet
To grow wings that'll cairry it
Ayont its native speck o' grit,

And I exult to find in me
The thocht that this can ever be, 2495
A hope still for humanity.

For gin the sun and mune at last
Are as a neebor's lintel passed,
The wheel'll tine its stature fast,

And birl in time inside oor heids 2500
Till we can thraw oot conscious gleids
That draw an answer to oor needs,

Or if nae answer still we find
Brichten till a' thing is defined
In the huge licht-beams o' oor kind, 2505

And if we still can find nae trace
Ahint the Wheel o' ony Face,
There'll be a glory in the place,

And we may aiblins swing content
Upon the wheel in which we're pent 2510
In adequate enlightenment.

Nae ither thocht can mitigate
The horror o' the endless Fate
A'thing's whirled in predestinate.

O whiles I'd fain be blin' to it, 2515
As men wha through the ages sit,
And never move frae aff the bit,

Wha hear a Burns or Shakespeare sing,
Yet still their ain bit jingles string,
As they were worth the fashioning. 2520

tine—*lose* birl—*whirl* gleids—*sparks, flames* ahint—*behind* aiblins—*perhaps* aff the bit—*off the (same) spot* ain—*own* bit—*paltry*

2497-2511. Perhaps as a result of space travel, the enlargement of consciousness may be sufficient for human enlightenment, even if no final answers can be formulated and there is no sign of a divine personality behind the universe, no 'one infinite, dumb, beseeching countenance of mystery, underlying all the surfaces of visible time and space' (Melville, *Pierre*, Standard edition, p.70).

2507. *Ony Face.* Robert Buchanan in *The Book of Orm* (London 1870, p. 8) staked everything on the conviction that

Seen or seen not,
The Face is *there.*

Whatever Scotland is to me,
Be it aye pairt o' a' men see
O' Earth and o' Eternity

Wha winna hide their heids in't till
It seems the haill o' Space to fill, 2525
As 'twere an unsurmounted hill.

He canna Scotland see wha yet
Canna see the Infinite,
And Scotland in true scale to it.

Nor blame I muckle, wham atour 2530
Earth's countries blaw, a pickle stour,
To sort wha's grains they ha'e nae poo'er.

E'en stars are seen thegither in
A'e skime o' licht as grey as tin
Flyin' on the wheel as 'twere a pin. 2535

Syne ither systems ray on ray
Skinkle past in quick array
While it is still the self-same day,

A'e day o' a' the million days
Through which the soul o' man can gaze 2540
Upon the wheel's incessant blaze,

Upon the wheel's incessant blaze
As it were on a single place
That twinklin' filled the howe o' space.

A'e point is a' that it can be, 2545
I wis nae man 'll ever see
The rest o' the rotundity.

winna—*won't* muckle—*much* wham atour—*(those) around whom* a pickle stour—*a little dust* thegither—*together* skime—*gleam* skinkle—*twinkle* howe—*void* wis—*believe*

2521-2529. Cf. Keyserling: 'In so far as one can speak of space at all in connection with thoughts, they are wherever one attaches them. There is no point in the universe to which I could not be as near as I am to myself. . . . With every thought which does not radiate into infinity, but returns to the body from which it emanated, man cuts himself off from his own wider reality'. (*The Travel-Diary of a Philosopher*, London 1925, I, 314.)

2535. *A pin*: a pinwheel?

2545. *A'e point is a' that it can be*—to the human observer.

2547. *The rotundity*: the celestial sphere.

Impersonality sall blaw
Through me as 'twere a bluffert o' snaw
To scour me o' my sense o' awe, 2550

A bluffert o' snaw, the licht that flees
Within the Wheel, and Freedom gi'es
Frae Dust and Daith and a' Disease,

—The drumlie doom that only weighs
On them wha ha'ena seen their place 2555
Yet in creation's lichtnin' race,

In the movement that includes
As a tide's resistless floods
A' their movements and their moods—

Until disinterested we, 2560
O' a' oor auld delusions free,
Lowe in the wheel's serenity

As conscious items in the licht,
And keen to keep it clear and bricht,
In which the haill machine is dight, 2565

The licht nae man has ever seen
Till he has felt that he's been gi'en
The stars themsels insteed o' een,

And often wi' the sun has glowered
At the white mune until it cowered, 2570
As when by new thocht auld's o'erpowered.

Oor universe is like an e'e
Turned in, man's benmaist hert to see,
And swamped in subjectivity.

But whether it can use its sicht 2575
To bring what lies withoot to licht
To answer's still ayont my micht.

blaw—*blow* bluffert—*blast* flees—*flies* drumlie—*dark, troubled* lichtnin'—*lightning* lowe—*glow* dight—*arrayed* glowered—*glared* benmaist—*inmost* withoot—*outside* ayont—*beyond*

2555-2556. This appears to assert that creation does have a race to run, a destination to reach. If so, 'lichtnin'' hardly seems an appropriate epithet for it, particularly in view of the image of the tide which follows.

2557-2559. Cf. the sea in ll. 1963-1967.

2560. 'Disinterestedness' is for Orage *the* key-word: 'Somewhere or other in its capacious folds it contains all the ideas of ethics, and even, I should say, of religion. . . . I venture to say that whoever has understood the meaning of 'distinterestedness' is not far off understanding the goal of human culture'. (*Readers and Writers*, London 1922, pp. 44-45.) Cf. MacD, 'Second Hymn to Lenin': 'Disinterestedness, / Oor profoundest word yet'.

2572. *Oor universe*: our view of the universe.

2572-2577. These lines were quoted by Professor Walter J. Moore as an epigraph for the Preface of the 1972 edition of his well-known textbook *Physical Chemistry*. He chose the passage because it 'summarizes so cogently the great problem of modern physics—is the world of science an interpretation of an objective reality or is it a reflection of the abstract structure of human thought? It is interesting that MacDiarmid saw this problem in 1926, since it was only in 1925-26 that quantum mechanics was discovered, with the resultant demise of strict determinism and materialism in physics'. Prof. Moore adds: 'I think "The Drunk Man" is one of the greatest poems in the world, but when I tried to get my students in physical chemistry to read it, they were unable either to understand the Scots or to see its relevance to their pragmatic interest in passing an exam'. (Letter to K. Buthlay, 22 Jan. 1986.) Nevertheless, ll.799-800 have a certain relevance: 'Guid sakes, ye dinna need to pass / Ony exam. to dee'.

But when that inturned look has brocht
To licht what still in vain it's socht
Ootward maun be the bent o' thocht. 2580

And organs may develop syne
Responsive to the need divine
O' single-minded humankin'.

The function, as it seems to me,
O' Poetry is to bring to be 2585
At lang, lang last that unity. . . .

But wae's me on the weary wheel!
Higgledy-piggledy in't we reel,
And little it cares hoo we may feel.

Twenty-six thoosand years 't'll tak' 2590
For it to threid the Zodiac
—A single roond o' the wheel to mak'!

Lately it turned—I saw mysel'
In sic a company doomed to mell,
I micht ha'e been in Dante's Hell. 2595

It shows hoo little the best o' men
E'en o' themsels at times can ken
—I sune saw *that* when I gaed ben.

threid— *thread* mell—*mix* gaed ben—*went in*

2581-2583. Cf. Orage: 'Are there in the subconscious, "yearning to mix themselves with life", faculties for which "humanity" has not yet developed end-organs? If this be so, as our fathers have told us, the next step in evolution is to develop them'. (*Readers and Writers*, p. 188.) The Nietzschean aspect of this is made explicit by Orage elsewhere: 'It is probable, indeed, that new faculties, new modes of consciousness, will be needed, as the mystics have always declared; and that the differencing element of man and Superman will be the possession of these'. *Friedrich Nietzsche*, p. 75.)'Single-minded humankin'' offers a parallel with Dostoevsky's 'pan-human'.

2584-2586. Again, the Nietzschean aspect of this line of thought is brought out by Orage: '[Art] is thus in the closest alliance with the process of Becoming; is . . . the mode by which that process is created, preserved—or destroyed.' (*Nietzsche in Outline & Aphorism*, p. 66.)

2590-2615. 'Mr. Yeats takes the Great Wheel of the Ancients, a cycle of *Anima Mundi* symbolised by the passage of the sun through the Zodiacal constellations, a period of about 26,000 years of our time, but in his system it is considered but as one year of that mightier being whose months and days, all with their own radiant vitality, influence our own evolution. One of its days may be the spiritual light of many of our generations. It moves from subjective to objective. There are cycles within cycles, action and recoil, contrasted and opposing powers, all of a bewildering complexity, and caught within this great wheel the lesser wheel of our life revolves, having phases as many as the days of a lunar month, all re-echoing the lordlier cycle and its phases. When he illustrates these phases of human life, thirty in all, by portraits of men and women, dead and living, typical of the phase, I suspect the author to be animated not only by a desire to elucidate the system, but by an impish humour. . . . I am a little uncomfortable with some of my fellow-prisoners in phase twenty-five. I welcome George Herbert, but am startled to find myself along with Calvin, Luther and Cardinal Newman, as no doubt the last three would be incredulous of their own affinities to associate pilgrim souls. I am inclined to think all the good qualities of Carlyle were pruned by Mr. Yeats' geometrical scissors to make him fit into his phase'. (A.E., Review of *A Vision*, p. 715.)

2596. *The best o' men*: evidently the author. A more complex piece of egotism than it might appear to be, since it was brought about by his habit of stealing from other authors.

The lesser wheel within the big
That moves as merry as a grig, 2600
Wi' mankind in its whirligig,

And hasna turned a'e circle yet
Tho' as it turns we slide in it,
And needs maun tak' the place we get,

I felt it turn, and syne I saw 2605
John Knox and Clavers in my raw,
And Mary Queen o' Scots ana',

And Rabbie Burns and Weelum Wallace,
And Carlyle lookin' unco gallus,
And Harry Lauder (to enthrall us). 2610

And as I looked I saw them a',
A' the Scots baith big and sma',
That e'er the braith o' life did draw.

"Mercy o' Gode, I canna thole
Wi' sic an orra mob to roll." 2615
—"*Wheesht! It's for the guid o' your soul.*"

"But what's the meanin', what's the sense?"
—"*Men shift but by experience.*
'Twixt Scots there is nae difference.

They canna learn, sae canna move, 2620
But stick for aye to their auld groove
—*The only race in History who've*

Bidden in the same category
Frae stert to present o' their story,
And deem their ignorance their glory. 2625

grig *(English)—a cricket or grasshopper (The phrase is traditionally applied to any lively person—OED.)* raw—*row* ana'—*as well* unco—*extremely, unusually* gallus—*reckless* baith—*both* thole—*bear, endure* orra—*nondescript* wheest—*hush*

2606. *Clavers*: John Graham of Claverhouse (1649?-1689), the scourge of the Scottish Covenanters. *My raw*: 'Among the solar and lunar cones that revolve in the circle of the great year are the cones of each separate nation'. (Yeats, *A Vision*, p. 171.)

2620-2634. MacD's condemnation of the Scots is reminiscent of Chaadaev's remarks on the Russians in the first of his *Lettres sur la Philosophie de l'Histoire*: 'Solitaires dans le monde nous n'avons rien donné au monde, nous n'avons rien appris au monde, nous n'avons pas versé une seule ideé dans la masse des ideés humaines, nous n'avons en rien contribué au progrès de l'esprit humain, et tout ce qui nous est revenu de ce progrès, nous l'avons défiguré. . . . Pas une pensée utile n'a germé sur le sol stérile de notre patrie, pas une verité grande ne s'est élancée du milieu de nous'. (Quoted, pp. 289-90, in Brückner's *Literary History of Russia*, which MacD had read.)

2623. *Bidden in the same category*. This is the basis of the statement (ll. 2644-2646) that a Scottish poet must lose his nationality if he wants to see another category.

The mair they differ, mair the same.
The wheel can whummle a' but them,
—They ca' their obstinacy 'Hame,'

And 'Puir Auld Scotland' bleat wi' pride,
And wi' their minds made up to bide 2630
A thorn in a' the wide world's side.

There ha'e been Scots wha ha'e ha'en thochts,
They're strewn through maist o' the various lots
—Sic traitors are nae langer Scots!"

"But in this huge ineducable 2635
Heterogeneous hotch and rabble,
Why am *I* condemned to squabble?"

"A Scottish poet maun assume
The burden o' his people's doom,
And dee to brak' their livin' tomb. 2640

Mony ha'e tried, but a' ha'e failed.
Their sacrifice has nocht availed.
Upon the thistle they're impaled.

You maun choose but gin ye'd see
Anither category ye 2645
Maun tine your nationality."

And I look at a' the random
Band the wheel leaves whaur it fand 'em.
"Auch, to Hell,
I'll tak' it to avizandum." . . . 2650

O wae's me on the weary wheel,
And fain I'd understand them!

And blessin' on the weary wheel
Whaurever it may land them! . . .

whummle—*overturn* bide—*remain* hotch—*swarm (of vermin)* dee—*die*
tine—*lose* fand—*found* tak' it to avizandum—*defer decision (MacD. In Scots law, this applies to a judge taking a case for private consideration outside the court.)*
wae—*woe*

2629. '*Puir Auld Scotland*'. 'While the Irish may envisage their national destiny as "the dark Rosaleen" and the thought of England may conjure up pictures of roast beef and stately homes, Scotland is always "puir auld Scotland" '. (MacD in *Scottish Chapbook*, I, no. 7 (Feb. 1923), p. 183.) The phrase is at least as old as Burns ('The Answer' addressed to the Guidwife of Wauchope-House), and has been much used by Scots sentimentalising over their lost causes. It is perhaps connected with Prince Charles Edward's cry when he started from his sleep in a hut on Raasay: 'O God! Poor Scotland!' Readers familiar with Burns's poem may recall, ironically in this context, the passage which follows his use of the phrase:

That I for poor auld Scotland's sake
Some useful plan, or book could make,
Or sing a sang at least.

The rough bur-thistle spreading wide
Amang the bearded bear,
I turn'd my weeding heuk aside
An' spar'd the symbol dear.

MacD was determined *not* to spare the thistle, 'the bur o' the world', as he called it in a letter to George Ogilvie concerning *A Drunk Man* (9 Dec. 1926).

2650. MacD had read, and deplored, George Saintsbury's evasion of the issue in the case of the Russian novelists when he suggested that the value of their work should be taken 'as Scotch judges say, to *avizandum*'. (*Periods of European Literature: The Later Nineteenth Century*, Edinburgh 1907, p. 389.) The case that has been made here against the Scots national poet is not answered, and MacD is likewise guilty of dodging the issue.

But aince Jean kens what I've been through 2655
The nicht, I dinna doot it,
She'll ope her airms in welcome true,
And clack nae mair aboot it. . . .

* * * * * * *

The stars like thistle's roses floo'er
The sterile growth o' Space ootour, 2660
That clad in bitter blasts spreids oot
Frae me, the sustenance o' its root.

O fain I'd keep my hert entire,
Fain hain the licht o' my desire,
But ech! the shinin' streams ascend, 2665
And leave me empty at the end.

For aince it's toomed my hert and brain,
The thistle needs maun fa' again.
—But a' its growth 'll never fill
The hole it's turned my life intill! . . . 2670

Yet ha'e I Silence left, the croon o' a'.

No' her, wha on the hills langsyne I saw
Liftin' a foreheid o' perpetual snaw.

the nicht—*tonight* doot—*doubt* clack—*prattle, natter* ootour—*out over*
hain—*preserve* toomed—*emptied* croon—*crown* langsyne—*long ago*

The Stars Like Thistle's Roses Flower, 2659-2670.

2667-2670. 'He seemed to crumple juist as if he'd gane fair through himsel', wi' the thistle hidin' the hole'. ('The Common Riding'.)

Yet Ha'e I Silence Left, 2671-2685.

There exists a holograph version of this poem with a few small variants and ending: 'O I ha'e Silence left, the croon o' a''. F.G. Scott claimed to have supplied the last two lines as published, but MacD, while not saying that this was untrue, did state repeatedly that he did not recollect it as having happened.

The mysterious suggestiveness of this fine poem, with which MacD rescued a work in danger at l. 2658 of petering out feebly, is aimed at eliciting as many responses as there are readers. The notes which follow are offered on that understanding.

The Silence may be associated with the Unknown God, the 'mysterious Infinite' of occult tradition, reigning unmoved above the voice which uttered the Word at the creation, and linked by MacD with Tyutchev's 'Silentium':

Silence—like Chaos ere the Word
That gar'd the Play enact
That sune to conscious thocht
Maun seem a foolish dream.
(*Cencrastus*, *Complete Poems*, p. 219.)

Carlyle, like MacD, was loud in praise of silence—e.g., in 'Characteristics' (1831): 'Well might the Ancients make Silence a god; for it is the element of all godhood, infinitude, or transcendental greatness; at once the source and the ocean wherein all such begins and ends. In the same sense, too, have Poets sung "Hymns to the Night"; as if Night were nobler than Day; as if Day were but a small motley-coloured veil spread transiently over the infinite bosom of Night, and did but deform and hide from us its purely transparent eternal deeps. So likewise have they spoken and sung as if Silence were the grand epitome and complete sum-total of all Harmony; and Death, what mortals call Death, properly the beginning of Life'. (*Critical and Miscellaneous Essays*, London 1899, III, pp. 16-17.)

2671. *The croon o' a'*. Cf. Coventry Patmore, 'The Child's Purchase':
Silence that crowns, unnoted, like the voiceless blue,
The loud world's varying view,
And in its holy heart the sense of all things ponders!

2672-2673. *Her, wha on the hills*: perhaps the Scottish Muse, as in MacD's early 'Sonnets of the Highland Hills'. Cf. the image in the Gaelic 'Aisling Air Dhreach Mnà': 'Her well-rounded forehead shone / Soft and fair as the mountain snow'.

No' her, wha in the how-dumb-deid o' nicht
Kyths, like Eternity in Time's despite. 2675

No' her, withooten shape, wha's name is Daith,
No' Him, unkennable abies to faith

—God whom, gin e'er He saw a man, 'ud be
E'en mair dumfooner'd at the sicht than he

—But Him, whom nocht in man or Deity, 2680
Or Daith or Dreid or Laneliness can touch,
Wha's deed owre often and has seen owre much.

O I ha'e Silence left

—"And weel ye micht,"
Sae Jean'll say, "efter sic a nicht!"

how-dumb-deid o' nicht—*the still centre of the dead of night* kyths—*appears; reveals herself* abies—*except (MacD)* deed—*died* owre—*too*

2674-2675. *Her, wha in the how-dumb-deid*: the Moon?

2678-2679. This conception of the alien natures of God and man goes beyond the general Gnostic view to the extreme position taken by Marcion, who said of the true God that men are 'entire strangers to him'.

2680-2682. Cf. 'Water of Life' (*Complete Poems*, p. 294):

> The ancient memory is alive to few
> And fewer when it is ken what they see,
> But them that dae fear neither life nor death,
> Mindin' them baith.

APPENDIX A

Author's Note
(1926)

This gallimaufry is dedicated to my friend, Francis George Scott, the composer, who suggested it, and to whom, during the course of writing it, I have been further greatly indebted for co-operative suggestions and for some of the most penetrating and comprehensive of modern European criticism.

I would gratefully acknowledge, too, the assistance I have received from my friend, Dr Pittendrigh Macgillivray, and from my wife, in the revision of proofs.

To the Editor of 'The Glasgow Herald' I have to tender the customary acknowledgements for his kindness in allowing me to republish here certain portions of my poem which originally appeared in his columns

Drunkenness has a logic of its own with which, even in these decadent days, I believe a sufficient minority of my countrymen remain *au fait*. I would, however, take the liberty of counselling the others, who have no personal experience or sympathetic imagination to guide them, to be chary of attaching any exaggerated importance, in relation to my book as a whole, to such inadvertent reflections of their own sober minds as they may from time to time—as in a distorting mirror—detect in these pages, and of attempting, in, no doubt, a spirit of real helpfulness, to confer, on the basis of these, a species of intelligibility foreign to its nature, upon my poem. It would have been only further misleading these good folks, therefore, if I had (as, arbitrarily enough at best, I might have done) divided my poem into sections or in other ways supplied any of those "hand-rails" which raise false hopes in the ingenuous minds of readers whose rational intelligences are all too insusceptible of realising the enormities of which "highbrows" of my type are capable—even in Scotland.

I would suggest, on the other hand, if I may, that they should avoid subtleties and simply persist in the pretence that my "synthetic Scots" presents insuperable difficulties to understanding, while continuing to espouse with all the impressiveness at their command the counter-claims of "sensible poetry."

The whole thing must, of course, be pronounced *more Boreali*.

H. M'D.

APPENDIX B

Author's Note to the Second Edition (1953)

I have to thank the original publishers of this poem, Messrs. Wm. Blackwood and Sons, Ltd., for permitting the Caledonian Press to publish this new edition. The poem has been long out of print, but continues in constant demand, and would have been re-issued long ere this but for the War and the consequent difficulties and high costs of printing, book-binding, and publishing.

I have also to thank Dr. David Daiches, Lecturer in English literature at Cambridge University, for his introductory essay, which should, I think, be read in conjunction with the opening chapter, on "The Scottish Literary Tradition", of his splendid book on Robert Burns which, together with his study of Robert Louis Stevenson and various other essays, has established him as the foremost living authority on our literature.

Dr. Daiches expresses the hope that there is no need to defend my "synthetic Scots" at this time of day. That is true so far as the small advanced poetry-reading public in England, America, and other countries is concerned, but that public is unfortunately limited to a few dozen people in Scotland—the most backward country in Western Europe aesthetically. We have the hopeless mass of our Anglo-Scots to contend with, the virtual monopoly accorded to English literature in our schools and Universities, and the fact that our leading newspapers (unlike those in the West Indies where they have opened their columns to and greatly encouraged recent literary developments) give no space to our younger writers but in so far as they give space to poetry at all continue to give it only to the traditional post-Burnsian rubbish. As my friend and fellow-poet, Sydney Goodsir Smith, says in his admirable "*A Short Introduction to Scottish Literature*": "It is very unusual to find the educated minority of a country objecting to their writers using the traditional language of that country". We still find that in Scotland, however, and though the *Times Literary Supplement* may observe that Scotland is now much more likely than Ireland or Wales to furnish an independent literature alongside English, and that the best work of living Scottish poets is now discerned as being of more lasting value than the much-publicised work of the English poets of the '30s (to which, of course, Scottish poetry-readers paid far more attention than they did to the work concurrently produced in their own country), Scottish writers and speakers are themselves as a rule apologetic, depreciatory, and defeatist about it. Only a minority have realised during these past thirty years that (as Mr. H.G. Woodley says in "*Scotland—Their Scotland*") "the time had not only come, but was swiftly passing, for Scotland to awake, and to return to the days before Burns, when poetry was poetry—and to repossess themselves of that which had been stolen from them, which was not so much the *Stone of Destiny*, as their first-class poetry and their native tongue. . . . It certainly seemed to him that unless Scots was taught in Scottish schools, even Burns would die the death of Ramsay, Fergusson, and the others."

Despite this pervasive cultural Quislingism in our midst, however, the Scots Renaissance Movement has made, and continues to make, great progress. I had occasion the other day to reply to a defeatist Scottish writer who wrote: "The burst of enthusiasm which carried it through its early days seems to have passed without showing any road on which advance is possible". Apart from the fact that practically every Scottish poet of any significance known to me has now turned to Scots instead of English, "think," I said, "of what is happening today in ancillary fields of Scottish scholarship—the Saltire Society's reprints of Scottish classics, the work of the Scottish Studies Department of Edinburgh University, the plethora of articles on Lewis Grassic Gibbon recently in learned reviews both in England and in America (and even in the *Aberdeen University Review*), the Scottish Dialect Survey, the Scottish National Dictionary, the changed policy of the Scottish Education Department in regard to dialect speech in our schools, and the many excellent books recently published in America on Robert Henryson, Robert Burns, and other Scottish writers, to say nothing of Dr. Baxter's excellent volume on William Dunbar in this country. Add to that work on Scots poets being done now in France, Germany, Russia, and elsewhere. If all these signs and portents do not indicate 'any road on which advance is possible' then your contributor must be looking in the wrong direction altogether. Probably his real trouble is that 'there are none so blind as those who *will* not see' "—a condition very general in Scotland today, especially among the so-called educated classes.

Fair-minded people who really study the matter will be compelled to agree with Mr. Sydney Smith where, writing about the state of affairs that obtained when I wrote this poem, he says: "In the early days there were only a few adherents to the cause. Today there are hosts of them. They are not all of the first flight, of course; many a crow squawks among our nightingales. But there are seldom more than one or two first-class artists, in any line, in one generation. What *is* a healthy sign, and a sign that this time the revival, the newly-captured tradition, is not so likely to prove a nine-days' wonder, is that the general *idea* is accepted by so many—the idea that the soul of Scotland can only be revived by a return to our true tradition—the idea that Scots is a language and not merely a hotch-potch of dialects (or even *one* dialect, as the foolish say); that it is a language capable of coping with any subject in heaven or earth or hell; the idea implicit in this belief that Scotland has a part to play in Europe as it had before, and the realization that Scots is a more expressive and potent medium for a Scottish writer than is English or American or Esperanto."

To the first volume of my Scots lyrics, "Sangschaw" in 1925 I put on the title-page, "*Habent sua fata libelli.*" And that act of faith has indeed been richly rewarded, especially in the work of the late William Soutar and that of Sydney Smith (of whose recent lyrics Dr. Edith Sitwell has said that some of them are *great* poetry, and among the best done by any living poet under forty), and Robert Garrioch. And the many new Lallans poets who have appeared in the last year or two shows that as Mr. Eric Linklater has said, "The Scottish Renaissance Movement has now got its second wind."

"*The Drunk Man*," unfortunately, has not been followed up by younger writers as my lyrics have been. With characteristic immodesty I am forced to agree with a correspondent who says: "The general attitude I adopt is that after Burns's strictly limited achievement there had to be a general widening of the horizons of Scots poetry if further development was to be possible at all. But the shoal of semi-literate versifiers who got into print by cashing in on the lowest level of the Burns vogue so discredited the whole vernacular movement that no one of real talents would take the movement seriously enough to apply these talents to the job crying out to be done. This, despite the fact that a few intensely patriotic individuals did see what was needed and a few interesting experiments like the Biblical translations of Waddell and Riddell, and Cameron's of the "*Imitation of Christ*" did take place, remained the depressing situation until you came on the scene a hundred and thirty years later. I can't see that anything in the interim is important enough to demand attention, though some of the attempts to follow your lead are certainly interesting in their various ways (notably Sydney Smith's) and the modern revival is not, thank God, entirely a one-man show. But yours is a highly individual achievement, and it will need big talents to digest it, let alone develop it, in Scots."

Crises in my personal life deflected me from following up the "*Drunk Man*" line myself, and I have only recently been able to recur to it. How much further I can carry it remains to be seen. My aim certainly is still what it was—and I know there is a steadily increasing number in Scotland who share that aim—admirably expressed by Mr. A.D. Mackie when he said of me: "What he socht was nae sma nerrie kinrik crynit intil itsel like a hermit crab intil its shell: he socht a Scotland sib and chief wi the warld-wide, shakan a luif wi France and Russia, shouther to shouther wi forrit-leukan folk o aa lands, whether Jew or

Gentile, black, white, or brown. That is the Scotland that is waukenan the day, that is the Scotland that will face the fecht o the years to come, and Hugh MacDiarmid has been, is, and will be the pyper on the parapet."

HUGH MACDIARMID.

BIGGAR.
March, 1953.

APPENDIX C

Note on the Text

ALL differences between the text of the present edition and that of the first edition (1926) are recorded in the lists below in the form: line number; emendation; first edition.

I. *Changes Authorised by MacDiarmid*

The following changes were made or authorised by the poet in the editions published in 1953, 1956, 1962 and 1969 and in the text of the poem printed in MacDiarmid's *Complete Poems* (1978; 1985). I am grateful to Kulgin Duval and W.R. Aitken for confirmation that the emendations in the 1969 edition and in the *Complete Poems* reflect the poet's wishes.

1 AMNA / AMNA'
2 wark / wark'
33 *Scotiae* / *Scotia*
44 gi'e / gie
50 pidgin / pidgin'
60 *Zeitgeist*! / *Zeitgeist!*
75 wurd / wird
82 Embro / Embro'
85 Burns / Burns'
87 isna / isna'
88 slip / slip,
96 mune. / mune
110 Burns / Burns'
120 no' / no
124 cup"? / cup?"
138 tak'n' / tak'n
174 *lie,* / *lie;*
190 *doun;* / *doun*
232 Tak'n' / Tak'n
241 *ha'e . . . ha'e* / *hae . . . hae*
250 *unkent,* / *unkent*
266 a'thing / a' thing
274 God / God.
295 ken / ken,
298 can / can,
349 Wissenschaftsfeindlichkeit / wissenschaftsfeindlichkeit
358 *hert,* / *hert.*
363 *life,* / *life*
382 Noo / Noo'
386 St. / St

452 s'ud / su'd
464 me; / me.
520 dae / da'e
558 ganien, / ganien.
607 hadna / hadna'
735 Brankstone's / Branksome's
782 *Maidenkirk / Maidenheid*
824 *no' / no*
828 din / din,
830 climacteric / climateric
831 ana' / ana
836 stude / stood
867 lug, / lug
877 e'e, / e'e
893 St. / St
909 back-hauf's / backhauf's
910 bean-swaup / beanswaup
926 hail / haill
981 ray, / ray
987 Daith / Daith,
1025 *hert! / hert*
1060 gars / gar's
1066 ancienne, / ancienne
1068 mêmes / même
1069 la / le
1069 de / des
1146 devise. / devise."
1150 seen." / seen"
1198 they've / they're
1249 life / life,
1266 God, / God
1279 ha'ena / haena
1362 soul— / soul,
1433 *specie / speciem*
1443 *lugs, / lugs*
1469 shasloch / skasloch
1537 shape / shape,
1542 show; / show,
1544 Angel; / Angel,
1659 [footnote] Herman / Hermann
1698 ken 't / kent
1708 hagger'd / haggar'd
1742 taste)? / taste?)
1759 big / bigs
1821 gi'e / gie
1914 intense / intense,
1934 it / it,
1936 insteed / instead
1942 bigger / bigger,
1944 grips / grips,

1953 in't. / in't
1993 *cratur* / *cratur'*
2091 is / is is
2111 cats' / cat's
2114 cats' / cat's
2118 pairt, / pairt
2125 abidin', / abidin';
2143 deceived; / deceived,
2230 *wund* — / *wund.*—
2237 humanity / humanity,
2289 per tal modo, / fer tal modo.
2291 Che / Ché
2310 s'ud / su'd
2348 evince / evince,
2370 rippit. . . . / rippit. . .
2372 th' owre / th'owre
2423 dae / dae,
2436 displayed.) / displayed.
2442 me! / me!)
2445 Infinity, / Infinity.
2448 aricht. / aricht
2455 't'll / 'tll
2473 oot-topped / oottopped
2526 'twere / t'were
2535 'twere / t'were
2559 moods— / moods,-
2564 bricht, / bricht
2590 't'll / 'tll
2594 mell, / mell.
2597 ken / ken,
2601 whirligig, / whirligig
2617 "But what's the meanin', what's the sense?" / *"But what's the meanin', what's the sense?"*
2679 he / he.
2683 left / left,

II. *Other Changes*

The changes listed below have been made to correct what appear to be authorial or printer's errors.

136 *animalcula* / *animalculæ*
309 [footnote] Georges / George
373 *hwyl* / *hwll*
817, 1749 bood / 'bood
1633 me. / me,
2044 were't / wer't